YOGA FOR PEOPLE WHO CAN'T TOUCH THEIR TOES

(AND FOR THOSE THAT CAN!)

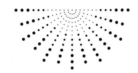

GORDON KANZER, M.D., K.Y.T.

With deepest gratitude

To my family and to my teachers and fellow students at Kripalu

You all inspired me to follow my passion

CONTENTS

INTRODUCTION

A gift consists not in what is done or given, but in the intention of the giver or doer.

Seneca

The oral traditions of yoga are felt to date back five millennia and were first written down in the Vedas and the Upanishads, the ancient, sacred Hindu religious texts, some three to four thousand years ago. My hope is that this book will provide both novices and advanced practitioners with a guide to the practice of yoga that is applicable to our modern day lives, while at the same time preserving the original, true essence of yoga that lies in self-realization and the development of a spiritual connection.

Physical limitations do not preclude one from the practice of yoga. Personal growth through yoga is available to all, whether flexible or inflexible, able or disabled and, of course, for those who can't touch their toes. The Sanskrit word *yoga* means to join or connect. While connecting the breath to the movement and uniting mind and body are all important to the practice of yoga, the most important connection is to your spirit and true authentic self. Finding clarity, however, requires patience and self-kindness. By developing the right mindset to develop a regular yoga practice, opportunities for transformation and self-fulfillment will unfold. Life is full of challenges. Yoga may not be the answer to overcoming them, but yoga can promote introspection and clarity that are valuable tools in any attempt.

This book consists of three parts. The first part identifies the obstacles to the development of a regular yoga practice, describes a positive mindset that will help you to progress on the path of yoga whether a beginner or a seasoned practitioner, and explores the possibility of personal growth through yoga. To add more meaning to your yoga practice, the second part of the book presents the many facets of yoga, including its benefits, philosophy, various schools and traditions, science, physiological effects and relevant human anatomy. The third part is an exploration of the postures and basic yogic breathing techniques to instill a greater sense of confidence tshrough familiarity as you embark on your journey.

I write this book from the perspective of a physician who embraced a second career as a yoga instructor. The knowledge I acquired during that transition helped me to realize that there is more to yoga than just the physical postures and movements. I have experienced a personal transformation with a new outlook on life based in gratitude. Faced with many obstacles, I embarked on the path of yoga three years ago. My career as a radiologist left me with extreme inflexibility from sitting in a chair in front of a computer for eight to ten hours a day over a period of thirty years. Assuming the responsibility for the wellbeing of my patients with a zero tolerance for errors and a need to constantly focus and concentrate without distraction for hours became the source of chronic anxiety and stress. Challenges that I previously faced in my career, however, are not important to my intention. Rather, what I wish to convey are the steps I have taken to develop a meaningful yoga practice that has opened my eyes to a future filled with hope. It is a true gift that I gave myself, one that I deeply wish to give to you.

PART I

1
THE JOURNEY BEGINS

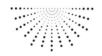

Faith is taking the first step even when you don't see the whole staircase.

Martin Luther King, Jr.

Bob, a middle-aged man in his early fifties, visits his primary care physician for his annual physical. He is in relatively good health. He tells his doctor that he is stressed out by his job, feels burnt out and is frequently depressed by his work situation. After discussing his symptoms with Bob, the doctor responds by offering him a prescription for Prozac, but tells him of the many potential side effects. As an alternative, she suggests that he try yoga. She tells him that she has several patients who found stress relief and a boost in mood from practicing yoga two or three times a week. Feeling that he doesn't need additional stress from worrying about the side effects of a medication, he decides to consider the alternative.

During the next several days, he starts to have some second thoughts about attending a yoga class at a local studio. He has led a relatively sedentary life and has worked for many years in front of a computer. He is extremely inflexible and stiff. He has trouble bending down to pick up things. He once left an extremely traditional Japanese restaurant because of his inability to sit cross-legged on the floor. He also doesn't wish to be the only man in a class of women. He imagines himself being surrounded by fit, in-shape and flexible women in spandex leggings. His wife, aware of the stress consuming her husband, convinces him to give it a try. She finds a website for a yoga studio in the next town. Bob notices a class on the schedule for Saturday morning that is described as "gentle Hatha" yoga. He doesn't know what "Hatha" means, but is comforted by the word "gentle".

As Saturday comes, he is not sure what to wear so he puts on black gym shorts and a blue Nike tee shirt imprinted with their slogan, "Just Do It". As he enters the studio, he notices that people are leaving their shoes on a mat near the door. He finds a chair to unlace his sneakers since he isn't able to bend down to untie them. As he approaches the front desk, his anxiety heightens as the receptionist asks him to fill out a medical release form, relieving the studio from all responsibility if he injures himself. He is then directed toward the classroom. To get there, he walks through the studio's retail shop filled with women's clothing, including yoga pants, spandex leggings and tank tops, as well as essential oils and jewelry. As Bob enters the classroom, he is greeted by a fit young woman wearing bright blue leggings and a tight-fitting yellow tank top imprinted with the Sanskrit word "*Om*". His fears begin to become reality. She instructs him to take a mat and a blanket from the shelves at the side of the room. The mats are all lavender in color and the blankets are striped in purple and white. Fortunately, he is early for class and is able to place his mat in the relative safety of the back corner of the room. One by one, women begin to enter. He is relieved that some of them are his age and overweight, but they are all wearing spandex in various colors and patterns. The room becomes crowded and, as he feared, he is the only man in the class.

The teacher instructs everyone to sit in *sukhasana.* He has no idea what that means, but notices everyone sitting on their mat cross-legged. Totally self-conscious at this point and unable to sit cross-legged, he sits with his legs out in front of him, slouched over with a rounded back. The teacher welcomes the students and instructs them to close their eyes as she leads them through a yogic breathing technique. So far so good. He knows he is capable of breathing. The breathing helps him to calm down. He tries to remember why he is there and is briefly reminded of the stresses of his job.

After the initial period of yogic breathing ends, the movement part of the class begins. The teacher instructs everyone to get into table position. "What is that?" He looks around in order to mimic the other students who are on their hands and knees. As he looks forward he is met with the site of a woman's rear end covered in flowered spandex.

The pace of the class picks up as the instructor leads the class from one posture to the next; cat and cow, downward-facing dog, three-legged dog, warrior, humble warrior, warrior II, triangle pose, child's pose, bridge pose. He quickly becomes lost and confused. He has no idea what these names mean. With each posture, he attempts to copy the teacher and the women surrounding him, but with little success. He feels inept and stupid. Because of his inflexibility and stiffness, most of the postures are uncomfortable and, at times, quite painful.

Stretching muscles and joints that were never stretched for years requires so much exertion that sweat begins to drip onto his mat, creating a slippery surface that limits his ability to sustain the postures and establish any sense of stability. He becomes even more self-conscious as it appears to him that no one else is perspiring. He assumes his uncontrollable anxiety is the cause of his excessive perspiration. He hopes that no one will see his sweat-stained T-shirt.

As the class progresses, the teacher walks between the mats throughout the room to assist students and correct their postures. In the worst way he doesn't want the teacher to come anywhere near him. He doesn't want anyone invading his space or reinforcing his sense of ineptitude. But, as the teacher instructs the students to reverse their warrior, she approaches him, noticing his arm isn't extended out over his head. Unsolicitedly and without asking his permission, she places her hand on his arm. She extends his arm out over his head unaware of his chronic rotator cuff issues. He winces in pain.

To his relief, the last ten minutes of class is spent in *shavasana* or relaxation, allowing him to lie on his back with his eyes closed as he tries to forget about the entire hour before.

So let's look at Bob's first experience with yoga. It was unpleasant, uncomfortable, and at times painful. He was self-judgmental and hyper-critical of his failings throughout the class. He not only hated that he was so inflexible, but worse, he hated himself for his inability to control his anxiety and stress, both at his job and during the class.

His first experience of yoga was his last. He never came back.

Susan, a woman in her late forties, married with two teenage children, regularly attends the local Weight Watchers meetings. She is fifty pounds overweight, and as a result has type II diabetes. She possesses a terrible body image. In fact, she tries not to look in the mirror, especially without clothes on. She hates herself for what she perceives as her lack of self-control when it comes to eating. She is constantly stressed by trying to take care of a family and a house while working full time at a job she feels is boring and unsatisfying.

During one Weight Watchers meeting, one of the leaders suggests that Susan might want to try yoga. She had a good experience and tells Susan that it made her feel relaxed, toned her muscles and lessened her need to stress-eat. Susan had never considered yoga before. She knew little about it, but always imagined it was for young, extremely flexible, fit women who sported expensive Lululemon fashion leggings.

The next morning, while reading the newspaper, she notices a promotion for a free class at a new local yoga studio. Reluctantly, she visits the listed website and notices a "gentle Hatha" yoga class on their schedule that is given right after she finishes her day at work. Fed up with just about everything in her life, she decides to sign up and give it a try.

During the rest of the day, she starts to have second thoughts. She feels that she has nothing to wear. She doesn't want to wear leggings that she feels would accentuate the shape of her figure. She settles on wearing sweatpants and a loose fitting tee shirt. Self-conscious about her body, she is worried about being surrounded by fit and flexible women all showing off their spandex-clad bodies.

She enters the studio dressed in her drab gray, baggy sweatpants and red, loose fitting Nike tee shirt imprinted with their slogan, "Just Do It". She notices that people are leaving their shoes on a mat near the door. She carries a lot of her extra weight in her belly. Unable to bend down, she finds a chair in which to unlace her sneakers. At the front desk, her heart begins to race as the receptionist asks her to fill out a medical release form, relieving the studio from all responsibility if she injures herself. She is directed toward the classroom. To get there, she walks through the studio's retail shop filled with women's clothing, including yoga pants, spandex leggings, and tank tops. As she enters the classroom, she is greeted by a fit young woman wearing bright flowered leggings and a tight-fitting lavender tank top imprinted with the Sanskrit word "*Shanti*". She instructs Susan to get a mat and a blanket.

Fortunately, she is early for class and is able to place her mat in the relative safety of the back of the room. One by one, women begin to enter. She is relieved that some of them are her age and overweight. The room becomes crowded. She feels closed in with little air to breathe. She is anxious and self-conscious.

The class begins. The teacher instructs everyone to sit in *sukhasana.* Of course, she has no idea what that means, but notices everyone sitting on their mat cross-legged. Unable to cross her legs, she sits with her legs out in front of her, slouched over with a rounded back. The teacher begins the class instructing the students to close their eyes as she guides them through a yogic breathing technique. So far so good. She knows she is capable of breathing. The breathing helps her to calm down. She tries to remember why she is there and briefly is reminded of the many reasons she dislikes herself.

After the initial period of yogic breathing ends, the movement part of the class begins. The teacher instructs everyone to get into table position. "What is that?" She looks around and mimics the other students who are on their hands and knees. She looks forward and is met with the sight of a fit woman's small rear end covered in purple spandex on the mat in front of her.

The pace of the class picks up, as the instructor leads the class from one posture to the next; cat and cow, downward-facing dog, three-legged dog, warrior, humble warrior, warrior II, triangle pose, child's pose, bridge pose. She quickly becomes lost and confused. She has no idea what these names mean. With each posture, she attempts to copy the teacher and the women surrounding her, but with little success. She feels inept and stupid. Most of the postures are uncomfortable and, at times, quite painful. Stretching muscles and joints that were never stretched requires so much exertion that sweat begins to drip onto her mat, creating a slippery surface and interfering with her ability to sustain any of the postures. She becomes even more self-conscious as she looks around and it appears to her that no one else is perspiring. She hopes that no one will see her T-shirt blotched with sweat.

As the class progresses, the teacher walks between the mats throughout the room to assist students and correct their postures. In the worst way, she doesn't want the teacher to come anywhere near her. She doesn't want anyone invading her space or reinforcing her ineptitude. But, as the teacher instructs the students to assume *Matsyendrasana,* a seated twisting posture with one leg extended and the other bent, she approaches Susan, noticing that her torso is barely twisted. She places her hand on her shoulder without asking permission. She pushes on her shoulder, attempting to get her to twist, but the only thing it accomplishes is pushing her belly fat into her thigh. She starts to cry.

So let's look at Susan's first experience with yoga. It was unpleasant, uncomfortable, and at times painful. She was self-judgmental and hyper-critical of her failings throughout the class. She not only hated that she was overweight due to stress eating, but worse, she hated herself for her inability to control her anxiety and stress, both during the class and throughout her daily life.

Her first experience of yoga was her last. She never came back.

Of course, many people have much more positive initiations into the practice of yoga. The aforementioned scenarios, however, are not dissimilar to my own story and to many others. I attempted yoga sporadically over the years, but never did it for long. It was sometimes unpleasant, uncomfortable, and yes, at times, painful. I was self-conscious and overly self-critical. I also hated myself for my severe inflexibility, but worse, I hated myself for my inability to control my anxiety and stress, unable to just relax.

My goals in writing this book are multifold. One is to suggest strategies to overcome the obstacles to developing a regular yoga practice that are often made more onerous by many studios and teachers, as well as by the marketing of yoga in Western society. I write from personal experience and with a passion for yoga. I had the perception that to "do yoga" correctly I had to position my body exactly as that of the teacher. A teacher who corrects your posture, either verbally or physically, reinforces that idea. The feeling that you are being watched or scrutinized can magnify negative self-judgments and interfere with gaining a sense of introversion, relaxation and peace. In addition, many of us believe, as I once did, that one must do whatever the teacher tells us to do. It took quite a while, but I finally realized that, as one of my teachers profoundly put it, "Yoga is not Simon Says!"

I firmly believe that there is only one right way to do yoga, which is to make it your own personal experience and self-expression. To attain the full benefits of yoga you must connect with your true authentic self, not with a version of what you think others wish you to be, including your teacher. You are in a yoga class for yourself and yourself alone, not for the teacher or anyone else in the room. It is your time, your moment, and your experience. Don't begin to establish a yoga practice with the goal of performing the *asanas* or postures flawlessly. Most of us can't and you will be setting yourself up to fail.

Yoga is the practice of self-observation without judgment. The inner critic can be silenced by objectively acknowledging one's limitations without any qualifiers. A statement such as, "I can't touch my toes like everyone else and I will never be good at yoga" doesn't serve you. Leave out the "and" in your observations. It is fine to just notice, "I can't touch my toes." That is who you are. Personally, I have relatively short arms, tight inner thigh muscles, and tight hamstrings. Do any of these limitations prevent me from having a meaningful yoga practice? Absolutely not, because by moving beyond any lamentations about those limitations I can focus on what I can do. I am left to enjoy my own experience by closing my eyes, enjoying the movements of my body, listening to my breath, and meditating. Yoga is the integration of the movements, the breath and meditation, all done simultaneously. I didn't believe at first that I could meditate while moving my body and listening to a teacher, but over time I developed the ability to achieve a state of introversion while practicing yoga. Introversion is turning inward. Focusing on one's inner self decreases one's awareness of what is external to the body, including the teacher and whomever is around us. The heightened awareness of the self connects one to his or her own personal experience.

It is always beneficial to create balance in life. We would like to have a good balance between work and play or sleep and wakefulness. For yoga, it is said that the most meaningful yoga practice is one where there is a balance between mind and body. The most inflexible person who achieves that balance will enjoy a more profound experience than the most flexible of people that does not. Think of your essential nature as a scale. On one side is the physical body that requires nourishment, the toning of muscles, and flexibility of joints. On the other side is the mind that requires a positive outlook on life, the experience of our full range of emotions, and the cultivation of thoughts toward the goal of gaining clarity. What connects the two sides of the scale in yoga is the breath.

In yoga, the spiritual connection of mind and body is the breath. In human anatomy, the actual physical connection between mind and body is the spinal cord. It is a fragile structure protected by a stack of thirty-three bony vertebrae that form beautiful graceful curves. Millions of messages are produced in the brain each second that travel down the spinal cord and throughout the body, some of which are instructions for the movements of the muscles and joints. Those movements initiate signals that are then sent back to the spinal cord and up to the brain, allowing us to react to what is occurring in the body with thoughts, emotions and feelings.

Both the novice and the most seasoned practitioner are both "doing" yoga if they are both connecting their unique movements to the breath. As we practice, we can breathe into a stretch, which heightens our awareness of and increases our focus on what is happening in the body. But, we can also breathe into an idea, a thought or emotion. Yoga is the body, breath and mind, all working in concert. It is your movements, your breath and your thoughts that are all unique to you. Access all three and you can overcome any self-judgments or preconceived notions of yoga.

In my yoga classes, I conclude by saying, "*Namaste,* the light in me bows to the light in you!" My hope is that by enjoying many profound experiences through yoga, the light within you and the light that is you will shine so bright for everyone to see. I am trained in the Kripalu yogic tradition. At the end of a Kripalu class we also say "*Jai Bhagwan*", which among other definitions, means "a blessed victory." How practicing yoga is a victory has individual meaning for each one of us. A meaningful yoga practice may bring you many victories, possibly helping to overcome whatever challenges or obstacles you may face in life. Of course, my hope is that from the words that follow you will overcome any obstacles to the development of a regular and meaningful yoga practice. I am humbled by your desire to read my words and entrust me with the privilege of being your guide on this wonderful journey, one that I hope is filled with feelings of peace, joy and contentment. To you, I say *Namaste* and *Jai Bhagwan*! Embrace life!

2
THE MINDSET

The secret of change is to focus all of your energy, not on fighting the old, but on building the new.

Socrates

I will start with just a few reasonable questions:

- *Do you wish to reduce stress from unresolved issues, physical or mental disease, or dysfunctional relationships?*
- *Do you want to enjoy a healthy lifestyle?*
- *Would you like more clarity in life?*
- *Would you like to experience peace and contentment?*
- *Are you open to new ideas?*
- *Are you humble?*
- *Can you move some or all parts of your body?*

- *Can you think?*
- *Can you breathe?*

If you answered yes to any of these questions you are ready to begin the profound journey on the path of yoga. As you will learn, yoga is not just exercise, but an avenue to personal growth. Embrace yoga with your heart and soul and it can become a way of life. It can allow you to experience a newfound sense of contentment and peace filled with love, compassion and gratitude. You can develop an ability to access a positive life force that can energize you throughout your days. Yogis talk of *agni,* the fire that burns deep in one's belly. Dedicate yourself to yoga and that fire can burn with the brightest of light that can fill you with a sense of hope and excitement for the future. A new and healthier perspective may better equip you to take on challenges you face.

Of course, if you are just beginning the practice of yoga or maybe just considering it, you may feel that I am getting way ahead of myself by discussing the potential end results, including the possibilities for personal growth. In fact, an important principle of yogic philosophy is nonattachment to end results and the possibilities of success or failure. Without considering yoga or any endeavor in life as a means to an end, one can enjoy the process and be fully in the present moment.

At this point, there are more practical matters at hand, such as how to overcome the obstacles that prevent so many from establishing or sustaining a regular yoga practice. I know those obstacles firsthand. When I first began my exploration of yoga, I read so many books written by seasoned practitioners and experts on yogic philosophy that talked about self-realization, enlightenment and the profound effects of a meaningful yoga practice. The same question constantly came to mind, "How can I think about enlightenment when I can't even sit on the ground with my legs crossed?"

Can you touch your toes?

As you will soon learn, it doesn't matter. Yoga is for everyone, regardless of physical limitations, from the most infirm person confined to a chair to the most flexible on a mat. Anyone can derive meaning from a yoga practice by discovering his or her connection of the breath to movement to create introversion and inwardness. The expression of the *asanas* or postures is particular to the individual. We all are dissimilar physically, with differences in inherited and acquired flexibility. But, with the exception of people afflicted with neuromuscular or pulmonary diseases, we all have a similar capacity to breathe. The yogic breathing techniques or *pranayama* are accessible to all. More importantly, we can all connect our breath to the unique movements of our bodies. That connection is yoga.

The first step to develop a regular and meaningful yoga practice is to consider your mindset. For me, changing my mindset, one that developed over many years, is a work in progress, and may always be one. Awareness of a problem and creating a plan, however, are the first steps toward change. When something "sets" it becomes rigid, hardened and fixed. A mindset is an attachment to one's fixed beliefs and habitual thoughts and behaviors. Changing one's mindset is a challenge, especially when it is mired in automatic and reflexive negative self-judgments. But is changing one's mindset necessary for personal growth or is there an alternative for self-realization? Practicing non-attachment to future outcomes and becoming mindful in the moment may be the work that needs to be done to become more receptive to new ideas and perspectives. Perhaps, that receptivity allows the mind to remain fluid, preventing it from becoming rigid, hardened and fixed, not allowing the mind to "set".

As you enter or continue on the path of yoga, drop all of your preconceived notions of what it is. Practice with the expectation of honoring your body and self. Physical limitations, including the inability to touch your toes, need not be limitations to practicing yoga. The only limitation that will prevent you from practicing yoga is the self-destructive effects of the inner critic that we seem to all possess to different degrees. Acceptance of yourself is the key. By acknowledging limitations, you can better concentrate on what is ultimately important to you.

Just like myself, you may be someone who previously shied away from trying yoga because of extreme discomfort arising from tight muscles, stiff joints and overall inflexibility. One of my yoga teachers referred to that inflexibility as hyper-stability, in contradistinction to hyper-mobility. Keep in mind as you read this book that it is arguably the most hyper-stable of us that will derive the most satisfaction from the progressive, albeit slow, development of newfound flexibility.

I was quite dubious about the benefits of yoga and likelihood of success when I first started my practice. But I tried to throw aside my skepticism, open up my mind to new possibilities and just take it one step at a time. Have faith in yourself. Know that yoga is for everyone regardless of ability or handicaps. Have patience. The process of mental and physical transformation takes time. It is also normal to get discouraged at times. Some days, you won't want to do yoga or it may not feel good. Acknowledge those feelings without self-judgment. Just like other experiences in our lives, we don't always enjoy everything we do all the time. One might have a bad golf game or see a bad movie and it likely won't be the last time that person plays golf or sees a movie. Having an expectation that yoga is always enjoyable is unrealistic. At those times, try to push through any dissatisfaction along the way and just congratulate yourself for practicing it anyway.

Yoga is about integrating our physical and mental selves. Honoring the mind is crucial to fostering personal growth. As it bears mentioning again, it is important to keep in mind that many times the most inflexible person who establishes a good balance between the mind and body has a more meaningful practice than the most flexible that concentrates only on the physical benefits of practice. The body is a conduit to gain access to our mind, emotions and our most profound ideas. We must cultivate the mind while we nurture our bodies.

Most important in the development of a healthy mindset is an understanding that a prerequisite for expressing love, compassion and gratitude for others is the possession of these same emotions in yourself. Love yourself for who you are and not someone else's idea of who you should be. Be proud of showing up on the mat instead of lamenting your inability to assume the full expression of a posture like your teacher or the person next to you. Your teacher should just be a guide, not someone there to correct you. This is not math class. A great teacher is one that guides a student into the expression of a posture that results in feelings of stability, balance, and strength and, most importantly, prevents injury. With time, your yoga practice will become more meditative and you will likely find that you are no longer looking at the person on the next mat. Strive to live as your authentic self. Make your yoga practice your own unique experience.

As you develop your practice of yoga, be kind to yourself, congratulate yourself often for making the attempt, and don't always take it so seriously. A good laugh from falling over during a challenging balance posture is often much better for reducing stress and connecting with yourself than doing it perfectly. I remember a time when I lost my balance and fell backwards onto the mat behind me. It was quite embarrassing at the time, but I still laugh about it to this day. It was the ultimate experience of instability. I always tell students that the only way to fully experience balance is to first know how imbalance feels and I surely experienced imbalance that day. A natural human instinct to move from a state of instability to one of stability arises from our balance centers in the brain. The brain does not want us to balance on one leg. So it is actually a wonderful thing to wobble or fall out of balancing because it means the brain is functioning, as it should. I, for one, am always overjoyed to be reminded that my brain is working! Feel free to laugh, smile and embrace your missteps. Most of all, as you practice yoga, enjoy yourself! Sometimes it is best not to overanalyze everything and just enjoy the ride. Enjoy your newfound energy, strength, and positivity. It is there for all of us. Yoga is the way to access it all!

3
OVERCOMING OBSTACLES

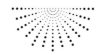

Patience and perseverance have a magical effect before which difficulties disappear and obstacles vanish.

John Quincy Adams

According to a Yoga Alliance/Yoga Journal Survey, in 2016 there were 36.7 million active practitioners of yoga in our population and 83.3 million people that are likely to try yoga. For any of those 83.3 million people, their first experience with yoga must be a positive one for them to return for more. It is somewhat analogous to trying a new restaurant. They have one chance to present you with a tasty meal or else you are never coming back.

This book is a sensible, pragmatic guide to the practice of yoga valuable to both beginners and seasoned practitioners. My intention is not to overwhelm the reader with excessive detail, but to enhance the reader's experience by offering an overall view and appreciation for the many facets of the practice of yoga. In one sense, the word "practice" refers to the active physical and mental application of the precepts and philosophies of yoga. But, it also refers to the act of performing something over and over again in hopes of realizing an ideal or developing mastery. In yoga, one ideal is non-distracted meditative consciousness, which may only be reached by a select few. So when we approach yoga we are always practicing, hoping for at least a partial realization of that ideal.

There are a multitude of reasons for practicing yoga. Since we are all individuals, my goals may be different than yours. According to many ancient yogis like Patanjali, one of the primary aims of yoga is to develop the ability to study a single idea or object without any distraction in order to gain complete clarity. He professed, "*yogash chitta vritti nirodhah*" or "yoga stills the fluctuations of the mind." I possess a more practical view. Simply, the reason I practice yoga is to figure things out and become clear as to how I wish to experience life. I gain awareness of the choice I have as to how I wish to approach my day. I am able to gain control over many things I always thought were out of my control. Your intention for practicing yoga may be very different from mine and may change and evolve over time. The path you take may lead you to profound meaning, even if you can't touch your toes.

So many people reject the idea of practicing yoga. As I alluded to previously, for years I refused to consider yoga because of my inflexibility, both physical and mental. I had tried it on occasion, but I dismissed it because of the muscular discomfort resulting from assuming the postures and my misconception that the end game was to gain enough flexibility to become a human pretzel. It was so very painful for me to stretch my hamstrings. Sitting cross-legged was even worse. Ironically, sitting cross-legged is known in yoga as *sukhasana* or the "easy pose", also known as the "posture of happiness". When I began, neither descriptor was very accurate as far as I was concerned.

One obstacle to developing a regular yoga practice stems from the female gender stereotype of the practitioner of yoga that is so pervasive in our culture. In the same 2016 Yoga Journal/Yoga Alliance report, 72 percent of active yoga practitioners were women. The Yoga Journal is a wonderful magazine with insightful articles, but as you leaf through the pages of any of the issues you will find that a lot of the advertisements are targeted to women, from clothing to feminine hygiene products. Most of the models in photos in the articles and on the covers are women. Yoga is a multibillion dollar business in the United States, including hundreds of millions of dollars spent on advertising. The retail business of yoga, including designer leggings from companies like Lululemon, is flourishing. Yoga as a business can be at odds with yoga as a spiritual practice.

Because of the marketing of yoga in the Western world, many men consider yoga to be a feminine pursuit. Many men would prefer to not think of being the only male in a yoga class surrounded by women in spandex leggings. During conversations about my newfound discovery of the benefits of yoga and my enjoyment of my daily practice, the first question asked by both my mother and many of my friends was, "Are you the only man in the class?" Of course, so many of the great yogis throughout history were men. It may not be the best analogy, but many men possess a misogynistic, gender-biased view that women belong cooking in the kitchen. Yet, a large number of the great chefs throughout the world are men. One of my hopes in writing this book is to bring more men into the world of yoga. If one aspect of being "manly" is having strength, I can assure you that after several weeks of daily practice you will feel stronger, both mentally and physically. Yoga tones the muscles of the body, especially the core. If you are a man worried about being judged as anything less than one, get over it. People will react more positively to your self-confidence and pride resulting from taking steps to improve your physical and mental health and establishing a profound dedication to a receptive attitude. Worrying about what others think of you adds to the negative energy that will interfere with your enjoyment of life. After strengthening my core, toning my muscles and improving my posture, I am overjoyed to enter into a yoga class, or anywhere else for that matter, with my newfound pride in my body and positive outlook on life.

Another obstacle in the pursuit of a yoga practice that many face is a poor self-body image. So many men and women fall prey to the image of the ideal body created by marketing and advertising that permeates all forms of media. From a very early age, girls are exposed to beautiful princesses portrayed in animated films and play with svelte Barbie dolls. Self-consciousness can arise from comparison to others in a class or feeling uncomfortable when compelled to dress in clothes that we have come to perceive as "the uniform" for yoga, namely tight spandex. This self-consciousness can be significantly magnified in a studio or other space that has mirrored walls. Watching oneself perform the postures can give rise to negative self-judgments when one's expression of an *asana* doesn't "match" that of the teacher or other classmates. The first step in overcoming this obstacle is the realization that yoga, as well as life, is one's own personal experience. It is healthier to become a version of yourself, rather than a version of what you perceive others or society wish you to be. Self-worth should not be dependent on the appearance of your body or your ability to perform all of the postures. Wear and do what is most comfortable for you. In class, practice self-kindness before practicing the *asanas*. Be kind to yourself by removing the self-inflicted pressure to perform everything without mistakes or failure. Yoga can be just as meaningful and profound for someone that doesn't do all of the postures "perfectly". Yoga is for everyone regardless of gender or body type or physical limitations. I have the privilege of teaching a blind, physically disabled woman with limited mobility in my chair yoga class. If she is able to connect her breath to her movements, she is "doing" yoga. Yoga is the connection of the movements to the breath to induce feelings of inwardness. A yoga teacher should honor you for who you are. If you feel a teacher isn't letting you be yourself by correcting you or entering into your personal space, find another teacher.

Yoga is meditation, breathing and postures, all done concurrently. The more you practice, the better you will become at integrating all three, not only in a class, but also throughout your entire day. They will become ingrained parts of your psyche that you will be able to access at any time. Through a regular yoga practice you will develop both muscle and cerebral memory that will reflexively trigger a sense of relaxation in times of stress. You might find that upon waking that breathing deeply and stretching elicits positive emotions, as if you just did a several second meditative yoga practice. Without conscious effort, you will deepen your breathing and relax and release tense muscle groups during a hectic day. When we rush through our busy days, often we tend to take shallow breaths. Allowing yourself to pause, take a moment for yourself and take a deep breath will result in a reboot of your day, thereby increasing your attentiveness, productivity and creativity. We strive to practice yoga on and off the mat, applying newfound perspectives to all aspects of our lives. It will be as if you have a sanctuary at your disposal that you may enter at any time when confronted by any external stressors.

As I will discuss in more detail in the chapter regarding the science of yoga, in more scientific terms, the responses of the nervous system to stimuli may be voluntary or involuntary. The involuntary responses are governed by the autonomic nervous system, which has two components, sympathetic and parasympathetic. The sympathetic nervous system elicits the so-called "flight or fight" response that increases the respiratory rate with more shallow breaths, diverts blood to the skeletal muscles and increases perspiration. The parasympathetic system is the "rest and digest" system. It functions in times of safety and low stress as respirations slow and deepen and blood is diverted to our digestive tracts and other maintenance systems. Chronic stress from which many of us suffer throughout our days for a multitude of reasons leaves us in a constant fight or flight response. We take shallow breaths, perspire and experience persistent muscle tension. Our back and neck muscles end up in knots, leading to chronic neck and back pain. A state of unrelenting stress leads to the release of inflammatory molecules, which can cause or worsen disease processes. Progressive stretching of muscles, meditation and the control and deepening of the breath that becomes habitual through a regular yoga practice promotes a shift from chronic sympathetic overload to greater parasympathetic tone. That shift lessens anxiety and stress that can become obstacles to relaxing while practicing yoga. A positive feedback loop is created; with stress reduction comes a sense of wellbeing that increases motivation to dedicate oneself to the practice of yoga.

In your practice you will learn all of the postures or *asanas*. You do not, however, necessarily need to know any of them to begin your practice. Knowledge is accrued over time. It also may be surprising that you will learn to breathe. There are ways to breathe that properly engage your diaphragm, stretch the muscles of your chest and abdomen and facilitate feelings of inwardness and introversion. An awareness of the senses leads to mindfulness. For example, as one breathes, focusing on the sensation and sound of air moving in and out of the mouth or nose, the movements of the ribs or abdomen expanding and collapsing or the image of breath filling your entire body with energy can bring one into the present with a greater appreciation of the moment. The ancient yogis believed that the breath is the portal to the soul. At the very least, becoming in tune with the wave-like sounds and rhythms of the breath will be the first step on the path to relaxation and peace. Learning and becoming comfortable with the *asanas* and *pranayama* can seem overwhelming. The old adage, "patience is a virtue", however, rings true. Ultimately, it is the psychological and physiological benefits of yoga that dissolve the impediments that you may face, whether it be inflexibility, issues with gender stereotypes or a poor body image.

Arguably the greatest obstacle to developing a meaningful yoga practice is the inner critic. It is a part of most of our personalities that if left unchecked can be quite consuming. So, leave it at the door of the studio or toss it out a window. An important tenet of the philosophy of Kripalu yoga is self-observation without judgment. This is easier said than done, but it is one of the prerequisites for learning yoga, without which you will be set up to fail. Our inner critic is the part of the brain that stymies our efforts, minimizes our achievements, compares us to others, beats us up and bruises our self-esteem. Understanding "self-observation without judgment" is paramount to attaining satisfaction and gratification in both yoga and life.

The inner critic develops at a very early age when one has yet to develop the abilities of abstract thought and the differentiation of right from wrong. We do not yet know that our parents might be wrong at times or capable of mistakes. We accept everything they do or say as "right." Anything that sparks the expression of disapproval sparks feelings of "being bad", shame and inadequacy in the young child. Thich Nhat Hanh described this phenomenon as "original fear". At a very young age, it is simply impossible to live up to what we perceive as our parents' ideals. Throughout childhood we will inevitably be confronted with parental disapproval. For some, that happens more often than for others, and perhaps for them, their inner critic represents a much more dominant and negative force later in their lives.

To be successful at yoga, you must silence your inner critic as much as possible. You wouldn't want to be constantly criticized by your significant other, a family member or a friend. You probably wouldn't want to have a relationship with them. If you let your inner critic take over, you won't be able to live with yourself. An important theme of this book is the control of negative self-judgments. Through yoga you can come to a crucial realization that you have control over what you thought you could never control. You have a choice as to how you wish to live, treat your relationships and titrate the balance of positive and negative energy in your life. As a medical doctor, I fully realize that many physical and mental diseases are incurable. I am not one to profess that yoga will necessarily cure you from whatever you suffer. With a meaningful, daily yoga practice, however, it will become evident that you can have some control over what seem like no-win situations, if at the very least through stress reduction.

One problem that can arise is that your inner critic can be fueled by your inability to silence your inner critic. This is a so-called "catch-22". As you try to suppress undesirable, negative self-judgments, you begin to hate yourself for lacking the capacity to do so. In fact, the more you find you can't suppress the mind chatter, the louder the inner critic becomes, possibly so loud as to consume you, lessening the potential for personal growth. The solution is to realize it takes two to wage a war. Stop fighting yourself. Congratulate yourself for taking the first step toward acceptance: awareness. Awareness results in the newfound ability to acknowledge the inner criticisms. When a self-critical thought arises, acknowledge it and then let it go as if you are throwing it into a river, watching it disappear downstream. In fact, you can even go so far as to embrace your inner critic. Love your enemy. The inner critic will attempt to make you feel "bad" for perceived inabilities and convince you that it disqualifies you from being "good" at yoga. It is easier to just say, "Hey, I'm good with that. That's who I am." and maybe try to divert your focus to all that you are capable of. Focus on what you can do and not what you can't. Accept yourself for who you are. Will your inner critic ever leave? Probably not, but without the expenditure of all of the negative energy it takes to wage the war, that inner critic will become more and more quiet with time. With the acceptance that you are enough as you are comes empowerment. You become empowered to make positive choices, choices that ultimately will allow you to embrace all the blessings in your life.

So how does negative self-judgment arise in one's yoga practice? A good example is that of the novice in a yoga class. I was once that novice. I made sure to get to the yoga studio early to get a spot for my mat in the back of the class so no one could watch me. Of course, I was under the misperception that everyone else knew what they were doing and could do all of the postures perfectly. I certainly couldn't. I had a defeatist attitude before I even began. As the class filled up, most people either sat or laid down on their mats and began to meditate. This made me feel even more uncomfortable and inadequate, as I had tried meditation in the past and absolutely hated it because of my inability to control all of the mind chatter. As class began, I concentrated on everyone in the room except myself. I neglected my own experience. Of course, it was necessary for me to observe the teacher to understand the various postures and how to perform them. While I watched the teacher, however, my thoughts of my own inadequacy worsened. Here was this teacher who was so flexible that there seemed to be almost no position she couldn't assume. Faced with physical discomfort and an awareness of my inflexibility, I decided right then and there that there was no way that I would ever come close to performing the postures correctly. I was certain that I would be unsuccessful at yoga. At times, the teacher came over and corrected my position in a particular posture, seemingly more than other students in the class. Of course, it came as no surprise to me at the time that I was in the "wrong" position. What magnified my negative self-judgment even more was comparing myself to other people in the class. I was so self-conscious. At the time, it seemed like they all could "do yoga." They all knew the names of all of the postures. The teacher even used the Sanskrit names at times for some of the *asanas,* and it seemed that everyone else knew them. I spent an entire hour and fifteen minutes comparing myself to everyone and beating myself up for being what I perceived as less than them. It is a miracle that I ever went back to a second class. Fortunately, I soon discovered that there is a lot more to yoga than meets the eye. I didn't know at the time what actually constituted a meaningful yoga practice, and I can assure you, it wasn't being able to touch my toes!

A constant need for some to compare themselves to others is not just particular to novices. Even many seasoned practitioners continue to do it, perhaps comparing their bodies or the performance of a posture relative to others. Our culture loves competition, from sports to reality television shows. We are compelled to compete with others and compete with ourselves, never dismissing a challenge because we can never just be satisfied with the way we are. Then, there is often that one person in a class who un-solicitously and spontaneously pops into an inversion posture, like a headstand. My competitiveness would cause me to say to myself, "Showoff!" Comparison is a cognitive distortion that diverts attention away from self and towards others.

Not infrequently, a yoga teacher will guide the class into a particular *asana*. He or she will then offer modifications. He or she might start you in a table position (on hands and knees). He or she might then instruct you to raise and extend one of your legs back at hip height. The teacher might then say something like, "You can stay here or if you feel you have more space you can raise and extend your opposite arm forward." Then, "If you really want more of a challenge, you can bend your knee and kick your hand into your raised hand." Since, we are comparing ourselves to everyone else and our natural tendency is to feel that we are part of this grand competition, we try to do whatever is the most extreme, difficult modification that the teacher suggests. I subscribed to this philosophy early on until I began to realize that some of these additional modifications were uncomfortable with the potential for injury.

Comparison and feelings of inadequacy can become even worse when you go from a reasonably paced *Hatha* yoga class to a rigorous, fast-paced *vinyasa* flow or power yoga class. The pace of the postures can be so quick that there is little time to breathe between them. A failure to keep up can result in more negative self-judgment. Now, add some heat to the room so everyone is sweating profusely and it might seem to you that yoga is a true competitive sport.

As we fall into the habit of the cognitive distortion of comparison, a lack of flexibility can allow our inner critic to eliminate the possibility for future success at yoga. When I first began, I was dismayed by the sight of fellow classmates sitting cross-legged with absolutely straight spines, while I sat with my knees high in the air with a rounded back and extreme discomfort in my inner thigh muscles. I beat myself up over my inability to sit properly. I was certain that yoga was not for me. I soon learned, however, that to properly sit cross-legged the knees should be below the level of the hips. This could be accomplished, or at least partially accomplished, by sitting on the edge of a bolster, which results in lifting the hips and dropping the knees. That insight allowed me to experience a small bit of progress. My knees were still up in the air, but now I could sit with a straighter spine. Unfortunately, my self-consciousness and competitive mindset got the better of me as I observed that no one else in the class was using a bolster. I felt that others must be watching me and that the bolster was a crutch. Ultimately, more important than the insight into how to straighten my spine was the realization that the only person watching me that mattered was myself.

Other cognitive distortions other than comparison to others can obstruct the path towards personal growth, clarity and development of a meaningful yoga practice. Cognitive distortions are misinterpretations of reality and patterns of negative thoughts that don't serve us, often leading to anxiety and stress.

Common cognitive distortions that can be obstacles to developing a yoga practice, or leading to abandoning any future attempts at yoga include:

Filtering: Magnifying all negative aspects of a situation while filtering out all positive ones. "I can't deal with my extreme ineptitude in attempting to assume the postures." "I look like a total fool!"

Polarized thinking: Everything is either black or white. There is no middle ground. "I am a failure!" "I will never be perfect like the teacher."

Mind Reading: Presuming to know what others are thinking. "The other people in the class are watching me and thinking I am inept." "They all can see that I don't have a clue as to what I am doing."

Substitution of positive affirmations, emotions or behaviors for those automatic negative thoughts can result in significant stress reduction. Thoughts of gratitude and appreciation might substitute for negative self-judgments. Once those feelings become habitual you are on the road to some peace of mind, increased self-esteem, and self-satisfaction. Of course, this is all easier said than done since our reflexive negative thoughts and behaviors are so ingrained and have been reinforced over many years. Similar to becoming more flexible both mentally and physically through yoga, a change in mindset occurs gradually and requires patience. Small "baby steps" can promote feelings of accomplishment that fuel a positive outlook.

Finally, with regard to challenges that need to be overcome to develop a regular yoga practice, we get to those who can't touch their toes. The misperception that yoga requires physical flexibility is an obstacle for those that aren't. Inflexibility can be acquired or inherited. We are all born with a certain range of motion in all of our joints that differs from person to person. The shape of men and women's pelvises differ. It may be that flexibility will be limited by the innate, restrictive, anatomical relationships in the body, preventing one from assuming certain positions, even after years of yogic practice. Due to inherited inflexibilities, I doubt that my knees will ever touch the ground in *supta baddha konasana* or reclining bound angle pose. This *asana* consists of lying supine with the soles of feet touching. As one lets their knees drop out laterally toward the floor, the groin spreads open and the hip adductor or inner thigh muscles are stretched. Can I still enjoy the stretch in my adductor muscles that this posture affords me? Absolutely! Should I lament my limitation as an obstacle to developing a meaningful yoga practice? Absolutely not! My self-observation without judgment consists of eliminating the word "and". Instead of, "My knees will never touch the ground and I will never be fully able to do this posture", I choose to alternatively say to myself, "My knees don't touch the ground." Or if I choose to use the word "and", "My knees don't touch the ground and I am enjoying breathing into the stretch in my inner thigh muscles". I accept that I don't possess the range of motion in my hip joints for my knees to drop all the way down to the mat. It is who I am. I inherited this particular trait just as I have dark brown hair. Fortunately, the word "modification" exists. Any yoga pose can be modified to suit the particular individual's physical situation. A modification is changing the expression of an *asana* to decrease discomfort or muscle strain. Modifying a pose can clear thoughts of discomfort that can cloud the mind. Of course, some of my hip adductor inflexibility has been acquired over many years of sitting in a chair throughout my career. I am overjoyed to say that I have made a little progress in increasing my range of motion. Possibly, over time I will realize more flexibility, but I must be patient and realistic at the same time. Awareness and acceptance are key. One should also realize that modifications are not challenges. Many of us adopt the attitude that modifying an *asana* is a failure to assume that posture due to the self-competitiveness that many of us possess and the need to compare ourselves to others. A modification is merely an option to express a posture in a way that decreases discomfort, possibly averting injury, and enhances one's experience.

The next question becomes how to deal with the discomfort that arises from stretching tight muscles, ligaments, tendons and fascia across relatively inflexible joints. I, for one, experienced extreme discomfort in the tendons of my hamstrings about my knee when I bent over and folded forward. Once again, the concept of "modification" comes into play. I learned that by putting a greater bend in my knees as I fold forward, the stretch moved from the tendons about my knee up into my hamstring muscle bellies in my thighs. Insights into the many modifications that exist to minimize discomfort and pain began my own self-exploration into what was best for my body, both physically and mentally. By simply listening to my body, I was able to turn discomfort into a wonderful stretch. Always listen to the body. It is always trying to tell us things. Let your brain hear everything it has to say.

Every *asana* requires the contraction of muscles, the stretching of tendons and ligaments, the tension and weight on joints and the opposing resistance resulting from the inelastic fascia or connective tissue that surrounds all of those structures. Pain receptors exist throughout all of the tissues of our musculoskeletal system. Over-engaging a muscle belly results in micro-tears involving individual bundles of muscle fibers, which cause pain. Over-stretching of tendons and ligaments also activates pain receptors. The body's complex network of neurons and centers in the brain devoted to the experience of pain, all mediated by neurotransmitters, is an exquisite warning system that alerts us to stop doing whatever it is that is triggering the alarm. Not heeding the warnings results in serious injury. Frank muscle tears, tendonitis and ligament and joint strains all result from ignoring the body's warnings. Evolutionarily through natural selection, the ability to experience pain decreased potential for injury and promoted survival of our prehistoric ancestors. Unfortunately, the irrationality of the ego can often supersede rational thinking. Not accepting the reality that inflexibility, either inherent or acquired, prevents oneself from assuming a posture like one's super-flexible classmate (whom you shouldn't be looking at in the first place) and neglecting the body's pain messages can lead to injury.

The flexibility that results from a yoga practice develops very gradually over time and requires patience. Patience is a virtue to which we all must aspire. What's the rush? It always seems we're rushing somewhere. Some feel that the most effective way to promote an increase in flexibility is to practice near the edge. The "edge" is the point where the stretch of a muscle becomes uncomfortable. Beyond that edge, discomfort turns into pain. The best way to approach the concept of practicing on the edge is to find it and then ease off just a little bit from it. The goal of yoga of finding clarity can be thwarted by thoughts of discomfort flooding the mind. The best way to find your edge for a particular *asana* is to enter the posture incrementally. Initially, ease into the *asana* possibly one quarter of the way from your edge, then halfway, and then three quarters, making sure to breathe into each increment. Finally, stretch and engage the muscles to the point of discomfort, beyond which would be frank pain. Then ease off just enough to enjoy the stretch. With time, your edge will begin to advance as you achieve greater flexibility. Once again, it takes time and patience. Muscles and, even more so, tendons, ligaments and fascia stretch slowly and incrementally. Gaining awareness of that progress initiates a cycle of positive reinforcement. Feelings of accomplishment and pride lead to positive energy and the desire for more.

Arguably, more important than increasing range of motion in the physical body is the development of flexibility of the mind. We are so often set in our ways with fixed beliefs that have solidified over many years. Yoga affords time for self-reflection and analysis of one's belief system. Personal growth comes from becoming receptive to new ideas and possibilities and welcoming different perspectives.

Of course, teachers are always important for learning the *asanas* and *pranayama*. Remember however, a teacher is only a guide. Never feel compelled to do exactly what the teacher is doing, but rather initiate the movements that your body is calling for. You are not taking a math test, which you must pass or achieve a high grade on. And the teacher should not be your proctor, assuring that everyone is obeying all the rules. Don't be a version of yourself that you feel someone else wants you to be, including the teacher. Be true to your authentic self with your own expression of movement and the emotions that arise from that movement. Ultimately, it is your efforts and discipline that lead to your success. The payoff for dedication to practice is a new clarity in all aspects of your life. You will better see your life with a new, exciting perspective with extreme gratitude for all of its blessings. Yoga becomes one of your blessings, and as such, it is important at the beginning and end of every practice to acknowledge your light and spirit that brought you to that moment. Cherish that moment. Allow yourself to soar. Enjoy yoga as it becomes your new way of life.

4
A LITTLE BACKGROUND

I am not what happened to me, I am what I choose to become.

Carl Jung

I believe learning becomes more meaningful when a student gains insight into their teacher's background and perspectives on life. A didactic lecture on any subject is transformed into a much more powerful discussion in the context of the teacher's life experiences. I can describe my passion and love for yoga, but it is much more impactful if you know how and why my passion developed. I have been on a transformative journey, both from physical and spiritual perspectives. I have made gains in flexibility and strength and have found clarity of mind. My hope is that my story will resonate and motivate you to strive for personal growth through your yoga practice.

I was born and raised on Long Island in New York. There has always been a nature-nurture debate regarding personality development. Suffice it to say, unfortunately I was an anxious, sometimes depressed boy with many psychosomatic symptoms, including disturbing muscle tension, all of which persisted into adulthood. I also possessed a fear of making mistakes, which served as a major motivator in my life. With an inability to tolerate failure, I was always at the top of my class in public school, went through undergraduate college with a 4.0 GPA, was inducted into Phi Beta Kappa and Alpha Omega Alpha, the medical honor society, became chief resident during my radiology residency and chief of the department of radiology at the local hospital.

As someone with a fear of making mistakes, ironically I became a radiologist. This is ironic because there is zero tolerance for error in the practice of radiology. One mistake could harm or even kill a patient. Radiology is the only field of medicine where everything is documented in pictures. There is always proof of a missed diagnosis. An arguably rational fear of making mistakes superimposed on a long-seated irrational fear of failure is not a healthy combination.

I don't wish, however, to lament my past. The aforementioned is simply a lead-in to how I developed the unfortunate inability to touch my toes. Quite simply, I sat in a chair with terrible posture for thirty years, fifty hours a week, slouching and hunched over a computer screen. As I alluded to previously, I suffered from chronic anxiety and depression. As I held my stress in my muscles, my muscles were often in constant states of contraction, my tendons became taut, ligaments constricted and my joints gradually froze. The range of motion in all of my joints became compromised. Working in a seated slouch translated into terrible posture with my head tilted forward, chin down, neck bowed, shoulders scrunched and chest closed. My posture placed undue stress on my back. I didn't think much about the inflexibility. It was just a part of life. I didn't have an expectation of it ever improving. After thirty stressful years, my hands could only reach down to my knees when I attempted to touch my toes.

After experiencing professional burnout, as many physicians do, I went to practice radiology part time. Then at the age of twenty-one, my son Aaron decided to run for state representative from our district. I became his campaign manager and treasurer. Together, we created a campaign with little knowledge of politics and with little help. We designed our own website, door hangers and lawn signs. We analyzed voting data to target our door knocking. We were faced with a challenger in the Democratic primary who was a fifty-seven year old lawyer and president of the school committee. Two hard-working and determined people knocked on over fifteen thousand doors. We went back to neighborhoods three times over in hopes of talking to voters that weren't home the first or second time we were there. We knocked on doors in the rain and during an oppressive heat wave. To everyone's shock, including our opponent's, Aaron won the primary election by twenty-two percentage points. Totally expecting victory, our opponent even went so far as to cater her own victory party at a local restaurant. We worked until the polls closed at 8 PM on election day. Our victory party wasn't catered. It consisted of eating Domino's Pizza and Cheesy Bread in our pajamas. Unfortunately, our district has turned red over the last few years, and along with the support of our popular Republican governor, our opponent beat us in the general election by ten percentage points.

The election was a liberating experience for me. It got me talking to people and out of the darkness and isolation inherent to the practice of radiology. Two months before the election, I realized that one is only given one try at life. I decided that it was time to take a risk and step into the unknown, not knowing in what direction life would now take me. Deprived of the opportunity when I was young, I decided it was time for self-exploration in the hopes of finding a passion. At the age of fifty-eight, I finally retired officially from the practice of diagnostic radiology.

Following the election, I was left with a lot of time on my hands. I honestly had difficulty occupying all of my newly found free time. I remained at this impasse for a couple of months. One day, I decided to attend a gentle yoga class at a local yoga studio. I had done yoga sporadically in the past, but as I discussed in the previous chapters, too many obstacles prevented me from developing a sustainable practice. Without a stressful job hanging over my head, I was able to relax somewhat during the class, although I was fraught with negative self-judgments and insecurity stemming from worries about my performance. Remember, honoring my mistakes was not a part of my toolbox. But my teacher was caring and compassionate. I appreciated her slow pace and her attempts to create a gentle, meditative experience. I decided to go to another class later that week, feeling more relaxed than during the one prior. My daughter Emily, who was already into yoga, also recommended a website, doyogawithme.com. She said that it was wonderful for beginners, filled with many basic and introductory tutorials. For me, practicing yoga with online tutorials proved to be a better way to learn yoga. I was in the safety of my home without any opportunity to compare myself to other students and without the uncomfortable sense that someone was watching me and scrutinizing my performance of the postures. In addition, the teachers on the video were much more explicit in their explanations of the different *asanas* relative to the teachers at the studio where it seemed a greater familiarity with the postures was assumed. The website also included a thirty day challenge for both intermediate and beginning students. It was a wonderful way to build my confidence.

I decided to attempt the thirty day challenge, of course for beginners. Suddenly I was practicing yoga from twenty to sixty minutes a day. At first it was uncomfortable. I wasn't able to do many of the postures. At times, I even fell over. At times, I cursed out the online instructor. It didn't matter because I was alone in my house. I eliminated the possibility of any self-judgments stemming from comparison to other students. The tutorials on the website were also wonderful from the standpoint that if I didn't understand something, I could "rewind" the video to hear it once again.

Soon, I developed curiosity as to what yoga was all about. The practice of yoga is one that is thousands of years old. I thought that there must be more to it than just its physical aspects. So, I began to read about yogic philosophy. The first book I read was *The Heart of Yoga: Developing a Personal Practice* by T. K. V. Desikachar. Desikachar was the son of Tirumalai Krishnamacharya, who is often referred to as "the father of modern yoga," and is credited with the revival of Hatha yoga. In his book, Desikachar professed the practice of *viniyoga,* an approach to utilizing the tools of yoga to individualize the practice to fit the needs of each practitioner. It takes into consideration both the student's physical and mental condition and limitations. The idea of *viniyoga* appealed greatly to me since I was becoming well aware of all of my own physical and mental limitations with regard to practicing yoga. I then went on to read the *Yoga Sutras of Patanjali. Sutra* literally means "string" or "thread". The work consists of 196 aphorisms on the philosophy and practice of yoga. It is considered the foundation of all classical yoga that followed. I then read Mahatma Gandhi's translation of the *Bhagavad Gita,* an ancient Hindu scripture examining the concept of nonattachment, eliminating any desires for possessing things or concern about outcomes. I also read several books by modern yogis.

My readings began to open my eyes to the profound meaning of yoga. I found that many of the precepts from the ancient Hindu scriptures continue to be applicable to modern day life. The explanations of many important yogic principles piqued my interest. One that was particularly enlightening was written by Desikachar. To paraphrase, he advanced the idea that the most important yoga practice is one where you balance mind and body, not one where you can do all of the *asanas* perfectly. A tremendous weight, the pressure to perform, was lifted and my predisposition to negative self-judgments lessened. I came to realize that I might achieve a more meaningful practice by becoming aware of and accepting my own limitations, both in yoga and life. My need to compare my performance to others lessened as I became more aware of my own experience.

Another impactful book that afforded me a new and healthy perspective was Richard Fauld's *Kripalu Yoga: A Guide to Practice On and Off the Mat.* His writings exposed me to the philosophy of the Kripalu tradition. I will discuss this philosophy in greater detail in a later chapter. For now, I will just say that it's tenets and precepts became, and still are, those that guide me through my daily practice and classes. They have reinforced the concept that yoga can be a way of life. Kripalu Yoga is about making yoga your own individual experience and self-expression, while practicing self-observation without judgment. I often say at the beginning of every class that I firmly believe that the only right way to do yoga is to make it your own experience. You are here for yourself.

I had also read about epiphanies and periods of clarity occurring during a yoga practice. I was skeptical of the existence of such "yoga experiences", but after about six weeks of daily practice, I began to develop some clarity as to how I wished to live each day. Although I remained somewhat mired in old habitual ways of thinking, I started to control the cacophony of negative thoughts in my head that prevented me from thinking about what was important in my life. I found myself more and more in the moment. I thought less about regrets of the past and worries about the future. With the lessening of the mind chatter, I could now enjoy my newfound ability to evaluate my life, including my desires, needs and goals. I realized that I no longer needed to be a version of myself that I thought others wanted me to be. I realized I had control over how I wished to spend my day, making a choice between a day filled with negativity or one full of positive energy. It was a very liberating experience that filled me with joy. I accepted that there would be days where I reverted back to anxiety and negativity, but those days became less frequent. Most importantly, my yoga practice afforded me a daily opportunity to acknowledge all of the blessings in my life. To this very day, it is gratitude that fills my heart. I pause during every class I teach or attend to experience that gratitude. I believe that gratitude is a prerequisite for all of the other positive emotions we experience. Your brain listens to everything you say. Positive affirmations become habitual after a while, replacing automatic and reflexive negative thoughts and behaviors.

With some of my self-judgments gone, my experience in classes changed for the better. I was not only less concerned about what others might think, but less aware of those around me. I got to a point where after a class I could not tell you anything about any of my fellow classmates. Oblivious is not a good word. I prefer to think that I was in my own zone, a place of serenity I could now access. I had opened the door to a whole new world. I also started to gravitate toward classes taught by more spiritual teachers. I wanted more than just a flow through the physical postures. I had a thirst for profundity and meaning. I wanted a slow-paced class that afforded me time to think, connect with my breath and experience introversion.

Four months after embarking on my regular, daily yoga practice, the stars began to align. One day in July of 2017, my wife Lauren told me about a fascinating podcast of an NPR program devoted to an organization called Encore.org. Part of their mission is to promote second careers for people in midlife that foster personal growth, while at the same time having social impact and a benefit to society. The podcast included an interview with a gentleman who spent thirty years in broadcasting. He always had an interest in ecology and conservation. He retired from his first career and went on to become a park ranger at Yellowstone National Park, living his dream. After listening to the podcast and reading information on the Encore.org website, it made sense that if I found my next career, similar to my first, it would be most meaningful for me if I could help others.

Later that day, a program catalog came in the mail from Kripalu Center for Yoga and Health in the Berkshires of Massachusetts. I had been to Kripalu a few times over the years, which was my initial exposure to yoga. Typically, since I know I can always access websites for information about organizations and their programming, I throw catalogs into the recycle pile. If it were up to me, I would make the world paperless. For whatever reason, however, I flipped the Kripalu catalog open on the kitchen table. It opened to the page devoted to the Kripalu Schools of Yoga. It was there and then that the crazy idea popped into my head; that this person who could not touch his toes could become a yoga instructor. I quickly became excited about this new possibility. As a yoga instructor, I would be in a position to help people while using my medical background and extensive knowledge of human anatomy. I also had the hope that the intensive instruction I would receive would deepen my own practice.

The very next day, I was walking my yellow lab, Bella, around a nearby pond when I bumped into Laura, as I often did. She is a friend of mine I know from the local concert band in which we both played. Our conversations were always about the band. This time the topic of yoga came up. Unbeknownst to me, Laura had trained as a yoga instructor at Kripalu. She enthusiastically assured me that the programs there were truly transformational.

Forest Gump is one of my favorite movies. The film is a masterpiece. Its genius lay in the sagacity of the main character disguised in the form of an intellectually challenged man. In an emotional moment towards the end of the movie and after a multitude of unique life experiences, he remarks, "I don't know if we each have a destiny, or if we're all just floating around accidental-like on a breeze. But I think maybe it's both." In yogic philosophy, the term *dharma* has multiple meanings. On a personal level, it can mean one's life purpose; what one is destined to do. Regardless of whether or not fate governs our lives, after only four months of a regular yoga practice I was determined to make into a reality this crazy idea of transforming from an inflexible, stressed-out radiologist to a relaxed yoga instructor.

As I aligned with the principles of the Kripalu philosophy from my readings, I knew the only place to learn was at Kripalu. From past visits there, I also knew of its idyllic setting and wonderful, healthy food. It was time to embark on my next career. In my prior career in medicine every step in my training was very structured and predetermined, from college all the way through my residency and fellowship. My journey to become a doctor was on a single, straight track. I decided this time I would let things simply evolve, taking one step at a time without attachment to any goals or expectations. I would enjoy every moment in the moment and just let things unfold. I submitted my application to the Kripalu School of Yoga and several weeks later I was accepted. In disbelief I realized that this crazy idea was going to soon become a reality.

I was accepted in July for a four-week, two hundred hour program that was divided into two two-week block periods. The first block started in the last week of November and the second, the third week in January, with a six-week recess between. I ramped up my efforts to gain as much flexibility as possible before my formal education began. I became like an athlete training for a big game. My expectation was that I would be in a class of hyper-mobile young women. I felt compelled to be ready. Of course, that attitude reflected a competitiveness and an attachment to future success or failure that I had always possessed, antithetical to what I was hoping to accomplish. It is difficult to break old habits that after so many years became part of the fabric of one's being.

After the long wait, I finally embarked on my journey into the beautiful hills of the Berkshires and the start of my new career. I arrived at Kripalu with both trepidation and enthusiasm. My expectation that my class would be composed of very flexible young women proved to be a false one. Although I was only one of three men in a class of thirty-two students, my classmates ranged in age from twenty-three to sixty-six years old. Many suffered from chronic conditions, including back pain, carpal tunnel syndrome and rotator cuff pathology. Although I had read that a meaningful practice did not require one to do all of the *asanas* perfectly, it was still a relief to no longer feel the pressure to perform or keep up with the other students. Once again, old habits are hard to break.

I will not describe the program in detail. It was, however, a transformational and emotional experience. I knew in advance that the curriculum would include lectures on yogic philosophy, anatomy and learning the ground up cues for the teaching of twenty-one *asanas*. The program was quite physically demanding. I participated in a minimum of three hours of yoga a day and sometimes as much as seven. Fortunately, I brought a physical therapy massage stick with me to iron out my tired and cramping muscles. My two teachers and five assistant teachers practiced love and compassion. They were nurturing, nonjudgmental and honored every question or idea expressed by any student.

The emotional climax of my entire experience occurred one week before graduation during a two day period of silence and meditation. I thought that intentional silence would worsen my mind chatter, but I found it afforded me the time to connect with my thoughts and feelings and undergo self-analysis. Before breaking our silence, the class participated in a Tantric ceremony. Although images of unbridled sexual activities are often conjured up when Tantric yoga is mentioned, it is actually an ancient yogic philosophy with rituals aimed at eliminating material and behavioral attachments. During our ceremony we tried to assuage our fears and doubts about becoming a successful yoga instructor. Subsequently, we were urged to take a thirty-minute walk through nature. The grounds at Kripalu are peaceful, serene and inspiring. There is a great lawn surrounded by woods throughout which are hiking trails that eventually lead down to a mountain lake. Our teachers told us to have no expectations on our hike. We were to see what might speak to us, and be fine if it was just a quiet stroll with no emotional impact.

I chose a fairly secluded trail that followed along a mountain stream. The slowly flowing water created a calming, bubbling sound as it washed over rocks and pebbles in the riverbed. As I walked, I began to reflect on my life, full of regrets, and the pain of past traumas. As I realized that I never knew my true authentic self, but instead lived a version of whom I thought others wanted me to be, I began to cry uncontrollably. The stress that I held in my physical body for all of those years seemed to release all at once with an emotional explosion. Through my tears, I noticed a beautiful silver and gold colored granite stone at a bend in the stream. I straddled the stream with one foot on each bank to reach the stone. I almost fell in the water, but my newfound flexibility allowed me to bend over just enough to grab it. As I held the stone in my hand, I felt a surge of energy fill my body and mind. I was at a turning point. As I walked on with both hands holding the stone, any regrets of the past were replaced with hopes for the future. Joy and love filled my soul. Most importantly, I experienced extreme gratitude, as all of the blessings of my life became clear images in my mind. I felt one with nature as it's beautiful shapes and colors became vividly sharp and crisp.

As I exited the woods, I began to climb up the great lawn towards the yoga center. I noticed my shoelace untied as I neared the top of the hill. I bent down on one knee to tie it. As I continued on my walk back, I realized that I no longer had my special stone. I went into a panic. Doubts arose as to whether my newfound positive outlook would be sustainable. The stone was a true symbol of my new life. Without it, I suddenly felt lost. I searched through the tall grass. I retraced my steps over and over. Then, as a Buddhist prayer bell sounded as a signal for us to return, all hope faded. I retraced my steps just one last time and there buried in the tall grass was my stone, the symbol of my personal transformation. As I reached the top of the hill, I broke my silence and let out a loud victory scream. I now knew where and whom I was supposed to be.

On February 2, 2018, I graduated as a certified Kripalu Yoga Teacher. I could now put the initials, K.Y.T. after my M.D at the end of my name. As I left Kripalu, I knew that I had so much more work to do. I needed teaching experience. My program gave me my training wheels. I now had to go and learn to balance on my own. But now, I possessed the tools to begin to realize my ultimate goal of helping others through yoga, as is the intention of this book. Yoga was quickly becoming a way of life. I was now on that wonderful path.

5
A SMALL TASTE OF THE PRACTICE OF YOGA

It is not the mountain we conquer but ourselves.

Sir Edmund Hillary

Before delving any further into the complexities and philosophies of yoga, it might be a good time to try an *asana* and give you a feel for yoga. Hopefully, this exercise will whet your appetite for more. If you already possess familiarity with the posture, possibly this discussion will offer you a different perspective. In order to best focus on this exercise, I would suggest that you find a peaceful and quiet place where you can minimize any distractions. Be sure to be barefoot on either a yoga mat or a hard, firm floor. Yoga is best done barefoot both to prevent slippage and to better and directly feel the bottoms of the feet grounding on the earth. Your feet are just like your hands. They are meant for gripping and exploring the world through the sensation of touch. Just as you wouldn't do yoga with gloves on, take your socks off. Using the five senses and focusing on those sensations can help you to be in the moment and gain feelings of introversion.

The *asana* that we will practice is *tadasana* or the mountain pose. The mountain pose is the foundation for all of the standing postures. It promotes good posture through the elongation of the spine and engagement of the muscles of the core. At the same time, we experience a strong sense of the ground, connecting us with the supportive, firm earth below. It is a posture full of positive energy that boosts self-esteem as we stand strong and tall. *Tadasana* is a posture to honor the spine. As the main energy centers and pathways are thought to be intimately associated with the spine, it is an important spiritual symbol in yoga.

From a health and wellness perspective, strengthening the spine is paramount as we age. There are deep paraspinous muscles that run the length of the spine. Picture those muscles as silly putty stuck to the posterior or back of the vertebrae. As those muscles contract, they pull the vertebrae back, bringing us upright. As we age those muscles lose tone and muscle mass and we lose that posterior pull. Consequently, the spinal column begins to round forward. Unfortunately, in extreme cases, many people are left kyphotic or chronically bent over.

Before assuming the *asana*, let's consider what a mountain might represent. It certainly is a symbol of strength. It has a large base that grounds it to the earth, and its peak majestically reaches toward the heavens. It might also represent a daunting challenge for those who wish to scale it. To face that challenge we must be deliberate and disciplined as we climb. As we start our journey, the sheer height prevents us from seeing the summit. We must have faith that our goal is attainable even though it is not visible or fully known to us. Along our climb, we will tire and may not want to continue, but as we rest we remind ourselves of our goal of reaching that summit, and then we resume our quest. What new knowledge will we acquire and what emotions will we feel when we attain our goal? As we get closer to the very top of the mountain, our climb becomes more arduous. It is at this point that we must dig deep within to access more energy. The energy we need is what in yogic philosophy is known as *prana*. *Prana* is the life force. We must bring *prana* into our bodies and minds. *Prana* is all around us, but we must internalize it to come to know contentment and peace. Our source of *prana* is the breath. With each step up the slope, we concentrate more and more on the breath. We listen to its sound and feel the sensation of the breath entering and exiting the nose. We become aware of the rhythmic expansion of the chest, as the intercostal muscles between our ribs stretch and relax. Life-giving oxygen fuels our muscles. Heightening our focus on what is happening in the body helps us to enjoy the moment, not regretting any previous missteps along our journey or worrying about what lies ahead.

When we finally accomplish our goal, we can thoroughly enjoy our experience at the top of that strong, towering mountain. From the summit, we obtain a different perspective of the world around us. We can gain clarity as to our true selves, our vision no longer blocked by the trees or rocks that once lined our path. We are closer to the stars scattered across the infinite universe. We realize that we are part of that same complex universe. Problems that seemed so monumental now look so very small from up on high. We salute both the light of the nurturing sun and our own light that has been fueled by our new abundance of all-important *prana* and ignited by our profound intention.

With deliberate analysis, our own profound meaning and symbolism for each of the *asanas* can be discovered. After consideration of the meanings of *tadasana,* we can now layer on the physical aspects of the posture. All *asanas* are built from the ground up. We must first root ourselves into the earth. Having a stable base leads to better balance and more effective engagement of the muscles of the body. Of course, for a standing posture, our base is our feet. So begin by placing the feet parallel and hip distance apart or approximately six to eight inches apart. As you stand, feel your weight evenly distributed on all parts of the feet, from the toes to the balls to the heels. Your feet, the mat and the earth are now all in continuity, becoming one.

Next, engage the muscles of your legs. Imagine that you are pushing your feet into the earth. Contract your leg muscles as if you are holding a block between your thighs. Engaging your thigh muscles, specifically your quadriceps muscles, will cause your kneecaps to rise up. The quadriceps muscles might feel as if they are wrapping around your femurs, the long thighbones. The legs are now both like strong trees with the feet becoming like roots extending into the earth.

The pelvis is next on our ascent up our mountain. Consider the pelvis as a large bowl that anatomically angles downward from the sacroiliac joints in the back to the pubis in the front. Imagine that there is water filling the bowl of the pelvis. In order to prevent the water from spilling out over the front edge, it is necessary to drop the tailbone and raise the pubic bone; the bone is located about six inches below the navel. We don't want any waterfalls on our mountain. By dropping the tailbone, the normal curve or lordosis of the lumbosacral spine lessens, resulting in a more straight and longer lower spine.

With regard to the entire spine, the spinal column is anatomically composed of five components: cervical, thoracic, lumbar, and sacral spines and the coccyx. There are seven cervical, twelve thoracic, five lumbar and five sacral vertebrae. The coccyx, usually composed of four segments at the very bottom of the spine, is the vestige of our tail that disappeared some time in evolution. The vertebrae of the sacrum are fused to add stability to the pelvis, but the other vertebrae more superiorly are capable of independent, although somewhat limited movements. Each vertebra articulates with other vertebrae, one below and one above, through the facet joints. The facet joints are located behind the spinal canal, the space in which lies the spinal cord. The facet joints are synovial joints that allow for movement of the spine in six directions; forward, back, laterally to the right and left and twisting to the right and left. Keep these six movements in mind, as we will later discuss how they are incorporated into almost all yoga postures. Again, one goal of our practice is to honor the spine both spiritually and physically. In front of the spinal canal, the round bony bodies of the vertebrae are separated from their neighbors by the intervertebral discs. The disc functions as a cushion to axial compressive forces on the spine. The intervertebral disc has a cushioning, gelatinous substance centrally, the nucleus pulposis, surrounded by supportive, stronger and less pliant tissue, the annulus fibrosus. Think of the intervertebral discs as shock absorbers between the vertebral bodies. Our spines are also not straight vertical structures. They have curves or lordoses. In the laws of physics, a curved or arched structure can offer more resistance to axial loading forces relative to a straight one. The cervical lordosis is convex anteriorly or toward the front of our bodies, the thoracic lordosis convex posteriorly or toward the back, and the lumbar and sacral lordosis convex anteriorly. Since the sacral vertebrae are fused, we cannot alter the sacral lordosis. We can only vary the angulation of it in relation to the lumbar spine above and the pelvic bones below.

The goal in maximizing length in the spine is the decompression or stretching of the intervertebral discs and the distraction or opening up of the facet joints, both of which result in the elongation of the spine.

The elongation then partially straightens the different segmental lordoses. The end result is a person standing straight and tall.

Let the arms be at your sides for now. In *tadasana,* although we try to emulate that strong mountain, the shoulders remain soft. If the shoulders move up towards the ears, the neck muscles contract and shorten the cervical spine. First, try scrunching your shoulders up to your ears. Notice your neck muscles engaging. Now release the shoulders and let the shoulder blades melt down your back. As they do, notice how much the neck and cervical spine can lengthen in the opposite direction. The other secondary effect of letting the shoulders drop down the back is a movement of the sternum or breastbone up and forward, as if you are about to salute the general. With dropped shoulders, fingertips can be pulled away from the body in order to engage the arm muscles, further adding to the strength of our mountain. The final step is to subtly drop the chin towards the chest.

To summarize the position of the body in *tadasana*:

1. The feet, parallel and at hip distance apart, are grounded on the mat with the body's weight evenly distributed on all parts of the feet.
2. The leg muscles are engaged, especially the quadriceps, wrapping around the femur and drawing the kneecaps up.
3. The pelvis is leveled by dropping the tailbone and raising the pubic bones.
4. The shoulders are soft and shoulder blades down the back causing the sternum to move forward and up and the neck to elongate.
5. The spine is elongated from the sacrum to cervical spine

> with one long line of energy extending from the feet to the crown of head. Imagine that there is a string attached to the crown of head, pulling it up toward the sky.

Congratulations! You are now standing strong and tall like a mighty mountain! The arms can now be positioned anyway that is meaningful to you or just feels good. Wherever they might be positioned, the arm muscles, however, should be engaged, with an attempt to drop the shoulders at the same time. Simultaneously contracting the muscles of the upper and lower extremities secondarily activates the muscles of the core. Except for the relaxation of the shoulders and the facial muscles, the entire body is active and working. The arms can be angled down at the sides, palms facing forward, and fingers spread wide, as if one is welcoming the life force of *prana* into their bodies. Spreading the fingers wide engages the forearm muscles. When I teach a class, I often instruct students to raise their arms above their heads and imagine that they are holding a big beach ball. This prevents the arms from coming close to the ears, scrunching up of the shoulders, activating the neck muscles and lessening the elongation of the cervical spine. Alternatively, the hands might come together at heart center in *anjali mudra* as you take a moment to create an image in the mind of someone for whom you are grateful. All that remains for the full expression of the *asana* is to breathe deeply into the stretch of the body. One might imagine a long line of positive energy coursing from the earth, up both legs and the spine and shooting into the heavens above through the crown of the head.

There is much meaning to be found in all of the *asanas.* Tools to make yoga your own expression and experience are components of the practice of *viniyoga,* allowing for introspection and finding individual, profound meaning in each *asana*. Common to all of the *asanas* is that they all arise from the ground up, involve engagement and release of muscle groups particular to that posture, and result in balance; the balance of the body relative to the force of gravity and the balance of the body relative to the forces of the mind. It is in the latter that lies the power of yoga.

PART II

6

THE PHILOSOPHY OF YOGA

Knowledge is a treasure, but practice is the key to it.

Lao Tzu

The word philosophy comes from the ancient Greek word *philosophia,* which translates to the "love of wisdom". An understanding of the wisdom of the teachings of the ancient yogis can add meaning to one's practice. The realization that yoga is not just a physical practice comes from an exploration of its philosophies. Applying yogic philosophical principles to present, everyday life can be challenging. Western society has created a system of morality built upon accepted Judeo-Christian beliefs and ideas that connect us to our community and society. One need not be a theist to participate in that system. Similarly, one need not ascribe to the more religious aspects of

Hinduism to embrace its ideals and perspectives on life. Many of the ancient yogic constructs are applicable to our modern system of morality. Similar to Judeo-Christian principles, yogic philosophical concepts can also promote a more ethical and meaningful life. In addition, as might be expected from the intermingling of cultures and dissemination of rituals and religious practices through the migrations of people and diasporas, there is some overlap amongst religions.

I believe that developing a new mindset is a prerequisite for personal transformation and growth through yoga. To embrace yoga on and off the mat, it is necessary to balance mind and body and not just rely on its physical benefits. Contained in the ancient Hindu scriptures and teachings of the various yogic traditions are ideas that can lead to the discovery of novel ways of thinking in the context of one's pre-existing habitual thoughts and behaviors. A complete, comprehensive discussion of this complex subject, however, is beyond the scope of this book. Words and meanings of terms have evolved through the ages. Stark differences and more subtle nuances exist between different philosophies and yogic traditions. My intention is to distill down centuries of yogic thought into a concise overview to deepen and expand the meaning of your practice. Yoga can be both a spiritual and intellectual pursuit and, in light of its existence for centuries, one that can also be both humbling and awe-inspiring.

This present discussion will also serve as background for the next chapter devoted to the philosophy of Kripalu yoga, which has guided my personal journey. Its tenets promote the idea of *viniyoga;* a practice of self-kindness and compassion in the pursuit of one's own meaningful experience.

The Sanskrit word *veda* translates to "wisdom" or "knowledge". The four *Vedas* are ancient Hindu scriptures that are believed to date back to 1700 BCE, representing some of the oldest books ever written. Yoga, however, predates the written word, arising on the Indian subcontinent as religious practices and rituals performed by nomadic tribes, preserved and handed down orally through the ages. The *Vedas* are a comprehensive resource containing the knowledge and principles for living a good and proper life. Their content includes texts on meditation, philosophy, ceremonies, rituals, sacrifices, mantras, and spiritual knowledge.

Written over a five hundred year period in the last century before the common era, the *Upanishads* contain the first written references to yoga. They are also called *Vedanta,* Sanskrit for "the end or last chapters of the *Vedas.*" The numerous works in the *Upanishads* introduced new practices and institutions. The word *Upanishad* translates, "to sit at the feet of the master." The masters handed down the oral traditions to their disciples until they were eventually transcribed in the *Upanishads.* In *The Tempest,* Shakespeare wrote, "What's past is prologue." The past written words of *Vedanta* would become the foundation for all Hindu societal rules and ethical principles to follow.

There are several important concepts and doctrines put forth in *Vedanta. Brahman* or the Absolute is the highest absolute reality of the Universe. It is the unchanging, infinite, eternal truth of the Universe. *Brahman* is invisible and not directly accessible to the human mind, as it is devoid of any discernible features. *Atman* or the Self is the true individual at its core that lies beneath the ego and the ever-changing state of the mind and body. It is similar to *Brahman* as being constant and unchanging. *Atman,* the true self, is identical to and one with *Brahman,* and as such qualifies *Vedanta* as a non-dualistic philosophy.

Maya or illusory power is the external world that can be perceived by the mind and senses. It is an illusion because we consider what we experience sensually as being permanent and everlasting, although truly only transient and fleeting. Only *Brahman* and *Atman,* which exist beyond our capacity to access experience, are unchanging and eternal. *Maya* is sometimes referred to as *avidya* or ignorance. Human suffering arises from that ignorance and the incapability of distinguishing what is real from the illusion of what we perceive as real.

Unlike *Vedanta, Samkhya,* another ancient Hindu philosophy is dualistic, regarding the Universe as consisting of two realities derived from *Brahman*: *purusha* or pure consciousness of spirit and *prakriti* or primordial matter. *Samkhya* formed the philosophical framework for most forms and traditions of yoga to follow. *Samkhya,* believed to date back as early as 1000 BCE, translates to the word, "list." It is a list of twenty-five *tattvas* or categories of human existence. *Purusha* and *prakriti* are the primary *tattvas.* From the primordial matter of the Universe that is *prakriti,* the other twenty-three *tattvas* exist in a hierarchy of downward steps. Through the descent through that hierarchy, *Samkhya* philosophy explains how one becomes bound in the material world. *Purusha* and *prakriti* are unmanifest, not seen or experienced. When they interact, however, the process of manifestation begins, as *prakriti* begins its descent into material form that one can experience with the senses.

One first descends through one's own witness or *buddhi* and one's sense of self or *ahankara.* The latter develops from early life under parental influence and continues to be molded by life experiences.

Next, one arrives at the level of the three *gunas: sattva, rajas and tamas.* All three are considered to be present in every individual, but differ in proportion at different times of the day or different days of the week. The *gunas* became an integral part of the practice of *ayurveda,* the traditional Hindu system of medicine dating back to the time of the *Vedas.* Both yoga and *ayurveda* arose in parallel from the ancient Hindu texts.

Tamas is a state of darkness, inertia, lethargy and materiality. *Tamas* arises from ignorance and deludes all beings from their spiritual truths. But the state of *tamas* also has positive attributes, such as the need for a low energy state to enter into restorative sleep.

In a sense, *rajas* is the antithesis of *tamas. Rajas* is a state of energy, action, activity, change and movement. It results in attachment, as it binds us to the results of our actions.

Finally, *sattva* is a state of bliss, joy, harmony, and balance. *Sattva* is the desired goal in the practice of yoga. With a greater component of *sattva,* there is a concomitant reduction in the contribution of *rajas* and *tamas* to one's present experience. We all fluctuate between the three states at different times. The three states are considered three threads that are wound together to fashion our perspective and outlook on life at any one moment. In order to enter into *sattva* from *tamas,* one must first pass through the state of *rajas.* At any one time, one might be *tamasic,* in need of being more *rajasic,* or vice-versa, as one might wish to lower one's energy level in order to enter into relaxation and sleep or shake off the lethargy of the day. Our hope is to spend more time in the state of *sattva.* Thus, a goal of a meaningful, regular yoga practice is to achieve those feelings of contentment, satisfaction, gratitude and peace.

The remainder of the *tattvas* at the lower levels of the hierarchy concern more concrete experiences of the self and the world, including the five organs of action (tongue, hands, feet, genitals, and anus), the five senses, the five subtle elements (sound, touch, color, flavor and odor) and the five elements (ether, air, fire, water and earth). The further down one descends through the layers of the *tattvas,* the more one becomes attached and grounded into the material and physical world.

Samkhya eventually gave rise to classical yoga. The advent of classical yoga can be traced back to the writings of Pantajali, a sage believed to have lived circa 200 CE. His *Yoga Sutras* are a treatise on the practice of yoga as a way of life. *Sutra* is the Sanskrit word for "string" or "thread". In the *Yoga Sutras,* these threads are short rules and aphorisms that are woven together into a system of ethics and philosophy. Interestingly, the *asanas* and *pranayama* are not extensively discussed and only comprise a minor part of Pantanjali's teachings. Rather, the *Yoga Sutras* concentrate on the ideas of accessing higher states of being through the cultivation of the mind, thereby freeing oneself from worldly attachments to experience higher states of clarity lying beyond the *ahankara* or one's sense of self.

In addition to incorporating the twenty-five *tattvas* found in *Samkhya* philosophy, the *Yoga Sutras* add one more, *Ishvara* or the surrender to the Divine. An essential concept of the *Yoga Sutras* is that of *samskara,* subliminal forces in the unconscious mind that when activated by external occurrences or conditions give rise to feelings of desire and attachment that are bound in our ignorance, egotism, desires, and aversions. The *Yoga Sutras* present a strategy to resist *samskara* in order to meditate with clarity in the pursuit of self-knowledge or *vidya.* Patanjali concisely states the goal of one's practice; *yogash chitta vritti nirodhaha* or "yoga is the cessation of the fluctuations of the mind." These four Sanskrit words are often chanted as a mantra for meditation.

Whereas *Samkhya* philosophy professes the descent of the soul down through the layers of the *tattvas* to become bound in matter, Pantanjali describes the ascent up a ladder to free oneself from material entanglement and experience spiritual liberation and enlightenment. That ladder is known as the Eight Limbs of Yoga, which arguably more so than other antecedent philosophies, best embody and conceptualize the practice of yoga in the context of our modern day world. These eight limbs are the rungs of the ladder that one climbs to attain the ultimate goal of yoga: achieving a deep state of meditation whereby one can observe a single chosen object without distraction, having a complete knowledge of every aspect of that object and becoming one with that object. I certainly don't have an expectation to ascend up to this highest limb, but I practice with the intent of clearing my mind to develop clarity as to how I wish to live my life and gaining insights into the qualities that constitute my true authentic self. Clarity can arise by eliminating distraction from thoughts that don't serve me, including regrets of the past, worries of the future and anxieties stemming from others' expectations that I feel I must live up to. The Eight Limbs of Yoga actually originally appeared in the *Upanishads,* however, it is through Pantajali's writings that this concept of yoga became more widely known. According to Patanjali, the eight limbs represent the path of internal purification for revealing the Universal Self.

The eight limbs are as follows:

Yamas ~ restraints

Niyamas ~ observances

. . .

Asanas ~ physical postures

Pranayama ~ breathing as a vehicle to balance *prana,* the life force

Pratyahara ~ the first state of introversion based on the flow of *prana*

Dharana ~ the initial stage of meditation arising from a single focus of concentration on a chosen object

Dhyana ~ the intermediate stage of meditation initiating the act of merging with the chosen object

Samadhi ~ the advanced and ultimate level of meditation devoid of distraction when the observer attains oneness with the object of observation and individual awareness dissolves

I like to think of the *yamas* and *niyamas* as analogous to the ten commandments. There are ten *yamas* and *niyamas,* five of each. Both the ten commandments and the *yamas* and *niyamas* represent tenets and principles that promote an ethical way of life, create moral standards in society and achieve long-lasting cultural strength and stability. The *yamas* include *ahimsa, satya, asteya, brahmacharya,* and *aparigraha* and *saucha, santosha, tapas, svadhyaya* and *Ishavara-Pranidhana* comprise the *niyamas*. All of these concepts have many meanings and have been subject to various interpretations throughout the ages. Simply, the *yamas* are restraints from what we should not do in order to lead an ethical life and the *niyamas* are observances, what we should.

The *yamas* are the first rung of the ladder on one's journey to a higher and clearer experience of consciousness. In ancient Hindu scriptures, when there is a list of terms, typically that which is mentioned first carries the greatest import. Such is true of *ahimsa,* the first of the *yamas. Ahimsa* represents the first and most important principle of the first limb of yoga, and as such, becomes a prerequisite for achieving all that follows. The practice of *ahimsa* must be embraced before attempting to master the *asanas* or *pranayama* or having any hope of entering into the four meditative limbs. One meaning of *ahimsa* is nonviolence. Mahatma Gandhi was a strict adherent to this principle that became the core of his moral center. *Ahimsa* also translates to non-harm. As we practice yoga with *ahimsa* we strive to neither harm the body nor the mind. With regard to the former, we honor the body each time we practice. Most of us have physical limitations and challenges. As we practice we must listen to our bodies. If a movement causes pain or, quite simply, just doesn't feel good, modify your practice. Clouding the mind with thoughts of discomfort is antithetical to gaining clarity. If the mind is flooded with disturbing thoughts arising from physical limitations and any associated negative self-judgments, any hope of finding clarity will be lost. One should never feel compelled to do everything the teacher or others might be doing. Our culture promotes a sense of competition with others and within ourselves. Yoga is not a competition, but rather your own personal experience with your own self-expression of movement. Pushing oneself into sensations of discomfort or pain in order to perform at the perceived level of others around you can lead to injury. One should practice yoga by finding one's edge. The edge is a point where discomfort arises. Once you determine your edge, ease off from it in order to practice without discomfort. Over time with much patience, gradually your edge will shift as flexibility increases.

In order to honor the mind through *ahimsa*, one must practice yoga with kindness. Compassion for self is difficult to realize if one adheres to perceived cultural norms and societal attitudes that can feed our inner critics. The inner critic is that part of the psyche that constantly judges our actions, thoughts and emotions. Negative self-judgments interfere with the positive outlook one needs to further one's practice. In both a yoga class and in life it is important to eliminate the word "and" from any self-observation. For example, when performing a balance posture like the tree or eagle, one might think, "I am wobbling and falling out of this pose, and I can't balance." Instead, one should observe that he or she is wobbling and falling out of the pose and eliminate the second half of the sentence. "I am wobbling and falling out of this pose" is more than sufficient. Depending on how you look at it, one could argue that wobbling is a wonderful thing. It means the brain is functioning as it should. The inner ear structures specialized for balance react to any instability in order to reestablish stability. Simply, the brain does not want us to stand on one leg. Just as flexibility is realized over time, balance can slowly be learned with a regular practice. In most circumstances in life, eliminating the word "and" is necessary to practice self-kindness. "I made a mistake at work" is preferred over "I made a mistake at work and I am a failure." If you had a friend who called you a failure every time you made a mistake, assuredly you would end that friendship quickly. Be a friend to yourself. Perfection is an unrealistic expectation as we are all imperfect. Making the choice not to engage the inner critic can result in peace of mind. When the inner critic rears its ugly head, acknowledge its presence and substitute any negativity with a positive affirmation. Throughout life, it is always better to focus on what you can do, and not on what you can't. *Ahimsa* is all about practicing self-love and kindness. Once they become habitual, you might develop greater empathy towards others and the battles they face against their inner critics. Although the concept of *ahimsa* was an important principle of ancient yogic philosophy, it remains a credo to live by today. We only have the opportunity to go through life once. Take advantage of all you can and cherish every moment. It all begins with love and kindness.

Ahimsa can also pertain to respecting our planet. This is especially true today where the health of the Earth is in decline and animal species are diminishing in numbers rapidly due to manmade abuses. We must all be reminded that we are all a part of nature. Natural beauty surrounds us, but also lies within. Through yoga, one may learn how to access it.

The second *yama* is *satya,* the Sanskrit word for truth. *Satya* is a restraint from lies and false representation in all of one's expressions and actions. *Satya* is not just about lying to others, but also to oneself by aspiring to become someone you think others want you to be, rather than living as your true authentic self. A yoga practice affords one the luxury of time for self-reflection in order to make genuine choices for living life. And just as flexibility and balance develop over time, so does the ability to access feelings of inwardness and clarity. As we come to understand the importance of the *yamas,* the practice of yoga becomes more meaningful and profound. Embracing the principle of *satya* fosters an awareness of one's true self and passion.

The next *yama* is *asteya,* the Sanskrit word for non-stealing. As with many other yogic terms, *asteya* has many layers and meanings. It of course refers to the restraint from stealing another's possessions or ideas or robbing precious resources from the Earth. *Asteya* can also refer to not stealing time. As I expressed previously, we have only a limited time to live. By not living in the present and becoming mired in regrets of the past and worries of the future, we are wasting precious time; stealing it from time we could spend cherishing the moments that fill our lives with meaning. We can also rob time needed to practice self-care and build resiliency in the face of challenges.

Brachmacharya in the ancient yogic tradition referred to the practice of celibacy and restraint from other worldly desires in order to redirect energy toward more enlightened, introverted states of being. More applicable to our modern times is a restraint from attaching to outcomes, and instead, staying in the moment to enjoy the process. Attaching to positive outcomes and successes in yoga is often fleeting. Attaching to the possibility of failure can reinforce pre-existing negative self-judgments. Practicing non-attachment facilitates single-pointed focus on the present and consequent clarity and introversion.

The final *yama, aparigraha,* translates to non-possessiveness. It is the restraint from coveting and desiring material possessions, especially at the expense of others. It is a restraint from greed, pursuing only what is necessary for a modest life. Similar to *brahmacharya,* embracing the principle of *aparigraha* promotes non-attachment to both material possessions and the potential outcomes of one's actions. Non-attachment is one of the primary themes of the *Bhagavad Gita,* an ancient Hindu scripture written in the order of 2,200 to 2,500 years ago. The story centers on the great struggle between two branches of a single ruling family, the Kauravas and the Pandavas and the personal struggle of the great warrior Arjuna, the leader of the Pandava army. Realizing that his enemies are his own relatives, cherished friends, and wise teachers, Arjuna is filled with doubt and sadness on the battlefield and refuses to fight. As the action of the battle freezes in time, Arjuna begins his analysis of what seemingly is a no-win situation. He turns to his charioteer, Lord Krishna, one of the principal Hindu deities and the god of love and compassion, in hopes of solving his moral dilemma. Krishna urges Arjuna to practice non-attachment. Krishna explains to Arjuna that his path in life or *dharma* is as a warrior and prince. Despite his misgivings, he has a duty to be true to himself . His predestined role in this world necessitates that he enter into battle. Non-attachment is a life strategy of acting in the present without any expectations as to the consequence of that action, thereby alleviating the self-imposed pressure to realize satisfaction from what we perceive lies only in our success. Non-attachment is the acceptance of either possibility of success or failure and being content with either outcome. The mind becomes clouded by anxieties of the future, but clears with greater awareness of the present. Although final outcomes are secondary, arguably, greater focus on the present moment with complete mindfulness might enhance performance and favor a successful outcome. One should not attach oneself to goals of increased flexibility, physical fitness, introverted states or performing all of the postures perfectly. Rather, yoga should be a practice of enjoying the process.

The *Bhagavad Gita* also professes the value of connecting with one's true authentic self, as evinced by this quote from the ancient scripture, "Far better to live your own path imperfectly, than to live another's path perfectly." Internal conflict is inherent to the repression of our true desires and passions. Living a version of ourselves that we think others want us to be can result in emotional turmoil. And as Polonius so eloquently says to Laertes in *Hamlet,* "This above all – to thine own self be true". Whether consciously or subconsciously, denial of one's identity with regard to sexuality, gender and career, amongst many others, can generate mental friction. It is the concept of one's actual life purpose and path or *dharma* that lies at the heart of the *Bhagavad Gita. Dharma* is a guiding principle in many Eastern religions. In

Hinduism, *dharma* has multiple meanings, many without direct English translations. *Dharma* is considered the moral order of the universe. Another meaning pertains to living by a code of morality, adhering to principles advanced through law, religion and personal duty and behaving according to *Rta,* the order in the universe that gives rise to life, all of which can potentially liberate oneself from *samsara,* the cycle of death and rebirth. *Adharma,* the opposite of *dharma,* are behaviors and thoughts that are immoral and evil, resulting in a disturbance in the universe, discord, and friction. *Dharma* also refers to one's predestined true calling and true authentic self. In the *Bhagavad Gita,* Arjuna must live life as a warrior and adhere to those qualities that define a warrior. It is his identity and true purpose in life. *Dharma* applies to all beings on Earth; mammals, fish, insects, etc.,which all possess predetermined life functions and behaviors.

The Sanskrit word *karma* translates to "action". Acting ethically, being morally principled and exhibiting behaviors that are rooted in altruism and kindness create so-called "good" *karma* that will instill one's next life with contentment and peace. "Bad" *karma* results from malevolent behaviors, egocentrism, and evil intent, all leading to pain and suffering in the next life. *Karma* is the force that compels individuals to behave morally and righteously in this life according to *dharma,* the moral order of the universe.

The *niyamas,* in contrast to the *yamas, are* observances; simply, what we should do, not what we shouldn't. *Saucha,* the first of the *niyamas* or observances translates to purity and cleanliness. It refers to the purity of body and mind that must be realized to establish happiness and well-being. In regard to the external purity of the body, *saucha* is achieved through daily washing, proper nutrition and other forms of self-care. Certainly, yoga can be considered a form of self-care. Internal purity of the body results through the practice of the *asanas* and *pranayama,* the yogic postures and breathing techniques, and their beneficial effects on a physiological basis. The mind can also be purified. An impure mind filled with anger, hate, greed, prejudice, and pride can be cleansed through yoga, meditation, and positive self-affirmations. Purity is realized through choices to live with a positive perspective and kindness toward others. Purity of mind translates to self-love and compassion, which in turn gives one the capacity for love and compassion toward others. Just as we count negative numbers backwards, becoming mired in negativity draws us back from a calm and peaceful life. Instead, anger and hatred destroy the spirit and the life within us. Positivity allows us to progress toward a meaningful and profound life with satisfaction stemming from the wonderful effects you realize as you love and care for others, especially the gratitude you feel in return.

The second *niyama* is *santosha* or contentment, which can be realized through the practice of non-attachment. By not attaching ourselves to any desired goals we can aspire to want what we have and not desire to have what we want. We try to practice yoga on and off the mat. Off the mat, acquiring material things may bring a sense of contentment, but that contentment may be fleeting. On the mat, attachment to the performance of an *asana* perfectly may set one up for failure and negative self-judgments. Even achieving that perfect posture ultimately may not give meaning to one's practice if not balanced with humility. It is interesting that contentment is one of the observances; what we should do. But, how do we "do" contentment? Perhaps, *santosha* can be realized through gratitude, as happiness does not bring gratitude, but gratitude brings happiness. In the Kripalu yogic tradition, we end our practice by saying, "Jai Bhagwan!", one definition of which is "blessed victory." How one's practice is a victory is up to individual interpretation. For me, the contentment that comes from being grateful for all of the blessings of my life is a true victory!

The third *niyama* is *tapas,* translated into English as "heat." It is also sometimes translated to "discipline." Like many yogic concepts, *tapas* can be interpreted many ways. One is the presence in the human spirit of a fiery passion, which through discipline can be harnessed to purify the mind and facilitate a connection with one's true authentic self. Dedication and hard work are required to habitually substitute positive affirmations and emotions for reflexive negative self-judgments. When the practice of yoga is done with passion, its beneficial effects become more far-reaching. Desires for peace and contentment fuel a passion for yoga, the heat of *tapas.*

One translation of *svadhyaya,* the fourth *niyama,* is the study or observation of self. Through yoga, we gain the capacity for introspection. Once again, we strive to create an authentic version of who we are. Conflict arises in the attempt to live up to someone else's expectation for whom we should be. Inner conflict is at the very least unsettling. In its extreme it causes depression and anxiety, sometimes leading to desperate acts. The resolution of that inner conflict puts one on the path to peace and contentment. Practicing *svadhyaya* is easier said than done, but without attempting self-realization, the process of calming the mind can never begin. Inertia is only disturbed through the application of energy to change the course of a moving object, in this case the mind floating through a state of unhealthy inaction. Yoga can provide that energy for change and transformation.

Finally, the last *niyama* is *Ishvara pranidhana,* which literally translates to, "Devotion or surrender to the Supreme Being or God". A secular interpretation of *Ishvara pranidhana* is the humility that arises from the realization that one is only a minute part of an expansive universe. It is this larger perspective that diminishes the importance of self and individual inner conflicts stemming from issues of the ego. Egoism can be replaced by both an intellectual and emotional exploration of our miraculous world. We are only a small part of the wonders of nature and our planet. Moving away from anthropocentrism, *Ishvara pranidhana* becomes a devotion to the protection of all of the species on planet Earth. Whether one believes in a supreme being or not, our universe remains mysterious. What we experience and confront on a daily basis may represent fated events or random coincidences. Distinguishing between the two is arguably impossible. Practicing *Ishvara pranidhana* is gaining an acceptance that much exists that is beyond our ken, but at the same time, not abandoning a pursuit of truth through inquiry with an open mind. Nature in and of itself is awe-inspiring, full of miracles and beauty. The realization that we are a part of nature creates a oneness and connection between self and the world.

With regard to Hatha yoga, it is the predominant tradition of yoga that is practiced today. It arose from Tantric philosophy. Tantra dates back to circa 500 CE. Tantra was a highly ritualistic practice. The purpose of these rituals was to eliminate the obstacles to achieving higher meditative states and worldly detachments. In our present day, a consideration of Tantra conjures up images of unbridled sexual activity, however, Tantric rituals took on many other forms. The purpose of many Tantric practices was to harness the energy of powerful emotions like fear, guilt, shame, anger, aggression and lust to dissolve the *ahankara* or one's sense of self and the ego mired in illusion or *maya* in order to achieve higher states of pure consciousness.

Much of Hatha yoga comes from the *Hatha Yoga Pradipika,* written in the 15th century by Svatmarama and based on the teachings of the great sage Matsyendranath, who is thought to have lived in the early 11th century. According to Hindu mythology, Matysendranath, also known as the Lord of the Fishes, was given the secrets of Hatha yoga from the deity Shiva. Seeing an ominous star in the sky when Matysendranath was born, his parents threw him into the ocean where he was subsequently swallowed by a fish. At the bottom of the sea, Matsyendranath overheard Shiva imparting the precepts of Hatha yoga to the goddess Parvati. For many years, Matsyendranath practiced his newfound knowledge of yoga inside the belly of the fish. He emerged twelve years later as an enlightened master of the practice of Hatha yoga. Gorakshanath, a disciple of Matsyendranath, developed a new system of yogic rituals: *asanas, pranayama* and *dhyana* or meditation. The word *hatha* literally means "force", which alludes to the physical aspects of the practice. Some sources consider *hatha* a compound word consisting of the word *"ha"* or sun and *"tha"* or moon. Masters of Hatha yoga advanced the idea of a life force or *prana* that activates the subtle body. *Prana* is received into the body with the breath, and then flows to the deeper self and spirit. Once *prana* is brought in from the external world, it then must be balanced throughout the body. To that end, an anatomical system of energy centers and channels was proposed that facilitate the flow of *prana* throughout the body. The energy network not only establishes a healthy balance of *prana* throughout the body, but also rids the body of an undesirable form of energy called *apana. Apana* is felt to control the eliminative functions of urination, excretion, and menstruation and the downward and outward flow of energy in the body.

The main energy centers and channels in the body are known as *chakras* and *nadis,* respectively. Whether or not you believe in the actual existence of *chakras* and *nadis,* at the very least they can serve as useful metaphors, allowing one to imagine an influx of positive energy of *prana* and its spread throughout the body through complex channels alive with energy. Depending on the particular source, anywhere from

72,000 to 350,000 *nadis* in the body have been described. *Prana* also activates the seven main *chakras* and fuels *agni,* the fire burning in the belly. Again, considering this concept as a metaphor, *agni* might represent one's zeal and enthusiasm for life, both of which increase with the development of a more positive outlook.

The reported number of *chakras* also differs from text to text. Often, seven are considered to exist in the body. The seven *chakras* are situated in the deep core of the body, the neck and head. The word *chakra* is Sanskrit for "wheel". From inferior to superior they are the root, sacral, solar plexus, heart, throat, third eye and crown of head *chakras*. One might consider the energy activating the *chakras* and subsequently traveling through the *nadis* and a multitude of more peripheral secondary energy channels analogous to electrical energy flowing throughout all parts of our living bodies through a complex neural network in the brain, spinal cord and peripheral body. A regular yoga practice provides the fuel to boost the energy of the *chakras,* causing "the wheels to spin." We accomplish this by creating the optimal balance between our body, mind and breath in order to maximize the influx of precious *prana*.

Each of the *chakras* is assigned a particular color of the rainbow. Sir Isaac Newton observed that light passing through a prism is refracted or bent, emerging as the specific individual components of the spectrum of visible light. Although we now know that the visible spectrum of light is a continuous range of colors, he divided it into seven primary colors. ROYGBIV (red, orange, yellow, green, blue, indigo, and violet) is the traditional mnemonic that we were taught sometime in our schooling to aid in remembering those colors. Many of us still rely on that mnemonic every time we witness and marvel at a rainbow. A rainbow is produced by a multitude of residual rain droplets suspended in the air that act as tiny prisms as the sun comes out after a storm, bending the sunlight into a beautiful arc of colors. The colors assigned to the seven *chakras* from inferior to superior range from red for the root chakra to violet for the crown chakra. Light is emitted in regular sine waves with peaks and troughs. The distance between two peaks of a wave is the wavelength. The shorter the wavelength, the more waves will occur in a given time and the higher the frequency of that light. Higher frequency light has greater energy. Therefore, violet light will have more energy than red light. Of course, ultraviolet light, which is just beyond the visible spectrum, has enough energy to be damaging to the skin. So keep in mind that as we proceed up through the seven *chakras* that the light energy associated with each one will possess incrementally greater energy than the preceding one as the frequency of light increases. This is fitting since the greatest energy lies in the high frequency violet light assigned to our crown chakra, the center of our spirituality. What a beautiful image of the energies of our souls. The energies that make up our unique personalities are all aglow with the colors of the rainbow. Your own glowing light illuminates the path to self-realization. Others will see that light in your expressions of love and compassion. The more you dedicate yourself to yoga, the brighter that path will become and the easier it will be to see all the wonders of life.

With regard to the specific chakras, the location of the *muladhara chakra or* root chakra is between the sitz bones and the perineum, the inferior most border of the pelvis and the site of our genitals and anus. The energy of this chakra grounds us to the earth. It is a reminder that we are part of this planet and we have a deep responsibility to treat the environment and nature with compassion and respect. Its energy also creates a sense of safety, diminishing fear and anger, which are felt to be part of *apana* centered in the pelvis. Without fear and anger, we can enjoy our meditation in peace. In addition, the energy of the *muladhara chakra* fuels our passion for living.

The *swadhisthana chakra* or sacral *chakra* is assigned the color orange. The energy of the sacral *chakra* fuels our sexuality and creativity and lets us experience the joy from both. From an anatomical standpoint, the sacral nerves that arise from the spinal cord and exit through the sacrum innervate our sexual organs and genitalia. The energy of the sacral *chakra* stimulates those nerves. Our sexuality stems from our primitive urges that promote survival. Perhaps similarly, our creativity also developed to allow our species to flourish. Man's creativity led to inventions such as tools and the wheel that significantly improved our abilities to hunt and farm.

Above the root and sacral *chakras* is the solar plexus or *manipura chakra,* assigned the color yellow. The solar plexus is located just above the navel and below the sternum. It is called the solar plexus because it represents a complex network of nerves in the abdomen that radiate out from a central point. Within that center is the energy that fuels our inner strength and wisdom. That wisdom leads to clarity, awareness and personal growth.

The ideal for which we strive is a balance of the energies of all of our *chakras,* but arguably the most important *chakra* that leads to contentment and peace is the *anahata* or heart *chakra.* Its energy fuels our love and compassion. Compassion for one's fellow beings, both human and otherwise, is necessary to generate positive energy. Negative energy arises from conflict, grudges, judgments and criticisms. The close companion of compassion is gratitude. We can experience gratitude to the greatest degree in our hearts. Gratitude is one of the most powerful emotions that we can express that is arguably a prerequisite for all other positive emotions that we feel.

The throat or *vishuddha chakra* is assigned the color blue. The throat *chakra* provides the energy for communication. Therein lies our ability to express ourselves. Outward expression of love, compassion and gratitude is crucial for the attainment of peace and contentment in our lives.

We will never fully comprehend the miracles of life, however, it is our third eye or *ajna chakra* that allows us to have a keen awareness of the world. The third eye is located just above the bridge of the nose and is assigned the color indigo. It is the portal to our higher consciousness, and through insight can help us along the path to enlightenment. Our two eyes allow us to see the external world. The third eye sees beyond the physical. It perceives the energies of all that surrounds us, especially those of living beings. Perhaps more importantly, the third eye can see inward, allowing for self-reflection and a connection to one's passions.

Finally, located above all other *chakras* in the body is the crown of head *chakra* or *sahasrara chakra,* assigned the color violet. Within this *chakra* lies the energy for our spirituality. What is spirituality? It is the connection of the external universe to our souls beyond its physical aspects. It is the driving force of life through the incorporation of ideas and emotions into our experiential thinking. The site of this *chakra* at the top of our head is fitting since by climbing up the ladder of the *chakras* we have gone from the Earth at our root to the Universe above our crown of head. With universal consciousness being the goal, ascending the seven *chakras* represents the process of liberation, whereas the descent results in manifestation and a greater awareness and connection to the present world. Through liberation the body becomes alive with lines of energy extending from the Earth, through the legs, up the spine and out the crown of the head into the heavens. The universe is vast and complex, but we are all a vital part of it.

The practice of yoga allows for *prana,* the life force, to enter into our bodies and energize the *chakras.* By balancing *prana* throughout our bodies, we can enjoy life to the fullest. As we develop a meaningful practice, accessing the energy of the *chakras* will allow us to feel grounded and safe, in touch with our sexuality and creativity, wise and strong, loving and compassionate, powerful through self-expression, in awe of the miracles and blessings of the world around us and within us, and spiritual and connected to the universe. The rainbow of color emerges as the storm of inner conflicts is calmed and the sunlight of clarity emerges.

The connection of the root to the crown of head *chakra* is through the main energy channel: the central *nadi* or *sushumna.* The *sushumna nadi* connects all of the *chakras* from the *muladhara chakra* to the *sahasrara chakra.* It is the pathway for the upward movement of the *kundalini shakti. Kundalini* is divine energy. Like a snake, it is coiled up near the base of the spine. The *Kundalini* is awakened through the practice of yoga, especially through vigorous forms of *pranayama,* the yogic breathing techniques, that employ *kumbhaka* or breath retention and *bandhas* or locks of certain regions of the body, including the perineum, belly and throat. *Kumbhaka* can be done following inhalation or exhalation, the latter being more energizing. The upward flow of the activated energy of the *Kundalini* dissolves the *ahankara,* the perceived sense of self that is learned through parental interactions and life experiences. Once the *ahankara* dissolves, enlightenment and the experience of universal consciousness are possible.

Two additional important main *nadis* are known as *ida* and *pingala. Ida* is the moon pathway or lunar energy channel. It lies in the left brain and the right side of the body. It is cooling, rational and feminine in nature. The freedom for interpretation of ideas, self-analysis, receptivity to new perspectives and expression that epitomizes the practice of yoga lie in the *ida nadi.* In contrast, the *pingala nadi* or sun pathway or solar energy channel is masculine, active and heat producing. It lies in the right brain and the left side of the body. Similar to the concepts of *yin* and *yang*, *ida* and *pingala* represent the duality of life, and as such are opposites yet complementary, one necessary for the existence of the other. The *ida* and *pingala nadis* extend along the *sushumna nadi*, criss-crossing at the level of each *chakra*. There is a constant interplay between *ida* and *pingala*, one possibly more dominant than the other at any part of the day. There are also *ida* type personalities that are more nurturing, but lack drive and determination, and vice-versa for a *pingala* type personality. Although *ida* and *pingala* reflect female and male qualities, each personality type is not limited to a specific gender.

Principal to the practice of Hatha yoga is bringing *ida* and *pingala* into balance. That balance clears the *sushumna nadi*, allowing for the flow of the energy of the *kundalini* skyward to higher levels of consciousness. *Nadi shodhana*, the channel clearing breath, which will be discussed in a later chapter devoted to *pranayama*, the yogic breathing techniques, is specifically directed at not only optimizing the flow of *prana* through the *ida* and *pingala nadis*, but also to bring them both into balance.

Both perspective and intention of your yoga practice may change through the development of a personal connection to many of these philosophical precepts presented. Many concepts, such as the *yamas* and *niyamas* center around the idea of fulfillment through the exercise of a healthy belief system. The practice of yoga can be a vehicle for personal growth through an analysis and exploration of one's personal belief system coupled with a willingness to change. It is important to understand that yoga is so much more than the physical postures. Connecting postures to the breath to meditation gives us the time and opportunity to think. That time is a true luxury, but also a necessity to become self-aware. Philosophy is truly the love of wisdom. Wisdom of one's true authentic self is the key to self-realization and personal growth.

The following chapter is an exploration of the Kripalu yogic tradition. I was drawn to its philosophy, which promotes the idea of inclusiveness regardless of physical limitations or mental challenges. I learned that yoga isn't about being good or bad, it is just about being. Connecting with the true self that lies deep in the soul is the heart of Kripalu Yoga.

7
KRIPALU YOGA

The highest spiritual practice is self-observation without judgment.

Swami Kripalu

More so than any other philosophy, Kripalu yoga embodies a methodology best suited to overcome the obstacles to the development of a meaningful yoga practice. One definition of the Sanskrit word *kripalu* is "compassion". Quite simply, Kripalu yoga is the practice of self-kindness and compassion. It is letting go of preconceived ideas, expectations and attachments to allow for the natural unfolding of one's experience. It is freedom from negative self-judgments and inner criticisms in the pursuit of clarity of mind.

Kripalu yoga is a type of Hatha yoga that integrates the principles of classic yoga, including Pantanjali's eight limbs of yoga, and blends ideas and concepts dating back to the ancient Vedic scriptures with modern day attitudes and practices. It professes an integration of movement, breathing and meditation to achieve self-realization. At its core is the principle of self-observation without judgment. Practicing self-kindness with positive affirmations and without self-criticism makes Kripalu yoga attractive to both beginners and advanced practitioners. It is a type of yoga for all levels that promotes continual self-discovery, reduced stress and increased health and wellbeing. From day one of practice, the novice is capable of experiencing yoga by connecting the breath to his or her unique individual movements to achieve feelings of introversion.

Swami Kripalu was born as Saraswatichandra in 1913 in Gujarat, India. In 1930, he began his exploration of yoga and the study of the ancient Hindu scriptures. He was initiated as a Swami in 1941 and given the name Swami Kripalvananda, meaning "compassionate one." He renounced all worldly possessions and lectured and taught throughout India. By making them applicable to contemporary life, Babuji or beloved father, as his students called him, gave new meaning to many of the ancient yogic principles. He stressed the integration of *asanas, pranayama* and meditation. Through his own intensive practices of Hatha *asanas* and *pranayama,* he gained unique insight into the nuances of both practices.

A close disciple of Swami Kripalu in India, Amrit Desai, came to the United States in 1960 and developed the tradition of Kripalu Yoga based on the teachings of his master. Desai was involved with yoga in the Philadelphia area until 1972 when he and his disciples created a yoga retreat in Sumneytown, Pennsylvania. In 1975, he founded a larger yoga center in Summit Station, Pennsylvania where he taught the Kripalu philosophy as a way of life. In 1977, Swami Kripalu came to the United States, inspiring thousands through his lectures and writings. In 1981, he returned to India, where he soon died.

In 1983, the Kripalu Yoga center moved to a former Jesuit seminary in Stockbridge, Massachusetts in the Berkshire Mountains. More than 350 disciples of Desai inhabited the ashram. Desai lectured worldwide, becoming a prominent figure in the world of yoga, disseminating the words of Swami Kripalu throughout the Western world. He had a huge impact on Western perspectives of yoga, professing the life-changing precepts of this practice of self-kindness. Unfortunately, many times power corrupts giving rise to lies and deceit. Following a scandal involving Desai in 1994, the center lost its religious affiliation and was converted from a religious ashram to a center for yoga and wellness. Despite initial financial hardships, the Kripalu Center for Yoga and Health was born. It developed a national reputation as a place for both education and retreat. Various perspectives and philosophies of yoga are welcomed there and presented in a vast array of programming, but the center remains based on the philosophy and teachings of Swami Kripalu. The reason for alluding to the scandal is that it demonstrates how a philosophy that advances the practice of love and compassion transcends and overpowers the insincere self-interests of the few. The Kripalu center is flourishing today because of that power.

From a practical perspective, a Kripalu class follows a specific methodology. Before performing any movements or breathing, creating a safe environment in which to practice is emphasized. Practicing with *ahimsa*, doing no harm, is paramount. And doing no harm refers not only to the prevention of physical injury, but also avoiding any detriment to the mind. From a physical perspective, it is extremely important to listen to your body as you practice. If you have any medical conditions, musculoskeletal issues or any physical limitations, it is critical to modify your practice. Flooding the mind with thoughts of discomfort is antithetical to the goal of gaining clarity of the mind. The motto for some exercise regimens is, "no pain, no gain." In yoga, it is, "pain, no gain." When I first began a regular practice of yoga, I had the misconception that by worsening the pain and discomfort I experienced from various movements and postures, I could accelerate the increase in flexibility that I so desired. That impatience led to many pulled muscles and joint strains. I have also injured myself many times in irresponsible attempts to perform certain postures. At one point, I tried to perform a headstand against a wall. My legs never made it above my torso. Instead, they fell quickly to the ground resulting in a bad joint sprain of my big toe. It is important to focus on what you can do, and not what you can't. By constantly listening to the body, serious injury can be averted. A teacher is a guide, not a drill sergeant, and is basically there to teach the postures with an emphasis on safety and balance. Yoga is not "Follow the Leader". One should make it your own personal experience, without an expectation of assuming all of the postures perfectly. By removing the pressure to perform, you can thoroughly enjoy your time in class. Experimenting with your own movements, maybe moving fingers or wrists as your body flows, creates novelty that becomes one's focus and clears the mind of other thoughts. Be kind to yourself as you practice. The "right" way to "do" yoga is to connect your breath to your movements. The connection of the breath to the *asanas* and the transitions between postures become points of focus necessary to achieve feelings of inwardness. Is the end result of introversion any less available to one that is physically limited? Absolutely not! We are all unique individuals capable of our own unique movements and thoughts. Connecting them all to the breath becomes your own version of yoga.

After setting a safe environment and a mindset of self-compassion for a Kripalu class, a period of centering ensues. It is a way of bringing oneself into the heart of energy in the class at that very moment. Centering can divert one's focus from any pressing issues of the day, becoming mindful of one's practice. It is an attempt to clear the mind of any thoughts that don't serve at the moment, although thoughts regarding stressful issues in life can be difficult to suppress. Recognize that thinking is normal and allow yourself to have thoughts. As any distressing thoughts arise, rather than fighting them, simply acknowledge their presence with self-kindness and then let them disappear, as if throwing them into a river, the current taking them away downstream. While centering, an intention might be set for one's practice that day, possibly one of improving the state of the body and/or mind. Often, no specific intention is necessary. You can just let your practice spontaneously unfold, seeing where it might take you. Whether setting an intention or not, non-attachment should be exercised. It is best to just be in the moment and flow through the movements and breathing without any expectation of accomplishing any goal or experiencing any beneficial effects. It is fine if nothing happens during your practice, including no epiphanies or revelations.

Centering is also a way to establish the breath for the remainder of the practice. It can be best accomplished through *pranayama,* the yogic breathing techniques. An instructor can guide students through *pranayama* at any time during a class or perhaps at multiple times. I prefer to guide a class through *pranayama* at the beginning of my class. Centering is achieved most effectively when one is in a position that is comfortable and stable to minimize awareness of the physical body. Elongation of the spine is critical for maximizing breathing capacity. During inhalation the diaphragm moves downward. If the torso is rounded, that downward motion will be restricted. Many people sit in *sukhasana* or cross-legged with a rounded back and the knees positioned above the level of the hips. Straightening and elongation of the back with more optimal downward movement of the diaphragm and a consequent greater breathing capacity is accomplished by sitting on the edge of a cushion or on a block. This action raises the hips above the knees. Even for the most flexible, such as those that can sit in a lotus position, sitting on the edge of a cushion drops the knees onto the mat, creating a stable tripod effect; the sitz bones and knees forming the three components. Another option that I enjoy, especially since I have lower back sensitivity from degenerative disease, is kneeling while sitting on two stacked blocks. This allows the knees to touch the ground and a nice elongation of the spine. The stable tripod effect in this case is created by the sitz bones on the blocks and both knees on the mat. In the third part of this book, in the chapter about *pranayama,* I will discuss in detail many of those yogic breathing techniques. Centering and relaxation can be effectively accomplished through non-distracted concentration and focus on the qualities of the breath; its sound, its sensation on the nostrils and the rhythm of the movements of the chest and belly.

In a Kripalu class, warming-up the body follows centering. As is true of any physical sport or activity, warming up muscles and joints is beneficial to prevent injury and increase strength and flexibility. Muscles of the body are more efficient if they are initially progressively stretched. Gentle stretching of muscles and movements of joints can counteract overnight stiffness, which is more frequent with advancing age. Warm-ups also increase the heart rate, allowing oxygen-rich blood to be delivered throughout the body. As blood vessels dilate to accommodate the increased volume of blood required to fuel active muscles, heat is produced.

In a sense, establishing the breath with an initial round of *pranayama* at the beginning of a class is a way of warming up the muscles of respiration. With each inhalation the intercostal muscles or the muscles between the ribs relax and, with exhalation, contract to force air from the lungs. By making each breath longer and deeper than the one before, the intercostal muscles are progressively stretched.

Warm-ups typically are flowing motions with quick transitions between postures. The breath is connected to these movements. The hope is to maintain awareness of the deep breath that was established during centering as one begins to move. Attention is focused on the spine, muscles and joints. The spine is stretched in its six possible movements: flexion or rounding forward, extension or arching backward, right and left lateral flexion and twisting to the right and left. Various movements are employed to activate the muscles of the core and extremities. Joints are moved repetitively to lubricate them with synovial fluid.

According to the Kripalu teaching methodology, sustaining the *asanas* follows the warm-ups. The amount of time for sustaining each posture is variable, but typically the *asanas* are sustained long enough that an awareness of the breath can be achieved. A non-distracted focus on the breath and the connection of the breath to the movements is paramount throughout the practice in order to experience meditative states. Postures can be standing, sitting, supine or prone. Again, the third portion of this book will describe each *asana* in detail to obtain familiarity with each one.

As a Kripalu class nears its end, transitions are created from the activation of the physical body to a state of release and relaxation and from an active mind to one at rest and stillness. Some teachers might accomplish this transition with a period of *pranayama* followed by *shavasana* or by guiding students directly into *shavasana,* translated into English as "corpse pose". This descriptor is quite morbid and I never use it in a class, but it does stress the goal of total unawareness of the physical body and the clearing of the mind of all thoughts. Before I guide students into *shavasana,* I suggest that they first make any movements or stretches that the body may call for, possibly stretching across any points of residual stiffness or tension. One's position during *shavasana* should be a comfortable one that allows you to divert all attention away from the physical body. One doesn't necessarily have to lie supine. Another position might prove to be more comfortable.

After several minutes in *shavasana,* I instruct students to begin to become aware of the body and the breath, breathing deeper while expanding the chest. I suggest that small movements can begin in the fingers and toes, allowing those movements to become larger as they spread up the arms and legs. Knees are then brought to the chest as one rolls over into a fetal position. It interests me that we transition from a corpse pose to a fetal position, almost as if our yoga practice is a rebirth into new possibilities. Traditionally, one rolls into the fetal position with the right side of the body on the ground. Many reasons have been proposed for this position, including maintaining the heart in the left chest above the other organs and positioning the left nostril above the right, honoring the *ida nadi,* which is calming and cooling. Students then gently push their way back up to the seated position where the class began. I typically have everyone bring their hands into *anjali mudra* at heart center with their eyes closed. I will close by returning to the theme I introduced at the beginning of class. Many teachers will end class by chanting the Sanskrit word "*OM*". I usually end my class with words of gratitude to my students and a final *Namaste.*

Namaste is a customary Hindu greeting of respect. *Namaste* is usually said while bowing with the hands in *anjali mudra;* hands pressed together at the heart center with fingers pointing upwards. *Namaste* translates to "The divine in me bows to the divine in you." To remove any religious connotation, I prefer the translation, "The light in me bows to the light in you." I believe the light is a beautiful metaphor for the energy that fuels our passions in life. *Namaste* is a common form of greeting in many parts of the world, similar to greetings like *shalom* or *aloha.*

The methodology of a Kripalu class serves as a framework for the implementation of a wonderful practical life philosophy that creates the potential for personal transformation. In many older schools of yoga, as well as in Pantanjali's *Yoga Sutras,* mastering *asana* was a prerequisite for practicing *pranayama.* The entry into higher meditative states was then predicated on the mastery of both. In Kripalu yoga, learning is focused on the concurrent integration of the postures, breathing and meditation. From the very early stages of building a yoga practice, introversion can be enjoyed by connecting the breath to movement. Through repetition, the brain can learn the feelings that arise during a meditative state, such that they can be accessed at any time during the day, for as short or long as desired. Many possess the misconception that meditation must be performed over an extended period of time. In a yoga practice, a meditative state may be of any duration, possibly for the entire class or just a few seconds while a posture is sustained. The more the brain experiences calmness and serenity, the easier it becomes to access both. Even short, "mini" meditations throughout the day, whether a deep breath at a red light or chanting a mantra with eyes closed for a few seconds at work, can promote relaxation and stress reduction. A meditative state should not be forced, however. Practice yoga without the pressure of meditating, but with the expectation that a meditative state is possible whether sustained or short-lived.

A practical technique known by the acronym BRFWA is taught at the Kripalu Center for Yoga and Health to both yoga instructors in training and participants in programs. BRFWA is an acronym that stands for *Breathe, Relax, Feel, Watch and Allow.* Many times during a busy day we become stressed or rushed or we become mired in thoughts that don't serve us, such as regrets of the past and worries about the future. Life can be a battle, but in your armamentarium, BRFWA can be a useful weapon. The first step is to notice the *Breath.* As we become stressed, breathing quickens and becomes more shallow. Focusing one's attention on deepening and slowing the breath is the first step to reestablishing a calm state. Deep belly breathing triggers the parasympathetic response, activating the rest and digest system, unlike shallow chest breathing that activates the sympathetic nervous system. The next step is *Relaxation.* Releasing and softening muscles while maintaining a deep breathing rhythm can dissipate feelings of stress. So many of us hold our tension in our muscles. Creating a focus on the breath and deliberately and consciously relaxing the muscles diverts attention away from the stress-inducing thought or event. After establishing a deep breath and a relaxed, physical state, we notice how we *Feel.* What emotions or sensations can you become aware of? Most important is to achieve awareness and clarity. The next step, *Watch,* refers to observing your entire experience without attachment, that is, not embracing what is positive and pleasurable or avoiding that which is negative or distressing. It is an attempt to step out of oneself and become an objective witness to what has transpired. Finally, you *Allow,* acknowledging the experience as it has unfolded, knowing that it was fine to react in your own way, and lifting any pressure of reacting according to a prior expectation you might have held. This self-analysis can become habitual with practice. It is a method to bring one back to the moment by understanding and embracing it. The end result is a revelation that you are enough as you are. It is simply an acceptance of yourself, your behaviors, your reactions and your emotions. In Western culture, there is a pervasive competitive attitude that too many of us possess. Making mistakes becomes fraught with negative self-judgments. Perfection, however, is an unrealistic expectation. Recognizing that we all make mistakes promotes a healthier attitude of self-acceptance. Imagine how easy it would be to take care of your landscaping if we all loved the look of weeds and had no need to grow grass or manicure a lawn. We need not try to manicure our expressions and behaviors for the sake of appearances. Embrace yourself as you are, not how you think you need to be. Embrace your mistakes as opportunities for learning rather than resigning yourself to failure.

Another technique for self-actualization that is taught at Kripalu is called, "Riding the Wave." The wave is composed of crescendoing anxiety and stress arising from a disturbing or distressing event. Before the wave crests, many of us "jump" off of it, reverting to reflexive and automatic negative thoughts and behaviors, including negative self-judgments, and defense mechanisms to lessen the stress. Learning more positive coping skills by having a full experience and a chance to understand the stressor is blocked. As a new wave of anxiety forms from another distressing event, one's response to stress remains unchanged. Each time one "jumps" off of the wave before it crests, opportunities for developing new perspectives and learning more positive attitudes and coping skills are lost. Anxiety begets anxiety as a vicious cycle ensues. Remaining on the wave is difficult. It requires tapping into one's inner strength to come face to face with painful and disturbing thoughts of feeling unsafe or out of control. Allowing the wave to crest, however, lets one appreciate the full impact of an experience, even if it is wrought with pain. As the wave begins to subside, we have an opportunity for self-analysis. Once the wave has fully abated and calm sets in, ensuing introspection might lessen future anxieties.

Perhaps, what seemed unmanageable before now seems reasonable. Rather than being left to speculation, riding the wave can allow for a full understanding of the experience and our reactions to the experience. New healthier perspectives and greater resilience are now possible. The practice of Kripalu Yoga can be transformational, as one learns both on and off the mat to ride the wave of a personal challenge. Through our practice we learn new strategies through introspection. Rather than triggering our ingrained, habitual responses that fail to serve us when faced with a stressor, we can first choose to breathe and relax, then access our feelings, watch, and finally allow ourselves to react in a way that better serves us.

When I attended my first yoga class, a plethora of emotions and thoughts filled my head, mostly negative self-judgments. I was raised to believe that success could only be realized through perfection. Mistakes equated to failure. I don't believe that particular perspective is peculiar to me. I believe that so many of us develop habitual anxiety from the possibility of making mistakes. Because perfection and success without failure are unrealistic expectations, inner criticisms arise. Lowered self-esteem may occur as we generalize experiences to global statements of "not being good enough" or "others can do what I cannot". I possessed the wrong mindset when I began to practice yoga. I compared myself to other students, was lost and confused as the teacher blurted out the names of the various *asanas,* and experienced pain and discomfort while I envied my limber and flexible teacher. I faced two choices. One option was to "jump off" the wave before it crested and succumb to my negative self-judgments and reflexive self-expressions of low esteem, defense mechanisms that developed over many years, never to move beyond my misconceptions of yoga or to return to another class. The other option, which I can assure you I chose, was to push on and see what would unfold. That wave took quite a long time to crest. Anxiety persisted as I remained mired in false expectations in many classes to follow and lamented over my ineptitude as I watched online videos. Once that wave crested, however, I was finally able to breathe. Through retrospective self-analysis, I came to identify and understand all of the factors contributing to my anxiety as a novice in the world of yoga. Reading about yogic philosophy and the benefits and different perspectives on the ultimate goals of yoga helped me to ride the wave all the way to the shore. With each class and online video, the waves of anxiety lessened in height and became more manageable over time. Even now, waves of self-doubt continue to crest as they roll into the shore, but the height of those waves are a magnitude less than when I first began.

If I had to identify the one guiding principle that more than any other allowed me to overcome the obstacles to a meaningful yoga practice, as well as served as an impetus to write this book, it would be Swami Kripalu's concept of "self-observation without judgment." This idea continues to be dear to my heart. If I didn't learn to free myself from my inner critic and the pressure to perform, I would have never been able to develop my practice. Initially, I thought the concept only applied to practicing yoga, but soon came to realize that it can be applied to every endeavor one attempts in life. "Self-observation without judgment" sounds like such a simple concept, but in actuality, it is quite complex with multiple layers of meaning. Taken at face value, self-observation simply means watching yourself. In a yoga class, a mirror on a wall can allow you to visualize the body. Sometimes mirrors, however, may worsen negative self-judgments if one possesses a poor body image or is unable to achieve the full expression of a posture. In addition, seeing the reflections of others can lead to undesirable comparisons.

Judgments that may arise with self-observation may be negative or positive. One might witness a teacher correcting a fellow student's posture. In many classes, you may experience a teacher who walks between the mats to correct students. The student being corrected inherently believes that they are "doing" something "wrong" that requires correction, whether or not they welcome the correction. The student on the adjacent mat who is not being corrected assumes they are "doing" the posture "right". Thoughts of "doing" the postures "right" or "wrong" are self-judgments. Positive or negative self-judgments have the power to cloud the mind and distract away from the clarity we desire.

In a yoga class, by using the other senses, observation need not be visual. You can use the sense of hearing to listen to the breath as it moves in and out of the mouth or nose, observing its rhythm that melds with the rhythm of your movements. With the sense of touch, you can experience the feel of the feet or hands grounding into the mat, creating stability, balance and greater confidence in attempting postures. We also possess the sense of proprioception. Proprioception is an awareness of where the body is positioned in space. Proprioceptive receptors in the joints and extremities send signals to the brain giving us an appreciation for the changing relationship of the body to gravity and space as we move.

Mindfulness of all sensations widens the scope of self-observation. Mindfulness brings you into the moment. It is difficult to have two thoughts at once. The brain is most efficient at processing information if presented with one stimulus at a time. A classic mindfulness exercise uses a Hershey's Kiss. Visually one can explore the appearance of the Kiss; the glint of light reflecting off of the silver, metallic, wrinkled foil wrapper and the wispy white paper ribbon sticking out the top. One can experience the sound of a finger running over the wrapper. The foil wrapper changes in appearance as it is unwrapped from the Kiss.

Once the Kiss is unwrapped, the scent of milk chocolate can be experienced. As the Kiss is placed in the mouth, both the evolution of the taste and the changing touch sensations on the tongue unfold as the chocolate slowly melts. Once the Kiss is almost liquefied, the feel of the teeth pushing into the soft chocolate can be appreciated. Swallowing the Kiss creates a taste sensation on the back of the throat. To take this exercise to an extreme, before the initial visual assessment is performed, one might consider the creation of the Kiss, from farming to manufacturing to delivery to the store. In the above exercise, focus and concentration are directed in succession to one sense at a time. Mindfulness is an awareness of each sensation in each moment. Mindfulness exercises can be done with yoga by individually focusing on each of the senses as they relate to the *asanas* and the breath. Meditative moments arise from non-distracted focus on one thing at a time. If the brain focuses on a single sensation, the mind clears as it becomes difficult for other thoughts to arise.

Consider *tadasana,* the mountain pose. Mindfulness can be practiced by shifting one's single point of focus while assuming the posture. First, one might focus on the feet, noticing the points of contact of the feet on the mat or the sensation arising from actively pressing down with the feet. Next, focus could shift to the thighs, noticing the contraction of the quadriceps muscles and the consequent gentle lifting of the knee caps. One might then concentrate on the shoulders, noticing if they are shrugged up towards the ears or relaxed down the back. Focus might then shift to the breath, listening to the sound as air travels in and out of the nose. Since it is difficult to concentrate on more than one thought at a time, deliberate, directed focus to one part of the body at a time is more effective at clearing the mind of other thoughts relative to a more global experience of the posture.

The pace of a Kripalu class affords opportunities for development of single-pointed concentration and mental clarity. In general, the tempo of a yoga class more often relates to the type of yoga being practiced. At one extreme is a fast-paced *vinyasa* class with a relatively continuous flow of movement and quick transitions between *asanas.* At the other end of the spectrum is restorative yoga in which postures are held for many minutes. Kripalu yoga falls somewhere in between that range. There is a flow with smooth transitions between postures, which are held long enough to focus on sensations and the connection of the breath to the movement. The luxury of time allows for experimentation with redirecting one's focus while sustaining an *asana,* creating the potential for a novel experience.

In the Kripalu tradition, we often end our classes by saying, "*jai bhagwan!*", which, among other things, translates to "a blessed victory." How one's yoga practice is a victory is up to each one of us to decide. We all face challenges in our lives, some more daunting than others. Whether through newfound spirituality or simply through stress reduction, the practice of yoga can help to better face the battle. Saying "*jai bhagwan*" is also a wonderful way to end a class on a joyful and celebratory note. To you I say "*jai bhagwan*" and may your yoga practice be a blessed victory in your life and may your life be full of blessed victories!

8

THE ANATOMY OF YOGA

The human body is first and foremost a mirror to the soul and its greatest beauty comes from that.

Auguste Rodin

Before delving into anatomy as it relates to the practice of yoga, it would be good to take a step back and marvel at the miracle that is the human body. Unfathomable complexity exists all the way from the microscopic to the macroscopic levels. At the subcellular level, atomic and subatomic particles intimately interact to create stability out of chaos, harnessing energy to overcome entropy, the randomness that exists in the universe. Elements form that combine to give rise to molecules. The various configurations of those molecules are limitless, yet they organize to become the structure of our cells. The number of cells in the human body is estimated to be in the trillions. That represents a number followed by twelve zeroes. Each cell contains a central information center, the nucleus, within which are chromosomes that contain the blueprints of life. Each chromosome is composed of genes consisting of beautiful helices of deoxyribonucleic acid (DNA), encoded with the information to ultimately produce proteins. Those proteins dictate the structure of tissues and organs and their specific functions. We all share many commonalities in gene structure, but the millions of variations and arrangements of genes also gives rise to individuality. Our cells organize into various structures, tissues and organs like the brain, heart and liver and become specialized for specific functions in each organ. Neurons in the brain conduct electrical signals, cardiac muscle cells contract and release to power the pump that delivers blood and precious oxygen throughout the body, hepatocytes filter toxins and produce bile, hair follicles produce keratin and cells in glands of the endocrine system produce hormones that regulate metabolism, digestion, and mood. As they develop, every cell in the body differentiates to perform a specialized function. They all have different roles to play, but also act in concert to sustain us. It is a veritable symphony made up of trillions of different types of instruments that together produce the music of life. And even more miraculous is that the cells in our brain, these neurons that merely function to transmit electrical signals, allow us to think.

Our thoughts occur both on subconscious and conscious levels. Hundreds of functions operate behind the scenes and out of conscious thought to maintain and sustain the body. Under the so-called "radar" are a myriad of physiologic functions that regulate the vital functions of our cardiovascular, pulmonary, endocrine, genitourinary and digestive systems. On the conscious level, we can analyze, examine, observe and react. The *asanas* are an integral part of yoga. Each posture requires the movement of particular muscles, tendons, ligaments, joints and bones. Those movements begin in the brain as thoughts. Often we are unaware of those thoughts. Each second the brain produces millions of signals that travel down the spinal cord and throughout the musculoskeletal system, instructing and guiding our limbs, torso, neck and head into orchestrated movements. Sensory receptors embedded throughout the muscles, joints and supporting structures react to movement, subsequently sending messages as electrical signals back to the spinal cord and up to the brain where we can react and feel. Every movement begins and ends with a thought.

Our senses also represent an integral part of the entire mind-body experience of yoga. Chemical reactions in the rods and cones of the retina convert light into electrical signals that are sent to the optic cortex in the brain, allowing us to appreciate whatever we see. By closing the eyes as we practice we can quiet the activity of the optic tracts and lessen visual stimuli. As we listen to the breath coming in and out of the nose, sound waves that strike the eardrum are transmitted through the ossicles or bones in the middle ear. Mechanical energy is then converted to electrical energy as the sound waves initiate chemical reactions in the hair cells of the cochlear in the inner ear. Electrical signals finally stimulate the auditory cortex of the brain, allowing us to appreciate the sounds we hear. Adjacent to the cochlear is the labyrinth of the inner ear that reacts to motion and imbalance, constantly updating the position of the body in space and activating centers in the brain that bring us to states of stability. If a studio uses incense or a diffuser to fill the air with a scent or possibly you are out in nature practicing yoga, your sense of smell will come into play. Molecules arising from the source of an aroma enter the nostrils as we breathe, eventually reaching chemoreceptors in the nose that also generate electrical signals to ultimately activate the olfactory cortex along the frontal lobes of the brain. As we ground our feet on our mats for the standing *asanas,* sensory receptors in the skin send information to the spinal cord and superiorly to the brain so we can appreciate the feelings of touch, as well as security, safety and balance as we connect with the earth. Proprioreceptors, organelles that relay information about the position of the joints, provide us with an awareness of the body as it moves through space.

Similar physiological functions are ubiquitous throughout the animal world. But, what separates us as unique beings is the capacity for conscious, abstract thought. We can interpret and analyze data. Our abstractions can trigger feelings and emotions. And whether you believe in an actual soul or consider it to be just electrical signals arising from the firings of neurons in the brain, it is that inexplicable part of our personalities that allows us to connect with ourselves and embrace life. Nourishing the soul and connecting with your true authentic self can lead to feelings of contentment, satisfaction and, ultimately, peace. That sense of peace begins with the relationships and interactions of atoms that give rise to the function of cells and complexities of the multilevel hierarchy of tissues and organs of the body. The human body is certainly a miracle. Through our practice of yoga we can honor that miracle. Yoga provides us with the luxury of time to ponder and wonder about all of the miracles of life and nature. We are a part of the beauty of nature. Accessing that beauty within ourselves leads to self-love. With self-love we can love others. Atoms to love ~ quite the miracle!

Definitions

- *Anterior* - towards the front of the body
- *Posterior* - towards the back of the body
- *Lateral* - to the side
- *Medial* - towards center
- *Flexion* - bending
- *Extension* - extending out straight

With regard to human anatomy as it pertains to yoga, for the sake of simplicity the physical body can be divided into three categories: the joints, the spine and the muscles. In actuality, all three are integrated and function concurrently. For example, the range of motion of the spine is dependent on facet joints between the bony vertebral bodies and deep paraspinous muscles that course along the back of the spine. We can also consider the body as consisting of the axial and appendicular skeletons; axial being the adjective form of axis and appendicular that of appendage. The axial bones, associated joints and attached muscles that form the central axis of the body are distinguished from those of the appendages; the arms and legs.

Just like any other physical activity or sport, in yoga we prepare by warming up the body for the *asanas* to follow. The specific targets of the warm-ups in yoga can be divided into the same aforementioned anatomic categories: the joints, the spine and the muscles, although all three are intimately involved in all of the movements. The teacher should select warm-ups appropriate to the *asanas* that he or she plans to guide, focusing on the spine, specific joints and muscle groups that will be employed for those specific postures.

As we warm-up the joints we wish to loosen, open and lubricate them. As we get older, our joints tend to stiffen and become more constricted and inflexible. A regular yoga practice can reverse that process. Almost all of the joints in the body are synovial joints. The joint complex allows for articulated movement of two or more bones. The bones at the articulation are covered with cartilage. Superficial to the cartilage is synovium. Synovium is a specialized type of tissue whose cells secrete a relatively viscous fluid. The fluid lubricates the opposing surfaces of the joint. With osteoarthritis, over time the synovium and cartilage lining the bony surfaces begins to thin and degenerate. Without the cushioning effect of the cartilage and the lubrication provided by the synovial fluid, the joint space narrows as bone contacts bone, and progressively the bone is destroyed. Once the bony surfaces become irregular, the full range of motion across the joint is lost and the joint loses functionality. The rubbing together of the irregular bony surfaces also induces pain. Eventually, pain and/or loss of function necessitates a joint replacement with a prosthesis.

The act of moving and opening the joints spreads the lubricating synovial fluid over all surfaces of an articulation, allowing for smooth gliding between the components of the joint. It is analogous to motor oil lubricating the pistons of an engine. As the engine warms up, oil is spread evenly over the surfaces of the pistons, assuring smooth motion while preventing wear and tear. Synovial fluid lubricates and spreads throughout the joint during our warmups to prevent undue stress while sustaining the *asanas*.

Often when we warm up joints, an audible "cracking" or "popping" sound is produced. This is a normal occurrence and not related to joint pathology, such as arthritis. It is merely the disruption of surface tension created by the synovial fluid being stretched as opposing parts of the joint are distracted. It is analogous to a soap bubble being stretched until it loses its surface tension and pops. "Cracking of the knuckles" occurs through the same mechanism. Applying pressure on both sides of the knuckle or metacarpalphalangeal joint distracts the bony surfaces to overcome the surface tension of the synovial fluid that lines the joint.

Throughout the musculoskeletal system, there are different configurations of joints that correspond to required functions. Movements of the body occur in different planes and through different mechanisms associated with the motion of specific body parts. These movements include flexion and extension. Flexion of the arms and legs brings the bones across a joint towards one another, while extension moves them apart. Considering the elbow joint, flexion draws the ulna and radius of the forearm towards the humerus of the upper arm; extension the opposite. Axial transverse movement of a joint represents a twisting motion, as is seen in the wrist and ankle joints. Rotational movement occurs at the shoulder and hip joints, which are ball and socket joints. Those joints are warmed-up with circular motions originating at the level of the shoulder and hip joints. Similar to the elbow, the knee and the joints of the fingers and toes are hinge-type joints and are warmed up with flexion and extension in one plane. The ankle and wrist are more complex, approximate a hybrid of both hinge and ball and socket joints, and are warmed up with both rotation and flexion and extension.

It is also important to note that the joints are all surrounded by a joint capsule consisting of an inner layer of synovial tissue and an outer layer of fibrous tissue, which in turn is surrounded by fascia. Fascia is a fibrous tissue that acts to support and stabilize a joint, preventing malalignments and dislocations. Imagining paper mache applied to a surface, the fascia is intimately attached to the external surface of the joint. Localized thickening of the fascia forms the ligaments of the joint. Therefore, ligaments are also composed of fibrous tissue. The tendons that attach muscles to bones are composed primarily of parallel arrays of collagen fibers. With inactivity, as well as advancing age, the tendency is for the fibrous tissues of the joint capsule, surrounding fascia and ligaments and the collagenous tissues of the tendons to become chronically stiff and contracted over time. Repetitive stretching of the structures of the joint through a regular yoga practice can reverse that process. Relative to muscle, the fibrous tissues of the joint and tendons are inherently inelastic. Therefore, increases in flexibility of joints occur much more slowly than muscles. Because increasing the pliability of the soft tissue components of a joint is a gradual process, extreme patience is required as one practices yoga. One does not become flexible overnight. As was discussed previously, the repetitive stretching of all the soft tissues triggers the release of "happy hormones." Patience is also required to feel the positive effects of those hormones, requiring time for the adaptation and autoregulation of the neurotransmitters and synapses of the brain.

The spine consists of thirty-three vertebrae: seven cervical, twelve thoracic, five lumbar, five sacral and four coccygeal. The coccyx is a vestigial remnant of a tail that disappeared during our evolution, hence the word "tailbone." It has little or no function and deserves no further discussion. Seen from the side, the spine forms an "S" shape created by three curves or lordoses. The cervical and lumbar lordoses are convex anteriorly or arced towards the front of the body and the thoracic lordosis is convex posteriorly or towards the back of the body. The physics of a curved structure is such that it can offer more resistance to applied forces than a straight one. This is true in all forms of architecture where an arch can handle a greater weight load than a straight horizontal element. The orientation of the curves of the spine allows it to withstand greater axial loading, that is, head to toe forces, than if it were straight. While in an upright position, as one progresses down the spine, more and more weight from more proximal segments needs to be supported. Thus, the lumbosacral spine experiences the greatest amount of axial loading while we are standing as it is required to support the weight of the more proximal vertebrae of the cervical and thoracic spines, as well as the head. Malalignments and poor posture compromise the lumbar spine's ability to withstand axial loading, thereby predisposing it to the development of lower back pathology with associated chronic back pain. The cervical spine functions to support the head, which weighs on the order of ten to eleven pounds. Similarly, malalignments in the cervical spine lead to chronic neck pain and other neck maladies. The thoracic spine is more protected from malalignment issues and pathology because of the stabilizing forces of the ribs. Except for the last two ribs, the ribs attach anteriorly to the sternum and posteriorly to the thoracic spine, thus forming the rib cage. In yoga, through paraspinous muscle strengthening and the muscle memory that is learned through assuming proper posture during the standing *asanas,* the tolerance for axial loading is increased and the potential for acute and chronic neck and back injury is minimized. As you have already experienced, elongation of the spine and proper upright posture is emphasized in *tadasana,* the mountain pose.

The spine is capable of moving in six directions: flexion, or bending forward, extension, or arching back, lateral flexion, or bending side to side to the right and left, and twisting to the right and left. Since the spine is involved in all of the *asanas,* warm-ups should always include those six motions. The spine has a relatively limited range of motion. Each vertebra articulates with those above and below it. The vertebral body, the larger, anterior, rounded part of the vertebra, is separated from the adjacent vertebral body by the intervertebral disc. These discs are like cushions filled with a gelatinous substance, the nucleus pulposus, and surrounded by a fibrous capsule, the annulus fibrosis. The discs can undergo a process of degeneration whereby the nucleus pulposus loses its water content or dessicates. The annulus fibrosis loses its firmness allowing the disc to bulge. If a tear develops in the annulus, a disc herniation ensues. The relatively fixed positions of the intervertebral discs and vertebral bodies decreases inherent mobility of the spine. Most of the range of motion of the spine is attributed to the facet joints. Each vertebrae has four facets posteriorly which articulate with those above and below through synovial joints. Despite the relative greater mobility of these joints, they are structured to maintain the stability of the vertebral column to protect the spinal cord it surrounds. Finally, the attachments of the rib cage to the thoracic spine in the back and the sternum in the front limit movement of the thoracic spine.

Intimately associated with the posterior or back of the spine are deep paraspinous muscles. You might imagine these as a scaffolding of silly putty running lengthwise on either side of the spine. As these muscles contract, they function to exert a backward pull on the spine, helping it to remain upright and elongated. As part of the normal aging process, muscles lose mass and atrophy. If those deep paraspinous muscles lose tone, their function becomes compromised. Without that backward pull on the spine, it can round forward. Many elderly people often have a chronic, forward rounding of the spine or kyphosis. With a regular yoga practice, the six movements of the spine result in strengthening of those paraspinous muscles, maintaining their posterior pull and assuring straight posture as we age.

Yoga is extremely beneficial for the health of muscles. Progressive stretching of a muscle over time, not only strengthens it, but also creates greater flexibility. The development of that strength and flexibility occurs slowly over an extended period of time. Yoga requires patience. Accept that positive change will come with work. Then, by focusing on what you can do and not what you can't at the present moment, dissatisfaction over what you perceive as physical limitations need not occur. One must not be impatient and feel compelled to rush the process. Overstretching of muscles can result in microtears or even frank tears on a larger scale. An impatient practitioner of yoga might develop an attitude of "no pain, no gain", believing that flexibility will only come and come fast if he or she is feeling pain and discomfort. In yoga it can be said, "pain, no gain!" Safe stretching of muscles in yoga requires one to find his or her edge. The edge is the point where discomfort occurs while stretching. When that edge is experienced, one should ease off to a safe point of minimal or no discomfort. In time, as the muscles progressively stretch you will find your edge moving in a positive direction.

There are antagonistic muscles and muscle groups in the musculoskeletal system. Antagonistic muscles do not hate each other, but occupy the same region of the body, possessing opposing functions. For example, the biceps and triceps in the upper arm are antagonistic. Contraction of the biceps muscle flexes the arm while the triceps is passively stretched. Contraction of the triceps muscle extends the arm out straight while the biceps is passively stretched. You can feel this effect by placing your hand on the biceps as you flex and extend the arm. The muscle will contract and release with the movement. Various muscle groups have opposing functions. The inner thigh muscles or hip adductors are antagonistic to the hip abductors, the former pulling the thighs together with contraction and the latter pulling them apart and rotating the hips out laterally as they contract. Once again, when the adductors contract, the abductors passively stretch, and vice versa. Similarly, muscles along the top of the forearm extend the wrist and fingers and are antagonistic to muscles along the bottom of the forearm that result in flexion. In all of the warm-ups and *asanas* we do throughout our practice, antagonistic muscles are constantly working and releasing as we move. These actions allow the muscles to have periods of active contraction and passive stretching. Periods of release and relaxation of the muscles protects them from overuse and potential tears. As anyone that has climbed a long flight of stairs knows, sustained contraction of muscles leads to a "burning" sensation caused by the buildup of lactic acid that occurs when the muscles are so overworked that they become deprived of oxygen. The periods of rest that occur as the antagonistic muscles work in opposition assure a more than adequate delivery of oxygen to the muscle fibers.

One need not be an anatomist to appreciate human anatomy as it pertains to the practice of yoga. This book is a practical guide to yoga with the intent of presenting information in limited detail, but at the same time offering the reader an overall view and knowledge of yoga to enhance one's experience. In that regard, knowing all of the names of the muscles of the body is not a prerequisite for developing a meaningful yoga practice. Many yoga instructors, however, will refer to specific muscles or muscle groups so I will discuss only the muscles or muscle groups that are more likely to be mentioned. Those muscles appear in italics.

Tendons attach muscles to bones. With regard to the description of a muscle's location and action, we define the origin of the muscle as the end that produces less or no motion of the associated bones and the insertion as the point of attachment that causes the associated bones to move to the greatest extent upon contraction. An example is the biceps muscle. Its origin is from the bones of the shoulder girdle, which when the muscle contracts remain relatively stable in place. Its insertion is on the radius, just distal to the elbow joint, which undergoes the greatest degree of motion as the muscle contracts, drawing the forearm toward the upper arm. The following descriptions of muscles, along with their origins and insertions, will proceed from superior to inferior, beginning at the level of the head and neck.

The largest muscle that supports the head and neck is the *sternocleidomastoid muscle.* You can palpate this muscle on the side of your neck. It becomes more prominent by tilting your head toward your shoulder. The origin of the muscle is from the superior portion of the sternum or breastbone and clavicle or collarbone, hence "sternocleido" and its insertion is on the mastoid process of the temporal bone, located just below the ear on either side of the skull. The muscle's action is rotation and lateral flexion of the head and neck. We designate the sternum and clavicle, which remain relatively motionless upon contraction of the muscle, as the origin of the muscle. The insertion is on the mastoid, which is drawn laterally and downward as the muscle contracts, pulling the remainder of the skull along with it. Beneath this thick muscle lies the carotid artery and internal jugular vein, the main blood supply to the brain. This protective relationship likely was an important factor in natural selection during evolution. This muscle is especially thick in dogs, protecting those two important vascular structures from a bite from a fellow canine or other toothed predator. Owners of larger dogs know that their dogs easily tolerate the strong pull of a choker collar owing to this broad and bulky muscle.

The *trapezius muscle,* sometimes referred to as "the trap", is a large trapezoid-shaped muscle responsible for the multidirectional movements of the scapula, or shoulder blade, and clavicle, or collarbone. This muscle is usually the target of a good neck and shoulder massage. It originates from the lower skull and cervical spine and inserts on the clavicle, scapula, and portions of the back, which undergo movement as the muscle contracts. There are some that hold a lot of stress in their muscles. The trapezius muscle, along with other deep muscles of the neck, is often a site of chronic tension. The electronic devices of the modern era create a greater potential for the development of "computer and cell phone neck". Unconscious, frequent contraction of the neck muscles triggered by anxiety and stress leads to chronic neck pain and poor alignment of the cervical spine. One function of the trapezius muscle is to pull the shoulder blades upward. With yoga, we can soften and release the trapezius and other neck muscles by dropping the shoulders, allowing the shoulder blades to melt down the back. One can create muscle memory of the feel of the relaxation of the neck muscles by frequently and consciously shrugging the shoulders toward the ears and then experiencing the downward movement of the shoulders and shoulder blades as the muscles release and soften.

The *deltoid muscle* originates from the clavicle and top of the scapula and inserts on a tuberosity located on the outer surface of the humerus or upper arm bone. The main function of the muscle is abducting the arm. Abduction refers to the movement of a body part away from the center axis of the body. One way to remember the term is to think of a movement stealing or abducting that body part away from the center axis. The opposite of abduction is adduction, a movement towards the center of the body. You can feel the contraction of the deltoid by placing your hand on the outside of the shoulder and upper arm as you lift the arm away from the body.

Deep to the deltoid is the *rotator cuff*. The rotator cuff, as it sounds, is responsible for the rotational movement of the shoulder, which again is a ball-in-socket joint. The muscles of the rotator cuff also have a significant role in stabilizing the shoulder, preventing dislocations and subluxations. The rotator cuff is composed of four muscles that originate on the scapula and insert on the humeral head, one anteriorly, one superiorly and two posteriorly. Although it is doubtful that your yoga instructor will mention them, for completeness sake, those muscles from anterior to posterior are the *subscapularis, supraspinatus, infraspinatus and teres minor*. As mentioned previously, the shoulder or glenohumeral joint is a ball and socket joint. As the muscular insertions are on the humerus, it is the upper arm that moves in a circular fashion with activation of the rotator cuff. During the warm-ups in my yoga class, I always guide students through circling of the arms or other rotational movements of the shoulders in order to stretch these very important muscles that are involved in so many of the postures. Many of the *asanas* require lifting the arm above the head or over the ear, which puts stress on the rotator cuff. Those particular movements can be quite uncomfortable or painful for people with rotator pathology and/or acromioclavicular degenerative joint disease , and therefore, modifications should be offered.

Distal to the shoulder in the upper arm are the *biceps* and *triceps*. The suffix "ceps" comes from the Latin for head. The biceps consists of two heads, hence "bi" "ceps" or two distinct, but intimately associated upper muscle bellies that each have their own tendinous origin on the scapula. These join distally to form a single muscle and tendon that crosses the elbow joint to insert on a tuberosity on the radius, one of the two forearm bones, the other being the ulna. The triceps consists of three heads, one originating from the scapula and the other two from the upper humerus, and similarly forms a single tendon distally that inserts on the olecranon process of the ulna. The olecranon process is the knob you feel as you cup the back of the elbow and is also what someone feels if you "give them the elbow." As noted, the biceps and triceps are antagonistic muscles that accomplish flexion and extension of the arm across the elbow joint, respectively.

The muscles in the forearm are characterized as *flexors, extensors, supinators* and *pronators*. Flexion and extension occur across the wrist joint. By grabbing the forearm, you can feel the flexors contract as you bend the wrist and the extensors engage with wrist extension. Rotational movements of the wrist are the function of the supinators and pronators.

The muscles of the chest, back and abdomen produce the six movements of the spine, some in concert and others antagonistically. They allow for flexion, extension, lateral flexion and twisting of the spine. Many of these muscles also contribute to the movements of the limbs, especially in adduction. They are located nearer to the central axis of the body, pulling the more peripherally located limbs inward as they contract. The names of these muscles that you will often hear in a yoga class are the *pectoralis muscles* or "pecs" in the chest, the *rectus muscles* or "abs", the *internal* and *external obliques* or just "obliques" along the front and sides of the abdominal wall, respectively, and the *latissimus dorsi* or "lats" along the back. These muscles all contribute to the "core". The core consists of superficial and deep muscles extending from the neck to the pelvis. Almost all of the *asanas* strengthen the core, however, the majority of the time we are unaware of the engagement and release of those muscles. Simultaneous contraction of the arm and leg muscles automatically activates the core. You can experience this by focusing on the chest and abdominal muscles while coming into a standing star position; legs spread apart and arms extended out at forty-five degrees. The arm and leg muscles contract from pressing the feet into the mat and pulling the finger tips away from the body. Secondarily, the core muscles contract. Conversely, relaxing the limb muscles relaxes the core.

The *gluteus muscles* or "glutes" are located in the buttocks. There are three gluteal muscles: *maximus, medius* and *minimus*. The gluteus maximus is most superficial and palpable. It originates from the sacrum and iliac bone that comprises the so-called wing of the pelvis. The muscle inserts, in part, on the greater trochanter of the femur, which is a protuberance on the lateral aspect of the upper thigh bone.

The muscle participates in external rotation and extension of the hip joint. Another important muscle, the *psoas muscle,* inserts on the lesser trochanter on the medial side of the upper femur, and helps with flexion of the hip joint. It is a long muscle that originates from the sides of the spine from the last thoracic level T12 and all five lumbar levels, extending down through the pelvis to insert on the lesser trochanter. Because the muscle is so extensive, psoas strains, tears or dysfunction can lead to lower back, pelvic, groin and/or hip pain, and therefore maintaining strength, flexibility and good tone of this muscle is paramount. The muscle contracts in any postures that flex the hip and stretches and releases with hip extension.

There are twenty muscles that cross the hip joint and are involved in all of its complex motions. Like the shoulder or glenohumeral joint, the hip or femoroacetabular joint is a ball and socket joint. The acetabulum, a cup-shaped portion of the pelvis, is the socket and the femoral head is the ball. As a ball and socket joint, it is capable of complex rotational motions coupled with flexion and extension. Strengthening and establishing good muscle tone of the muscles around the hip promote flexibility and decrease the potential for osteoarthritis and other degenerative processes.

The main bones of the leg are the femur or thigh bone and the two main bones of the lower leg, the tibia and fibula. Similar to the arms, the muscles of the legs are antagonistic with opposing functions. In the upper thigh, the *quadriceps muscles* in the anterior thigh oppose the *hamstring muscles* posteriorly. The quadriceps muscles represent four distinctive muscles ("quadra" "ceps") that originate from the bones of the pelvis with a common distal quadriceps tendon that inserts on the patella or kneecap. An additional tendon, the patella tendon, arises from the lower pole of the patella and inserts on a tuberosity on the anterior aspect of the upper tibia. The patella is a sesamoid bone, a specialized, independent bone that develops within a tendon that does not articulate with any other bony structures. The quadriceps muscle group creates an extensive, complex extension of the leg from the pelvis to the tibia via the quadriceps and patella tendons that hold the patella in space. The quadriceps muscles are the extensor group of the thigh. When the muscles contract, tension is applied to the patella and tibia as the knee joint straightens. The antagonistic flexor group of the thigh are the hamstrings, three distinct muscles that originate from the ischial tuberosities of the pelvis or sitz bones. A yoga instructor often mentions the sitz bones. While you are sitting, if you slip your fingers under the buttocks, you can palpate the sitz bones. These bones are actually called the ischial tuberosities, but sitz bones seems much more descriptive and easier to say. The hamstrings extend from the ischial tuberosities and insert on the posterior aspects of the upper tibia and fibular head. When the hamstrings contract, pull is applied to the backs of the tibia and fibula causing the knee to flex or bend. A common misconception arises when one bends over from the hip crease with a straight, extended leg and experiences discomfort in the hamstrings along the back of the upper leg. The discomfort may lead one to believe that the muscle is working and contracting, but in actuality, the muscle is relaxed and undergoing stretching. It is also the stretch on the distal tendons that can create the most discomfort. Similarly, discomfort may arise from stretching the quadriceps, such as can occur with crouching or squatting, however, the discomfort is solely from passive stretching of the muscular and tendinous fibers, rather than contraction.

Additional muscles that are found in the thigh are the *hip adductor* and *abductor* groups. The hip adductor group or inner thigh muscles pull the thighs together. Passive stretching and potential discomfort in the hip adductor muscles come from pulling the legs apart, the antagonistic function of the abductor muscles. One of the abductors is the *tensor fasciae latae* that originates from the iliac bone of the pelvis and is continuous with the *iliotibial tract* or *band,* which runs down the side of the thigh to insert on the lateral tibia. The tensor fasciae latae is foreshortened in a sitting position so it easily becomes tight, especially in so many of us that sit for hours at work. Tightness and stiffness of the muscle can lead to knee problems. Stretching and strengthening the muscle occurs as we practice yoga.

As you see, antagonistic muscles function to move joints in opposite directions. In the lower leg, there are flexors and extensors. The primary flexors of the calf are the *gastrocnemius muscles,* deep to which is the *soleus muscle.* These three muscles arise from the upper tibia, occupy the back of the calf and form a common tendon, the *Achilles tendon.* The Achilles tendon inserts on the back of the calcaneus or heel bone. The heel is pulled up as the calf muscles contract resulting in flexion of the ankle joint. For the ankle joint, flexion results in the toes pointing away from the body. If the calf muscles are chronically tight, persistent tension is applied to the Achilles tendon, promoting degenerative changes and potential tearing of the tendon. The extensor muscle group in the anterior lower leg produces the bending of the ankle joint to an acute angle, toes pointing up to the sky. The flexors and extensors in the lower leg, along with shorter intrinsic muscles of the foot, also create flexion and extension across the joints of the toes. The flexors bend the toes downward, while extensors pull them upward.

Much of the physicality of yoga involves opposing forces in the body. Throughout our practice, we contract and stretch antagonistic muscles. Repetitive contraction results in muscle strengthening, while progressive stretching leads to increased flexibility. The antagonistic movements occur in the poses and counterposes we sustain. A pose is a particular posture we assume that requires the contraction of numerous muscles, while others are soft, relaxed and passively stretched. We can see this in the cow and cat postures, which represent a pose and a counterpose. These are both done from a table position where the knees and hands are on the mat and directly under the shoulders and hips, respectively. The cow requires the lifting of the tailbone and sternum as the gaze comes up, resulting in extension or arching of the spine. assuming the appearance of an old cow. The cat is the counterpose whereby the back flexes or rounds, as the tailbone drops and gaze comes down towards the belly, assuming the appearance of an angry cat. Although the extension and flexion of the back may seem like simple movements, they are actually quite complex with many muscles and muscle groups involved. The poses and counterposes result in the muscles successively working and relaxing, engaging and softening. As we practice, we are often unaware of these complimentary muscle actions, but over time they promote strength and flexibility.

In the aforementioned discussion, the musculoskeletal system was divided into three categories: the spine, joints and muscles. It is important to realize, however, that this was done to facilitate the discussion of human anatomy as it relates to the practice of yoga. In actuality, all parts of the body act in concert. Muscles stretch across joints and support the spine. As joints move, muscles contract and relax. The facet joints allow for the six movements of the spine. All of the structures of the musculoskeletal system also work as a unit to provide stability and strength throughout the body. The extreme tensile strength of tendons assures that the muscles are firmly attached to the bones. Muscles that cross joints help to stabilize those joints. Ligaments "tie" bones together and assure proper alignment and optimal functionality of the joints. Adding to joint stability is a fibrous capsule, within which is the synovial fluid that allows the articulating bones to glide smoothly over one another. Finally, there is the strong fibrous fascia that spreads over all of the joints, tendons and muscles like a firmly adherent blanket. The act of stretching in yoga not only acts on the muscles, but also on the tendons, ligaments and fascia. Flexibility and strength are achieved by engaging and stretching all of the soft tissue structures of the musculoskeletal system.

By employing the laws of physics, we can take the most advantage of the anatomical relationships in our bodies. Effective grounding during the *asanas* is paramount in maximizing strength and achieving balance. As you experienced in *tadasana,* the mountain, distributing the weight evenly over all parts of the feet from heel to toe and separating the feet about a hip distance apart, affords greater balance and leg strength relative to other leg positions. You can experience the difference by coming into *tadasana,* but with the inner edges of the feet touching and weight shifted onto the heels or balls of the feet. Now quickly flail the arms back and forth. Then try to do the same with the feet and legs in proper position with good weight distribution. The difference in stability is striking. In fact, proper grounding of the feet optimizes balance in all of the standing postures. The realized stability allows you to assume a multitude of different positions with the upper body. Multiple possibilities open up for upper body movements by being well grounded. Our legs become like supporting girders for our upper body. Just as strong grounding in yoga improves balance, being well grounded in life leads to stress reduction from feelings of stability and safety.

Now, it is time to explore the most important part of the body from a functional and anatomical standpoint, as well as from a yogic perspective: the human brain. It is estimated that there are 100 billion neurons in the brain and 1 trillion glial or supporting cells. Miraculously, these neurons form complexes that become specialized for particular functions in the body. Some parts of the human brain are similar to those of species lower on the evolutionary scale. These more primitive brain structures include the cerebellum and brainstem. These components of the brain regulate basic functions such as balance, hearing, sleep, blood pressure, heart rate and breathing, to name just a few. What separates us from lower species is a large, developed cerebral cortex. The complexity of the cortex is astounding. Numerous convolutions increase the surface area of the brain potentiating a greater density of neural cells without increasing the size and weight of the skull.

Our cerebral cortices consist of four main paired lobes: frontal, parietal, temporal and occipital. Located in the parietal lobe is the motor cortex, adjacent and anterior to which is the sensory cortex in the frontal lobe. The motor cortex sends signals down the spinal cord that dictate movements and the sensory cortex receives information from the body that allows us to interpret and react to each movement. Along both of these cortices is a map of the body, called a *homunculus*; from the Latin for "little man". With regard to movement, parts of the body requiring fine movements correspond to a proportionately larger area of the motor cortex. For the sensory cortex, larger areas are devoted to regions of the body with the greatest density of touch receptors, like the fingers and lips, such that the image of the "little man" that represents the cortical map is disproportionate with large hands, fingers, feet, toes, lips and face and a small back and torso where the sense of touch is more muted. As we touch, millions of electrical signals travel from sensory receptors in the skin to the spinal cord via peripheral nerves and then up to the brain. Those electrical signals spread from neuron to neuron throughout the brain, allowing us to interpret our experience and react accordingly. If part of that reaction is movement or if we wish to initiate movements, electrical signals from the motor cortex spread down from the brain to the spinal cord and out through peripheral motor nerves that innervate muscles. The simultaneous production of millions of neural stimuli allows for extremely complex movements of the musculoskeletal system. It is this constant flow of electrical energy that allows us to practice yoga. Our bodies and very beings are filled with energy. Yoga is all about harnessing that energy and directing it to nourish the soul.

Finally, a word about neuroplasticity, the ability of establishing new neural connections in the brain. On a cellular level, this ability is related to the formation of proteins. A regular yoga practice promotes the relaxation response, which over time leads to alterations in gene expression. The genetic code lies in DNA (deoxyribonucleic acid). RNA (ribonucleic acid) is the messenger that delivers the information encrypted in the code to cellular sites, thereby directing the production of specific proteins. Some of those proteins are involved in the formation of memories. In addition, repetitive elicitation of the relaxation response over time leads to the creation of new synaptic connections between neurons. In essence, the stress-reducing effects of a regular yoga practice alters the brain for the better. Although these changes occur on the cellular level, we develop a global awareness of better coping skills and a whole new way to embrace life. As you practice, make sure to take some time to honor your body and marvel at the miracle that you are!

9

THE SCIENCE OF YOGA

The most beautiful experience we can have is the mysterious. It is the fundamental emotion that stands at the cradle of true art and true science.

Albert Einstein

From the very first day of medical school, I was taught that evidence-based data was the foundation for determining the efficacy of treatments and necessary for the conversion of theories into practical therapeutic applications. Great medical scientists in history recognized the need for controlled studies that minimize confounding variables. They created reproducible experiments that led to discoveries that eradicated disease that was often epidemic. Emil von Behring, the discoverer of the cure for diphtheria and the first recipient of the Nobel Prize for Physiology or Medicine, and Alexander

Fleming, who developed the antibiotic penicillin, were just two of the many of these great thinkers. The acceptance of the many benefits of yoga and other meditative practices has primarily been based on empirical evidence and observational data. There is a trend, however, toward the study of these practices through more formal variable-controlled research studies.

I admit a bias toward Western medicine, which should not be surprising. I practiced medicine for over thirty years. Over that time period I witnessed thousands of patients benefited by medical treatments and interventions. Over the years, however, I have also come to understand and appreciate the practices and benefits of many alternative medical therapies. Regardless of the effectiveness of any therapy, however, most care providers believe that stress can create a susceptibility to disease, as well as worsen pre-existing disease states. Think of stress as water in a bucket. If the bucket is full to the brim, it only takes one more drop of water for the bucket to overflow. Yoga and other meditative practices lead to greater resiliency to external stressors. This is especially important for many mental diseases that inherently decrease tolerance for negative outside influences. For physical illnesses, stress can lead to an influx of inflammatory molecules into the bloodstream, interfering with the body's natural immune defenses. The goal is not the prevention of that last drop of water from overflowing the bucket, but to decrease the amount of stress so that the bucket can never overflow.

I had the pleasure and privilege to be associated with the Benson-Henry Institute for Mind Body Medicine at Massachusetts General Hospital in Boston. Its founder, Dr. Herbert Benson, studied physiologic changes in the cardiovascular status of transcendental meditators. He demonstrated that they were able to reduce metabolism, rate of breathing, heart rate, and brain activity through meditation. Dr.

Benson labeled these physiological changes the "relaxation response." The Benson-Henry Institute (BHI) considers overall health as a three-legged stool. One leg is surgery and interventions, the second is pharmaceuticals and the third is self-care. The decline in wellness in our country as evidenced by an increase in obesity, increasing BMI, heart disease and diabetes is reflected in the progressive shortening of the third leg. The goal of the BHI is to promote and teach self-care to lengthen that leg and level out the stool. To that end, it offers an eight-week group program called Stress Management and Resiliency Training or SMART. I initially enrolled as a participant of the program in 2013, and subsequently served as a peer mentor for two additional sessions. At the beginning of the program, a primary care physician and a nurse practitioner who leads the eight-week session assess the participant's health issues. In conjunction with the participant, they arrive at the individual's three main issues that are in most need of improvement to serve as indices to map out progress throughout the program. Possible issues to be assessed include chronic back pain, recurrent headaches, insomnia, anxiety, panic attacks and depression, among others.

The SMART program stresses the implementation of all forms of self-care, including restorative sleep, proper balanced nutrition, and exercise. The sessions primarily present and implement some of the basic precepts of cognitive behavioral therapy and explore the various forms of meditation. With regard to the former, through a step-by-step analysis of specific, individual life situations, participants discover habitual, automatic negative thoughts and behavior patterns and assign them to a particular category of cognitive distortions. They then practice conscious substitution of positive affirmations. The end result is a replacement of negative thoughts that don't serve the individual with beneficial positive ones, consequently with a significant reduction in stress. The hope is that those positive thought processes will also become automatic and habitual with time.

Over the eight weeks of the program, students are guided through many different types of meditation and are instructed to meditate at home at least twenty minutes each day. A particular form of meditation may speak to someone more than another. Types of meditation presented include meditation on the breath, repetition of a mantra, guided imagery, insight meditation and yoga. From this "menu" of meditation options, participants can adopt a type of meditation practice that best suits them, hopefully continuing that practice well into the future.

One commonality amongst all forms of self-care, which include restorative sleep, exercise, proper nutrition, positive thinking and affirmations and meditation is the elicitation of the relaxation response, the term coined by Dr. Benson. As noted above, the relaxation response includes a reduction in metabolism, rate of breathing, heart rate, and brain activity. The relaxation response has also been shown to enhance the expression of genes related to mitochondrial function, chromosomal telomere maintenance in the cell and insulin secretion by the pancreas, as well as reduce the activity of genes associated with the inflammatory response and stress pathways throughout the body.(1)

Meditative practices, including yoga, also have a direct positive effect on the autonomic nervous system. The autonomic nervous system is always operating on an involuntary level during both wakefulness and sleep. It consists of two components, the sympathetic and parasympathetic nervous systems. Traditionally in layman terms, the sympathetic nervous system elicits the "fight or flight" response, in contradistinction to the parasympathetic system, which allows us to "rest and digest". The fight or flight response can be understood by considering the plight of the proverbial caveman, who while out hunting is confronted by a saber-toothed tiger. In a split-second, he has to assess his odds of survival if he stays to fight this dangerous animal or attempts to flee. It is the sympathetic nervous system that will increase the odds in his favor. During a sympathetic response, the heart rate accelerates, pumping more needed blood and oxygen to engaged skeletal muscles. Breathing becomes faster and more shallow. Blood is shunted away from non-vital organs, including the digestive tract, which undergoes a virtual shut down. Blood vessels feeding muscles dilate to increase blood flow. Superficial subcutaneous capillaries dilate and perspiration ensues to cool down the heat generated from increased muscular activity.

The parasympathetic response has an opposite effect on the body's physiology. Without the need for increased oxygen to activate skeletal muscles, the heart can slow down, respiratory rate can decrease and blood can be shunted back to the digestive system. We can literally rest and digest. There is no perceived threat to our survival. Our caveman is back in the safety of his cave enjoying his family.

The sympathetic response occurs when we feel unsafe or out of control. Anxiety is the expression of both of those states. Unfortunately, many are in a constant state of feeling out of control or worrying about the future, precipitating chronic feelings of anxiety, even though not facing any immediate danger. Some might be anxious about their performance at work because there is a perception that one's job is in jeopardy or they possess a fear of disapproval. Some worry, and even obsess, about the future because they feel out of control of future events. Many also have regrets of the past, possibly feeling that past decisions were also out of their control or feeling that they cannot control the rumination over those regrets. Those ruminations can cloud one's present sense of self-worth. The nervous system has difficulty distinguishing between different types and grades of stress. Whether we are in mortal danger or we are worried about a bumpy relationship, the sympathetic nervous system will kick in. In both instances, heart rate increases, breathing becomes shallower, palms become sweaty, and digestion is inhibited resulting in the so-called feeling of a "pit in the stomach." If we are constantly stressed and anxious, we become chronically stuck in the sympathetic response. We enter into a state of allostatic loading. Allostatic load was a term coined in 1993 by McEwen and Stellar (2). Allostasis is the process whereby the body responds to stressors in order to regain homeostasis, a healthy state of equilibrium in the body. With allostatic loading, the system becomes overwhelmed, in essence stuck in a sympathetic overload state, leading to a chronic decline in the health of the organs and tissues of the body, a reduction in resiliency, the inability to react to stressors, and the eventual development of disease states. One might consider the relationship of the two components of the autonomic nervous system as two sides of a scale, sympathetic on one side and parasympathetic on the other. Allostatic loading is analogous to a huge weight pressing down on the former. This chronic stress state results in a whole cascade of detrimental physiologic changes, including the activation or deactivation of genes, a flood of stress hormones like cortisol and epinephrine into the bloodstream, a rise in inflammatory molecules and a weakening of the body's immune status. These negative effects can promote a multitude of diseases, including atherosclerosis, hypertension, and heart disease, among numerous others.

Our perceptions of stress and our habitual automatic negative thoughts and behaviors elicited by stress initiate and sustain this process of chronic sympathetic overload and a disruption of normal physiologic homeostasis. In essence, we become unhealthy. The question arises as to how those pervasive negative thoughts and behaviors serve the individual. They are, of course, defense mechanisms that offer protection against external stressors. When those thoughts and behaviors become reflexive to all stressors, regardless of import or severity, generalized anxiety ensues. One solution to break that cycle is to retrain the mind to develop appropriate and graded responses to stressors. A more acute sympathetic response is beneficial when faced with a real danger, but chronic sympathetic overload is not. Our bodies need a homeostasis or balance between sympathetic and parasympathetic processes. It is appropriate for our proverbial caveman to increase his heart and respiratory rate and divert blood to his skeletal muscles when confronted by the ferocious tiger, but not for that sympathetic response to continue while in the safety of his cave.

How does one break this chronic stress cycle that will gradually erode the body and spirit? Of course, as I mentioned previously, practitioners of cognitive behavioral therapy stress the substitution of positive affirmations for negative judgments to increase self-esteem and achieve stress reduction. The brain listens to everything you say and you have a choice as to what to tell it. But, this book is about yoga and the reasons to pursue a regular yoga practice. Yoga quiets the mind and gives us the clarity to more realistically assess the stressors in our lives. It allows us to enter into a safe place. A regular practice of yoga can become your own personal sanctuary. It allows one to be in the moment, clear of regrets of the past and worries of the future. Even a single deep belly breath is enough to trigger the parasympathetic response. In addition, implementing the yogic philosophical principles, can foster a healthy outlook on life and feelings of contentment, satisfaction and peace that trigger beneficial physiologic changes in the body and reestablish the desired autonomic balance. The integration of the postures, breathing and meditation allows for interplay between the mental and the physical on a physiological level. That interplay is the balance between mind and body that we strive for as we practice yoga. The study of that balance is the essence of mind-body medicine.

There has been a considerable increase in yogic research studies in recent years, which is occurring concurrently with the surge in the practice of yoga in the general population. There is, of course, the ideal of the pursuit of science for science sake and for the betterment of society, but somehow, money always enters into the equation. Insurance companies and corporations have shied away from financially supporting many healthy mind-body practices. A shift of the financial onus from the individual to the health insurance companies and corporate America will facilitate the more widespread implementation of those practices. By publishing reproducible and statistically significant research data that demonstrates that mind-body medicine and other practices such as yoga lead to a reduction in hospital stays, emergency room visits and repeat doctor visits, health insurance companies should be interested in supporting these healthy practices, those that ultimately lower healthcare costs and, of course, the amount of money required to reimburse providers. Corporations should also be interested in implementing mind-body medical practices to promote health and wellbeing, which leads to an increase in worker productivity and decreases absenteeism and burnout. We can only hope that both the health insurance companies and corporate America might also have a profound interest in improving the quality of life for people, not just their bottom line or fiduciary responsibility to shareholders. It is a shift of the paradigm from a reactionary illness-focused healthcare system to a proactive health-focused one.

Hartfiel and others (3) demonstrated a reduction in perceived stress and back pain in the workplace in those that practiced yoga over an eight-week period versus a control group. It was also shown by comparative scores on questionnaires that the yoga group experienced a greater sense of psychological well-being, with lesser feelings of sadness and hostility and substantially greater self-assuredness, attentiveness and serenity. More studies such as this one are needed to convince corporations to implement self-care programs for their employees, which might include yoga classes in the workplace.

One of the most interesting physiologic effects of yoga occurs at the hormonal level. Yoga, as does many forms of exercise, boosts levels of serotonin, dopamine, oxytocin and endorphins and decreases levels of cortisol and monoamine oxidase. Increased endorphins, of course, are felt to be responsible for the runner's high. Alterations in oxytocin levels may be involved in mood disorders. Imbalances of serotonin, dopamine and monoamine oxidase levels as the etiologies of many psychiatric illnesses have all been extensively studied. Monoamine oxidase inhibitors (MAOI), such as Nardil and Parnate, have been used in the treatment of depression since the 1950's. Medications such as Wellbutrin boost brain dopamine levels. Selective serotonin reuptake inhibitors (SSRI) are the most widely prescribed antidepressants. SSRIs, such as Zoloft, Prozac and Paxil, block the reuptake of serotonin by cells in the brain, thereby increasing the amount of available serotonin. Quite simply, serotonin, dopamine, oxytocin and endorphins are the so-called "happy hormones". The mechanism for the release of these hormones is complex and multifactorial. It is uncertain as to how the practice of yoga leads to an increase in brain levels of "happy hormones". Whether it be activation of mechanoreceptors in fascia and muscle that initiate hormonal release, factors relating to changes in autonomic balance or conscious perceptions and expectations of peace and contentment, the practice of yoga gives us a literal emotional lift as it causes the influx of "happy hormones" into the neural synapses of the brain. In this regard, might yoga be considered an antidepressant? Might a regular yoga practice function as a dosing schedule of a natural antidepressant? One might even speculate that the spiritual awakenings and feelings of bliss experienced by the ancient yogis, who formulated the many philosophies and schools of yoga, were a direct consequence of elevated levels of "happy hormones." This physiologic perspective on enlightenment is not meant to discount the power of human thought to gain spirituality, but our thoughts and experiences are ultimately the result of electrical and chemical activity coursing through the neuronal networks of the brain.

Yoga provides significant, demonstrable physical and psychological health benefits that one can realize through a regular yoga practice. The beneficial effects of yoga on the physiologic level can best be approached on the systems level. The consideration of the nervous system, especially establishing autonomic balance between sympathetic and parasympathetic activity, and of the endocrine system through the release of "happy hormones" were discussed above.

With regard to the cardiovascular system, a regular yoga practice builds endurance. During a yoga class, the heart rate typically increases. Similar to other "cardio" exercises, over time the heart becomes stronger and more effective at delivering oxygen throughout the body, including to the muscles and joints. With stronger and more effective contractions of the heart, the pulse rate drops, as less "beats" are required to deliver oxygen throughout the body. There is also a lessening of resistance to blood flow in the blood vessels reflected in a decrease in blood pressure.

With regard to the respiratory system, the breath is central to the practice of yoga. Listening and connecting to the breath promotes meditative states. From a physiological perspective, yogic breathing techniques teach one how to optimize breathing capacity, thereby bringing more precious oxygen into the body that is necessary for the optimal functioning of all of the organs and muscles. Since the heart is also a muscle, more effective breathing also promotes more cardiac efficiency. Diaphragmatic breathing also activates the parasympathetic nervous system.

With regard to the digestive system, as yoga activates the parasympathetic nervous system, the delivery of blood and oxygen to the stomach, small intestines and colon is optimized. Chronic anxiety stimulates the sympathetic nervous system, reflected in poor bowel functioning. Yoga allows one to rest and digest.

With regard to the immune system, a regular yoga practice can boost immunity and the body's defense mechanisms against disease by decreasing cytokines and other circulating inflammatory molecules that cause and worsen disease, while at the same time altering the expression of genes involved with immunity. Regardless of the cause or symptoms of a disease, stress can interfere with our ability to cope both mentally and physically.

With regard to the musculoskeletal system, yoga has widespread benefits that are realized in increases in flexibility, strength and posture. Flexibility arises from the progressive stretching of muscle fibers, tendons, and ligaments. The stretching of the stiff connective tissues that hold our joints together increases mobility and range of motion. Strength arises from the isometric effects of sustaining the postures. Although we are often unaware of it as we practice, almost all of the postures activate and engage the core. Strengthening the core results in better posture, along with the conditioning of the spine, which can result in feelings of pride and confidence. One learns balance and grounding through yoga, both of which can prevent falls.

The science behind yoga supports the idea that a regular practice has widespread beneficial effects on our health and wellbeing. Understanding this evidential-based perspective on yoga can be a valuable tool to enhance one's practice and add motivation to dedicate oneself to this path to a healthy lifestyle. One must be so fortunate in life to be blessed with good health. Self-care increases your odds of enjoying that blessing. Take care of yourself. Your loved ones, friends and community depend on it. Embrace yourself and embrace life!

1. Bhasin MK, Dusek JA, Chang BH, Joseph MG, Denniger JW, et al. (2017) **Relaxation Response Induces Temporal Transcriptome Changes in Energy Metabolism, Insulin Secretion and Inflammatory Pathways.** PLOS ONE 12(2):e0172873
2. McEwen BS, Stellar, E. (1993). **Stress and the individual. Mechanisms leading to disease.** Archives of Internal Medicine 153 (18): 2093-101
3. Hartfiel N, Burton C, Rycroft-Malone J, Clarke G, Havenhand J. (2012) **Yoga for reducing perceived stress and back pain at work.** Occupational Medicine 62(8):606-12

10
MEDITATION

When meditation is mastered, the mind is unwavering like the flame of a lamp in a windless place.

Bhagavad Gita

Yoga is the integration of movement, breath and meditation. Perhaps, the latter is the most difficult of the three to achieve. Pantajali's eight limbs of yoga described in the *Yoga Sutras* represent the rungs of the ladder necessary to ascend in order to achieve the final goal of *samadhi*. As discussed previously, the first rungs of the ladder are the mastery of the five *yamas* and *niyamas*. Feelings of introversion are only realized by leading an ethical life guided by the *yamas: ahimsa* or nonviolence, *satya* or truthfulness, *asteya* or non-stealing, *brahmacharya* or discipline, and *aparigraha* or non-greed, and by the *niyamas: saucha* or cleanliness and purity, *santosha* or contentment through non-attachment, *tapas* or discipline and enthusiasm, *svadhyaya* or the study of self and texts, and *Isvara pranidhana* or the consideration of a higher power. Once one has accepted the responsibility to lead a moral life, one may then progress to learning the *asanas* and *pranayama,* followed by the ascent to the fifth limb, the beginning of the process to delve deeper into self. The last four limbs of yoga are *pratyahara, dharana, dhyana* and *samadhi*. As one ascends the rungs one enters into deeper and deeper meditative states.

The Kripalu tradition embraces a more pragmatic view of the eight limbs. Rather than a ladder with a hierarchy of levels, Kripalu Yoga believes that all of the limbs can be potentially accessible at any time regardless of one's level of mastery, although the deepest meditative states may still be difficult to achieve. One can strive to be a moral, compassionate person while at the same time, learning the complexities of the *asanas* and *pranayama* and developing the ability to meditate. In the Kripalu tradition, yoga is the integration of *asanas, pranayama* and meditation, all performed concurrently.

What exactly is meant by meditation? One definition of *samadhi* is the achievement of single-pointed concentration without distraction in order to comprehend every facet of the object of meditation. I do believe that this is the essence of what it means to meditate; focusing on one thing to gain clarity of thought. The goal of meditation is drawing oneself into the present by letting go of thoughts that don't serve, including regrets of the past and anxieties about the future. This can be accomplished by diverting all attention to a single focus, such as the sound of the breath, with consequent suppression of other thoughts. Being fully in the moment is a learned skill, one that is often an elusive one for many of us. The reality is that the mind is constantly generating thoughts. Mind chatter is difficult to silence. Loud and dominating mind chatter is one reason people fail to develop a meditation practice. I possessed the stereotypical image of a meditator as someone at total peace and in full control of their thoughts. Initial attempts to meditate are met with negative self-judgments regarding an inability to rein in the pervasive chatter seemingly filling the entire mind. Similar to developing a regular yoga practice, meditation can be fraught with initial obstacles that are unpleasant. It is difficult to pursue anything that causes one to feel uncomfortable. Overcoming those obstacles requires a change in mindset.

It may not be an absolute truth, but anything beneficial or worthwhile requires work. Just as an increase in flexibility requires patience and an acceptance that change occurs gradually over time, one needs to recognize that the ability to achieve a quieting of the mind through meditation develops slowly. I believe that the first step towards that end is to accept that thinking is a normal function. Constantly throughout our lives, millions of brain waves are generated every second, both those regulating primitive processes such as breathing and blood pressure and those that create thoughts in higher centers of the brain. The goal of meditation is to decrease the latter through single-pointed focus and concentration.

Mind chatter is a flood of thoughts that have no pertinence to the present moment. These often are lamentations and regrets of past experiences and failures. These sometimes take the form of the "shoulda, coulda, woulda" scenario. Regrets of the past are often accompanied by worries of the future. Anxiety stems from feelings of being unsafe or out of control. Since we are no longer in control of the past and, for the most part, cannot control the future, we become stressed. As discussed previously, stress and anxiety activate the sympathetic nervous system, the flight or fight response. Being in a state of fleeing or fighting in the face of an unsafe situation only worsens feelings of anxiety. In addition, mind chatter can become more magnified as one enters into a quiet place in which to meditate.

The key to meditation is to not flee from or fight with anxiety-provoking thoughts. Accept that these thoughts will arise. Don't try to negate them. Most of us don't possess a switch in the brain that allows us to suddenly shut off all of our thoughts at any given moment. Accept that it is normal to think. The quality of thought reflects our personalities and behaviors that have been shaped by past experiences over many years. Meditation is simply allowing oneself time to rest the mind as one might rest a muscle that is overworked. Working at a meditation practice entails teaching the mind what it feels like to be at rest. Success at a meditation practice allows one to access that feeling effortlessly.

Teaching the mind to rest begins with acknowledging a thought when it arises and then letting it go, rather than giving into rumination. Regardless of the content of a thought, recognize it, let it go and then return your attention back to your desired object of meditation. Some employ imagery in this regard. One might acknowledge a thought and then imagine it disappearing into the air like a puff of smoke pulled away by the wind, floating away like a balloon into the sky or thrown into a river, only to be taken downstream by the current. Each time a thought disappears, return back to the object of your meditation. The practice of meditation can be summed up as, "Think, acknowledge and return." If I am meditating on the sound of my breath and I begin to worry about a future responsibility, I acknowledge that worry although it is an undesirable thought, let it go and return back to the sound of my breath. The sound of my breath is occurring in the present moment. By focusing on that sound, I am in the present.

There are a multitude of ways to meditate other than focusing on the breath. I have found guided meditation to be a wonderful method to focus the mind on the present. Guided meditation consists of someone taking you on a journey filled with imagery. Suggestions are made along the way to invoke all of the senses: the sights, sounds, scents, touch sensations and tastes. I enjoyed a transformative guided meditative experience during one of my visits to Kripalu. Our guide was a woman who studied Peruvian Shamanism from tribal shamans in the Amazon rainforest. Over an hour, she guided us above tall trees swaying in the wind, into a meadow filled with colorful wildflowers, through a path in the forest bathed in filtered sunlight and into a cave through which flowed a stream. There are myriad guided meditations available on CD and YouTube. It is necessary to "shop around" to find a guide that speaks to you with a voice you find soothing. In a guided meditation, your attention is directed toward the suggested imagery and away from the noise of the inner critic. An effective guided meditation can seem like a beautiful dream during a period of restful sleep. It can be both restorative and energizing. The guide simply makes suggestions, but you are the one that produces all of the beautiful images you experience.

Although similar to guided meditation, insight meditation is directed towards a particular personal issue or quality that is chosen before the meditation begins. One might choose to address a prior trauma or a perceived personal failing. Once the specific issue to be addressed is determined, the guide then transports you to a place where negative thoughts can be replaced with positive ones. For example, an insight meditation might consist of a guided meditation through a forest, taking you to a hollow in a tree. The guide might tell you to take the troubling issue you face and place it in the hollow, putting it to rest, and then extract a positive affirmation or an object of gratitude in its place. Both guided and insight meditations are very effective, for not only do they focus one's concentration on images, but they also have the power to take one on all types of wonderful and meaningful journeys.

A specific type of meditation, which typically employs guided meditation is *yoga nidra.* The Sanskrit word, *nidra,* translates to "sleep". The concept of *yoga nidra,* a state of consciousness somewhere between waking and sleep, first appeared in the *Upanishads.* A guide takes you on a journey. A common experience for many is an alternation between sleep and wakefulness. It is felt that even when asleep, you maintain a conscious awareness and continue to hear and process the words of the guided meditation.

As long as you can accomplish a single-pointed focus on something in the present, you can succeed at developing a meaningful, meditation practice. Arguably, one could focus on anything. Even the sounds in a crowded subway car could serve as the single object of meditation because those sounds exist in the present moment. A visual or audible point of focus can also be used, such as meditating on a picture, a flame or music.

With regard to yoga, there are many possibilities and opportunities to establish a point of focus on which to meditate. Certainly, the breath is one. Meditation might be directed toward the sound or feel of the breath as it comes in and out of the nose or toward the rhythm of the chest and belly as they expand and contract. As we shall see later on in this book, *pranayama,* the yogic breathing techniques, are designed to optimize and facilitate the focus on the breath. As we practice the *asanas,* focusing on the movement of the body, the action of joints and the stretch and engagement of muscles can also promote feelings of inwardness. I often tell students to close their eyes to become more aware of their movements and the position of their bodies in space. Closing the eyes removes any visual stimuli that might distract the mind and allows for the other senses to become more hyper-acute. A wonderful alternative is to maintain a *drishti* throughout one's practice, choosing points or lines on which to focus appropriate to a particular *asana*.

I once asked, "Why should I go through all this effort to learn to meditate and how will it benefit me?" Motivation to develop a yoga or meditation practice has to be more than just being told that it is good for you. Both practices carry over into the rest of life. The ability to access a state of relaxation at any time is a wonderful tool to help cope with everyday stresses with greater clarity and a useful perspective. Both practices lead to a positive cycle, whereby the experience of the relaxed state makes you want to come back for more. The positive effects of both yoga and meditation are not just limited to the self. You will be better equipped to step outside yourself and be there for others. Meditation and yoga should not just be about improving oneself, but about finding oneself. Connecting with one's true authentic self allows one to connect better with others. We all possess a light within us. It is all about fueling the light with positive energy and thoughts that will allow everyone to see it and feel your warmth.

11
THE FORMS AND TRADITIONS OF YOGA

The essence of the beautiful is unity in variety.

Felix Mendelssohn

This book primarily focuses on the practice of **Hatha Yoga** for two main reasons. One is that many classes that you will encounter at a yoga studio or other venue, such as a community center, health club or YMCA, are described as Hatha Yoga. Typically, these classes are qualified as either gentle or moderate. A moderate class might include more advanced or vigorous poses or have a faster pace relative to a gentle class. I believe that "meditative" should be substituted for "gentle", as the slower pace affords more time to connect the movement with the breath. Second, I, your humble author, am formally trained in Kripalu Yoga, which is part of the lineage of Hatha yoga. Kripalu yoga and Hatha yoga in general are wonderful for all levels, both advanced and beginners. It is a wonderful way to start on your path of yoga and begin to develop your regular, meaningful practice before venturing out to explore other yogic traditions.

The Sanskrit word *Hatha* means "force", reflecting the physical nature of the practice. Matsyendranath or Matsyendra, a Hindu prophet from the 10th century, is considered the founder of Hatha yoga. In Hindu mythology, it is believed that Matsyendranath received all the secrets of Hatha yoga from Shiva, the Hindu deity known as the destroyer and transformer. The seated spinal twist posture, *Matsyendrasana,* derives its name from that ancient prophet. Hatha yoga, as it is used in the Western world, is a general term that encompasses many other types of yoga taught in classes. It refers to a type of yoga that stresses both the physical postures and breathing techniques. Another translation of the Sanskrit word, "*Hatha*" is "the sun and the moon", *ha* meaning sun and *tha* meaning moon. As was touched upon in the chapter regarding yogic philosophy, the sun and the moon are complementary energy channels, the *pingala* and *ida nadis,* respectively. The sun produces heat and activity and has masculine properties. The moon is cooling, rational and receptive with feminine properties. In a *Hatha* yoga class, you will access both the energy of the sun and the moon; periods of activity coupled with periods of stillness and rest.

The 18th century English poet, William Cowper, wrote, "Variety is the spice of life, that gives it all its flavor." Yoga is only one path to take for practicing self-care and establishing wellbeing. Certainly, for some, other activities might prove more beneficial to reduce stress and improve health. Intention is also a major factor in one's choice. For me, my intention in regularly practicing yoga is to reduce stress, improve my strength and flexibility and gain clarity of thought by accessing meditative states. An intention for a body builder may be an increase in strength or achieving a desired self-image. For a runner, he or she might want to increase endurance and improve cardiovascular health. And just like yoga, for both the bodybuilder and runner feelings of introversion are attainable as both practices can be meditative. Potentially, all self-care activities may possess a common thread of stress reduction, feelings of inwardness through non-distracted concentration on repetitive motions and similar physiologic and hormonal changes. Most important is to find a regular activity that is interesting, stimulating and enjoyable, and thus sustainable. Too often people invest in exercise equipment or health clubs, soon only to find their experience dull, repetitive and boring. That certainly could be the case for someone trying yoga. What works for one person may not work for another. The critical denominator for whatever you might choose is to practice self-care, however you can accomplish it.

With regard to yoga, different types may prove more interesting, and thus better suited to produce desired results for some than others. The remainder of this list of the various forms of yoga is not meant to be an exhaustive or comprehensive one. It is not meant to be a detailed discussion of the philosophies behind each one, but rather focuses on the common forms that you may encounter when searching the web for local classes to attend or online videos to watch.

Ashtanga Yoga

The precepts of Ashtanga yoga are complex with many nuances. *Ashtanga yoga* means "eight-limbed yoga"as put forth by Pantanjali in the *Yoga Sutras.* It was first described in the *Yoga Korunta,* an ancient manuscript attributed to Guru Vamana Rishi. His teachings are philosophical, but also describe different groups of *asanas.* In the early 1900's, the Guru Rama Mohan Brahmachari passed down the teachings of the *Yoga Korunta* to his disciple, Sri T. Krishnamacharya. He then taught them to his disciple and Indian scholar, K. Pattabhi Jois, who ultimately formulated the principles of Ashtanga yoga. During the 20th century, Jois developed Ashtanga yoga as a modern day form of classical yoga. He is one of the yogis most responsible for the dissemination of yoga throughout the Western world. Ashtanga yoga follows a specific set of posture sequences, usually beginning with two sets of sun salutations, five repetitions of each, followed by a standing sequence, then a choice of one of six possible postural sequences, and finally, a closing sequence. From a practical standpoint, it is a physically demanding practice with a flow from one posture to the next, and so is not ideal for beginners.

Vinyasa

The Sanskrit word *vinyasa* literally means, "to place in a special way", *nyasa* denoting "to place" and *vi* "in a special way". It arose from Ashtanga yoga in the 1980's. Similar to Ashtanga, the practice consists of a flow from one *asana* to the next, while at the same time, linking the breath to that flow. Unlike Ashtanga, the teacher is not confined to a specific set of posture sequences. Rather, the instructor has the freedom to design and individualize a class according to his or her style and the abilities of the students. Along with Hatha yoga, Vinyasa is one of the most common descriptors of a class that you will encounter at a yoga studio. From a practical standpoint, like Ashtanga, it tends to be more physically demanding with a faster pace and may not be suitable for beginners. Some Vinyasa classes stress the physical aspects of yoga and deemphasize the importance of the breath. Their intention might be solely improving the physical body through strengthening and toning. As I stated previously, different types of activities for self-care speak more to some than others. Most important is participating in an activity that can be sustainable.

Power Yoga (Power Vinyasa)

In the 1980's, Brian Kest, a yoga teacher who studied Ashtanga yoga, developed Power yoga. Power yoga focuses on the physical aspects of yoga. It tends to be fast-paced, athletic and strenuous. There are also many yoga studios named Power Yoga. In nearby Boston, there are numerous studios springing up with Power Yoga in their names, many appealing to the younger crowd interested in a vigorous, physical workout, but also in meditation through breathwork. Many of the postures can be physically challenging, allowing for some students to tap into the self-competitive part of their psyches. As is true with Ashtanga and Vinyasa, Power yoga may not be a good starting place to begin a yoga practice. Starting with a gentle or meditative Hatha yoga class might be analogous to learning a foreign language; starting with the basics before becoming immersed in conversation or texts.

Heated Vinyasa or Hot Yoga

Heated Vinyasa and Hot Yoga refers to any type of yoga performed in hot and humid conditions. There are both pros and cons to practicing yoga at high temperature and humidity. The temperature of hot yoga classes can range anywhere from 90 to 105 degrees. A common misconception is that sweating profusely removes toxins from the body. From a physiological perspective, the kidneys, liver and intestines are responsible for filtering toxins that eventually are excreted into the urine and feces. Toxins are not released from our sweat glands in any appreciable amounts. Sweating is simply the body's evaporative cooling mechanism, functioning in two ways. First, the secreted fluid cools down the skin. Second, evaporation of the fluid removes heat from the body. Under hot conditions, greater perspiration is required to cool the body's core temperature. The body requires more cooling relative to practicing yoga at room temperature. Furthermore, as perspiration builds up on the skin surface, it can drip on a yoga mat, potentially leading to slippage and injury. In very humid environments, large concentrations of water vapor in the air can interfere with the evaporative cooling function of perspiration, causing the body to overheat.

Losing fluids from perspiration necessitates adequate hydration during a hot yoga class. As anyone that has watched a professional football game played at high temperatures, such as in places like Arizona, dehydration can lead to muscle cramping. The dehydrated football player is often seen on the sidelines on his back being worked on by a trainer or on a stationary bicycle, peddling out his muscle cramp. Proper hydration is paramount while practicing hot yoga. One proviso, however, is that overhydrating can have a deleterious effect by diluting the body's electrolytes. One should consider hydrating with a sports performance drink like Gatorade or Powerade to replenish and maintain electrolytes at normal levels.

Another misconception is that activities done in the heat promote greater weight loss. Decreases in weight are short-lived, returning back to baseline after proper hydration. In general, weight loss is best accomplished through good nutrition, exercise and eating low glycemic index foods to lower one's set baseline weight, not through excessive perspiration.

One benefit of hot yoga is that at high temperatures muscles stretch more easily. Warm muscles are inherently more pliable, which is why we do warm-ups before engaging in any physical activity. Certainly, stretching muscles is one of the pleasures of yoga and makes hot yoga attractive to some for this reason. Another benefit is psychological. A perceived greater challenge and a visible and tangible effect of exercise, such as perspiring profusely, can lead to positive feelings of accomplishment and satisfaction with a subsequent reduction in stress.

Hot yoga and heated vinyasa are good for some and not for others. We all have varying tolerances to heat. Just like any yoga you might practice, most importantly always listen to your body. Certainly, if you feel light-headed, stop, hydrate and sit or lie down in a cooler place.

Iyengar Yoga

B.K.S. Iyengar, who was also a direct disciple of T. Krishnamacharya in India, was also one of several yogis responsible for the dissemination of yoga throughout the Western world. His yoga is a type of Hatha yoga that adheres to the precepts of Patanjali and his eight limbs of yoga. Iyengar developed a yoga that is very precise and detail oriented, focusing much of the time on alignment. Props are frequently used to facilitate the full expression of the asanas. Iyengar introduced the use of props to allow beginners to assume more advanced postures, as well as to aid those with physical limitations and inflexibility. There is also an emphasis on breath control. *Asanas* are sustained for relatively long periods of time, during which subtle and precise corrections are made to optimize the full expression of a posture. Iyengar systematized over 200 yoga postures and 14 types of *pranayama*. The *asanas* and *pranayama* vary in complexity, allowing the novice to progress gradually towards more advanced techniques. Iyengar yoga is relatively slow-paced with an emphasis on the integration of the breath with both movement and the sustaining of postures. Instructors receive rigorous training in order to master the multitude of postures, breathing techniques and the very detailed-oriented approach that is specific to Iyengar Yoga.

Kundalini Yoga

Kundalini is a Sanskrit word meaning snake. In Hinduism, it refers to latent and primal female energy that lies coiled in the *muladhara* or root *chakra*. Kundalini awakening occurs when energy is released to travel sequentially up through the *chakras* until it reaches the *sahasrara* or crown of head *chakra,* the energy center for spirituality. The awakening manifests as feelings of enlightenment and bliss, emotional and spiritual transformation, and a multitude of physiological changes. There are many methods and techniques used in the attempt to realize the Kundalini awakening, including various forms of meditation and yoga practices. The precepts of the Kundalini are quite complex with a myriad of interpretations and meanings.

Most Kundalini yoga classes in studios consist of postures, breathing techniques, meditation and the chanting of *mantras*. Classes will differ, but more commonly begin with a "tuning in " with the chanting of specific Sanskrit *mantras. Ong namo guru dev namo,* translated to "I bow to the teacher within" is often chanted three times at the beginning of a Kundalini yoga class. A combination of *pranayama, asanas* and *mantras* called a *kriya* or "completed set" follows. *Shavasansa* is then assumed. Following relaxation, a period of meditation of varying length ensues. Meditation is done to *mantras* and *mudras* or specific arm and hand positions. It is typically customary to close every Kundalini yoga practice by chanting the "May the Long Time Sun Shine Upon You" blessing:

"May the long time sun shine upon you,
All love surround you,

And the pure light within you,
Guide you on your way."

Typically following the blessing are three repetitions of *Sat Nam*. Like many Sanskrit terms *Sat Nam* has many different meanings, including "truth is God's name" and "truth is my identity". Kundalini yoga uses similar postures as found in a typical Hatha yoga class. It is relatively slow-paced, but differs from Hatha by a larger emphasis on meditation and chanting.

Yin Yoga

The concepts of *yin* and *yang* come from the Chinese religious and philosophical traditions of Taoism. Although *yin* and *yang* could be considered opposites, they are actually complementary states of being that are inseparable. Similar to the *ida nadi* in yogic philosophy, *yin* represents traits that are feminine, passive, cool, stable and downward moving, in contradistinction to *yang*, which similar to the *pingala nadi,* reflects those that are masculine, active, hot, changing and upward moving. Some *yin* yoga classes incorporate more active *yang* postures to act as a contrast to the *yin asanas*. The *yang asanas,* more often done first, generate heat in muscles and throughout the body, complemented by the cooling effects of the *yin* postures that follow. Sustained for relatively long periods of time, *yin* postures focus on the passive stretching of tendons, ligaments and fascia, which are more firm and inflexible relative to muscles. *Yang* practices, such as *Hatha, Vinyasa,* and power yoga focus on dynamic movement of the body coupled with the breath. *Yin* classes have a much slower pace, as the *asanas* are sustained from anywhere from one to five minutes. Many of the *yin* postures are similar to those in a Hatha class, but often are referred to by different names. Because *yin* yoga targets the stiffer and more inflexible connective tissues, tendons and ligaments, a novice practitioner may experience discomfort. Adhering to the strategy of "finding your edge" is critical in a *yin* yoga practice since postures are sustained for relatively long periods of time. Patience is necessary to gradually achieve greater flexibility in and across joints. As previously discussed, "finding your edge" is finding the point where discomfort is experienced and then easing off to no or a minimal degree of discomfort. Gradually, through a regular practice of *yin* yoga, your edge will advance as greater flexibility and strength are realized.

Since *asanas* are sustained for such long periods of time, a *yin* yoga class affords the opportunity for meditation through the awareness of the breath. Entering into a meditative state requires non-distracted focus on a sound, object, mantra, idea, or a guiding voice in an attempt to clear the mind of thoughts. Accessing meditative states and creating new connections through neural plasticity allow the brain to more easily enter into those states. *Yin* yoga affords one with the luxury of time to strive towards that goal.

Restorative Yoga

One definition of "restorative" is "possessing the ability to reestablish health and well-being." Restorative yoga is focused on the healing of both physical and mental issues or ailments. It is not limited, however, to addressing disease states. It can also serve to enhance meditative states, reduce stress and increase parasympathetic tone. Induction of the parasympathetic nervous system on an immediate basis slows the heart rate, lowers blood pressure and promotes good digestion. Regular yoga practices that stimulate parasympathetic processes over time decrease circulating inflammatory molecules and boost the immune system.

The practice of restorative yoga is an opportunity to slow down and relax into the postures with as little physical effort as possible. In a restorative yoga class, there is a minimum of physical movement with an emphasis on the passive stretching of muscles and connective tissues coupled with an awareness of the breath. Props are extensively used for each posture. Props rather than your musculoskeletal system are used to support your body. Postures are usually similar to seated or supine Hatha yoga poses, but with the addition of blocks, bolsters, and blankets to eliminate unnecessary straining and tension in the body. Although one's body is supported, there remains an awareness of the stretch of the body. Breathing into the stretch can foster feelings of inwardness. The teacher guides students to arrange the props in relation to the chosen pose or possibly physically assists you both with the props and the proper positioning of the body. Each pose is held for an extended period of time, possibly ten or twenty minutes. A class may only consist of four or five postures. The instructor may dim the lights, play gentle music or lead a guided meditation.

Restorative yoga can be a great complement to any of the aforementioned types of yoga, especially the more active and physical ones, by promoting meditative states with both an awareness of passive stretching and the breath.

Music

Before moving on to the specific details and expression of the *asanas* and *pranayama,* I feel compelled to discuss something that is dear to my heart: the use of music in a yoga class. Some instructors choose to lead a class in silence. They feel, and arguably so, that music distracts one's focus from the breath. Others, including myself, consider music as a wonderful adjunct to a yoga class. Music may serve many functions. It can be emotional, and at times meditative, especially when it explores the interrelationship of sounds. My oldest son Bryce, who is a composer with expertise in sound design, created an album of meditative music that accomplishes just that, called *Reflections.* I often play his music not only because it allows my students to experience those intimate interrelationships of sounds, but it also fills me with overwhelming pride and gratitude for my son.

In many Eastern religions the repetition of mantras is often a source of meditation. Mantras can also be chanted with a melody. It is felt that the chanting of mantras produces a vibratory energy with frequencies that when experienced create calmness of the mind. One example of a chanted mantra is, *"Ra Ma Da Sa Sa Say So Hung".* This is a Kundalini yogic mantra for healing that awakens the Kundalini life force and drives it up the spine to activate all of the *chakras*. Each of the seven words chanted represent each of the *chakras*. The words also have meaning. *Ra* means the sun, and chanting it allows one to harness the energy of the sun. *Ma* is the moon, which is calming and cool, allowing one to become more receptive to new ideas and perspectives. *Da* is the earth, which is grounding. *Sa, say* and *hung* represent different aspects of the infinite. *So hung* translates to, "I am thou". The chanting of a single mantra can last for a relatively long time to maximize its meditative effects. In yoga, those meditative effects might be realized by connecting the movements of the body with the tempo of the music of the mantra.

A wonderful mantra that can be chanted comes from Pantanjali's *Yoga Sutras; "yogash chitta vritti nirodhah"*, meaning "yoga stills the fluctuations of the mind." The mantra epitomizes the goal of yoga; creating an ever-changing single point of focus to clear the mind of thoughts that do not serve in the moment. By fully being in the present moment, clarity of mind can be realized. And becoming clear that you do have a choice as to how you wish to live your life is quite liberating. The fluctuations of the mind are like ripples on a beautiful mountain lake. When those ripples abate, what lies beneath the surface becomes crystal clear.

Yoga can be a wonderful path to gaining clarity and undergoing personal growth. The mental clutter caused by mind chatter can create a dense fog that obscures any glimpses into our true authentic selves. Finding that clarity is easier said than done. It takes patience to train the body and mind to release and relax. But the path to all of the benefits of yoga is there for you to take. It is both the process and the destination that can be transformative, filling your life with contentment, satisfaction and peace.

As this is a practical guide to yoga, it is time to move on to the so-called "nuts and bolts" of the *asanas* and *pranayama.* My hope is that what I have presented to you so far will enhance your experience, and hopefully reinforce the idea that there is so much more to yoga than just its physical aspects. My discussions of the various aspects of yoga are not meant to be exhaustive analyses. There are entire books devoted to human anatomy, science, yogic philosophy and each of the various forms of yoga. My intent is to offer an overview of yoga to instill more meaning into your practice and give you more motivation to appreciate all that yoga has to offer.

We always try to practice yoga on and off the mat. On your mat, or in your chair, thoroughly enjoy your practice with self-kindness and gratitude. Be grateful for yourself, for others in your life and for all the blessings of your life. Once you treat yourself with kindness and experience gratitude, you can have love and compassion for others. And when you have love and compassion, the world will be yours. Embrace life!

Jai Bhagwan!

PART III

12
THE ASANAS AND PRANAYAMA: AN OVERVIEW

What would life be if we had no courage to attempt anything?

Vincent Van Gogh

The Sanskrit word *asana* literally translates to "sitting down". In the hierarchy of Pantajali's eight limbs of yoga, *asana* and *pranayama* constitute the third and fourth limbs, respectively. In Patanjali's *Yoga Sutras, asana* refers to sitting in a position for *pranayama* that is firm and steady, but at the same time, relaxed and comfortable. The original concept of *asana* referred solely to a seated position in which to meditate that, by being steady and comfortable, would divert attention away from the physical body. In later Hatha yogic texts, especially the *Hatha Pradipika,* eighty-four classic *asanas* are described, believed to have been handed down to the yogi Matsyendranath from the Hindu deity Shiva.

The practice of yoga is not limited to just the expression of the classic *asanas.* The *asanas* merely serve as a reliable, transferable and consistent system of communication that serves as a common ground on which practitioners can learn and instructors of yoga can teach. In reality, any series of movements connected to the breath on which to meditate constitutes yoga; the integration of body, breath and mind. As you attend classes and establish a familiarity with the classic *asanas,* you will begin to notice teachers modifying them and creating variations. In addition, after a time, through your regular practice, you will enjoy finding individual postures that are your own self-expression, ones that provide enjoyable stretches. It is wonderful to experiment with your own movements in a class. Adding movements, such as flexing the wrists, moving the fingers or changing the position of arms and legs can create novelty that becomes the focus of your attention, rather than maintaining a posture in a typical, familiar way that may allow the mind to wander. In addition, sustained postures need not be static. Creating a dynamic, flowing posture with your unique movements can become your version of an *asana.*

Part of the Kripalu yogic philosophy is the concept of *Meditation in Motion.* Through a regular practice of yoga, over time the ability to access meditative states becomes so fine-tuned that rather than consciously entering into postures, the body moves spontaneously on a subconscious level. It is no longer the will of the mind that directs the movement of the body, but it is *prana,* the life force, that guides one through the postures. Removing conscious thoughts directed at specific movements of the body heightens the single-pointed concentration necessary for deep meditation. When set to music, *Meditation in Motion* becomes a wonderful, flowing dance that engages mind and body.

The following discussion of the *asanas* is limited to the more basic poses that you will likely encounter in a yoga class. It is a practical guide to instill feelings of confidence in your practice. Feeling lost with a need to constantly look at the teacher or fellow students for guidance detracts from enjoying all of the wonderful benefits that yoga has to offer. Be kind to yourself as you learn the *asanas.* Practice nonattachment on the path to *santosha,* contentment, not attaching to the end result. What is most important is to be in the moment and enjoy the process regardless of the outcome. We all have limitations. What might be considered the "ideal" expression of an *asana* may not be possible for many. Whether genetic or acquired, I have many physical limitations that prevent me from assuming the full expression of every *asana.* This is particularly evident in an advanced class that might include postures like half splits, the crow posture, hand or head stands or deep squats. In such a class, I have three choices. One is to feel compelled to attempt postures that potentially may lead to injury and negative self-judgments about my abilities. The second is to remain in the class and create my own variations of the postures that allow me to practice at my edge or substitute other *asanas* for those I don't wish to do. The third is to find another class that is more appropriate to my practice. Attaching to any final outcome is a "set up" for potential self-criticism.

Always keep in mind while learning and performing these *asanas* that the only "right" way to practice yoga is to make it your own personal experience, not to do all of the postures perfectly. Perfection is an unrealistic goal that many of us possess. Further, the satisfaction derived from the perfect expression of an *asana* likely will be short-lived and won't sustain one's practice. Accepting any outcome removes the pressure to perform. Finding satisfaction in your own distinctive expression of a posture should be one's intention. We are all unique. We all think and move differently. Connect with that uniqueness.

Consider the performance of the *asanas* as an opportunity for self-expression.

Learning the cues to enter into and express *asanas* is like learning a language. We are all taught to write according to the rules of grammar, but each one of us possesses a capacity to create poetry or prose that is faithful to our emotions and ideas. As I write these words, I am enjoying the process of writing through the lens of personal experience. Regardless of whether or not this book is published, I have already succeeded in connecting with myself through self-analysis and exploration. I also find deep meaning in the process of teaching yoga, allowing my own personality to shine through. I am fine if someone does not connect to my words and moves on to another class. Removing the pressure to perform for others' approval or recognition is liberating. Immerse yourself in the process of creating your own movements. Enjoy creating your own unique version of yoga. If you come to my class, you are experiencing my version of yoga. If you attend another instructor's class you are exposed to their version. And as a student, you have the freedom to create your own version of yoga. Consider this from another perspective. As a student in a class, you may never be able to express an *asana* exactly as the teacher does. But on the other hand, as your expression of the *asana* is unique, the teacher or anyone else will never be able to do it quite like you.

Undistracted involvement in the process and sensations of movement also keeps us in the present moment. Expectations and worries about future results do not serve us. Living in the present with an awareness of each moment is a prerequisite for cherishing those moments and embracing life. A yoga class is not a game of Simon Says or Follow the Leader, but an amazing opportunity to be guided through the process of self-exploration. Yoga is freedom from self-imposed expectations. The *asanas* are a road map laying out the course to personal growth. Learn these *asanas* with the utmost self-kindness and be proud of yourself in the attempt. At Kripalu, we end each class by saying, *Jai Bhagwan,* which along with other definitions, means "a blessed victory." The victory does not lie in success or failure, but in the expression of deep self-love and compassion along your own unique path of yoga, and ultimately through life.

Finally, in a yoga class, pay attention to the pauses between the postures. Very often, the magic of yoga occurs in the spaces between the *asanas.*

The following descriptions of each *asana* includes its Sanskrit and English names, a discussion of any historical origins and meanings that may exist and a step-by-step guide to its expression. The Sanskrit names for all of the postures are compound words that incorporate the word *asana,* simply meaning "position". For example, *tadasana,* the mountain pose, consists of the root *tada* or mountain and *asana* or position. One proviso is that many of the names of the *asanas* may differ from one school of yoga to the other. There is not complete consistency among the various yogic traditions. For example, the standing crescent or standing half moon crescent pose in Kripalu yoga is called the half moon or *ardha chandrasana.* In other schools *ardha chandrasana,* the half moon, is an advanced balance posture. More commonly, the standing crescent or half moon crescent goes by the Sanskrit name, *indudalasana.* I will try to present the more common expressions and names of the *asanas* that you more likely will hear in a typical Hatha class and not those of the Kripalu tradition in which I trained. In addition, I have placed an asterisk next to any Sanskrit name that you are more likely to hear a teacher say in a yoga class.

In the practice of yoga, safety is paramount. There are many contraindications to the performance of many of the *asanas.* A contraindication is a reason not to do something. For example, pregnancy is a contraindication to performing a supine *asana.* Rotator cuff pathology is a contraindication to *asanas* requiring the lifting of the arm above the head. Uncontrolled hypertension or a predisposition to orthostatic hypotension are contraindications to inversions where the head is positioned below the heart. It is impractical as an instructor guides a class to list the contraindications for every *asana.* There would be a lack of flow and transition from posture to posture if each one was interrupted by a list of pathophysiologies that represent contraindications. Therefore, it is so very important to listen to your body as you practice yoga. If something is uncomfortable or painful don't do it. Creating pain and discomfort clouds the mind with disturbing thoughts, distracts the mind from experiencing clarity and creates a potential for injury. One should never feel compelled to do what an instructor suggests or does. As was said previously, "Yoga is not Simon Says." Yoga is also not a competition. Never look at an instructor's suggested modifications of an *asana* as challenges. Modifications or options are simply different ways to experience an *asana.* It is up to you to choose the one that most enhances your experience. In short, protect yourself from physical and mental harm. Practice at your edge, not your instructor's. Honor your body and mind. We are all individuals with different thoughts and varying physical abilities, some limited by injury or disease. Become aware and then accept your individuality.

Before we embark on our journey to the wonderful world of the *asanas* and *pranayama,* a word about the illustrations of the various postures used in this book. I choose to use charcoal drawings of art figure mannequins for each pose. Many sources, including magazines and books, use photographs of people expressing each *asana.* Once again, an important guiding principle in yoga, as well as in life, is self-observation without judgment. It is difficult to look at a photograph and not draw comparisons to oneself. If the model is extremely fit and flexible, my mind wanders to my own inflexibility and feelings of envy. Regardless of the body habitus of the model, whether thin, average or of larger body size, potential exists for judgments about oneself and comparisons to the model.

The charcoal drawings of the full expression of the *asanas* serve the purpose of illustrating the relationships of the joints, arms, legs, torso, pelvis, spine and head as they exist in space, while eliminating any potential for negative self-judgments arising from comparisons. As you explore the *asanas,* imagine yourself transported into each illustration, breathing life into each drawing as it transforms into a version of the special individual that you are. Each one of us has the unique power to express oneself in body and mind. Enjoy that power. It is there for you in each and every *asana* and *pranayama.*

13
THE STANDING POSTURES

Be sure you put your feet in the right place, then stand firm.

Abraham Lincoln

Yoga accessible to everyone regardless of physical limitations or mental challenges is one of the main themes of this book. For those with limited mobility or confined to a chair, it is important to note that many aspects of these standing postures can still be enjoyed. There are specific arm movements inherent to all of the *asanas* that can be done with or without movements of the lower body. Accessing meditative states by connecting the breath to movement can be equally achieved by both the most physically limited and the most agile.

The practice of standing *asanas* can help improve posture over time. Developing correct posture promotes feelings of confidence, strength and pride whether standing or sitting in a chair.

Arguably, the two most important prerequisites in yoga necessary to master any posture are grounding and balance. I will consider balance in the next chapter. Grounding is quite simply creating a firm connection to the earth in order to achieve stability. Creating stability in the lower body allows for the freedom of movement of the upper body. Grounding of the feet on the mat also strengthens the legs, and we never want to miss an opportunity in our practice to strengthen the body.

From a yogic philosophic perspective, the standing postures begin with the acquisition of the energy of the Earth. To transmit that energy upwards to activate the *chakras,* the legs must always be engaged and working. In the process of liberation, energy of the *chakras* flows upwards, from root to crown of head through the *sushumna nadi,* the main central energy channel. The root *chakra* is the energy center for safety and grounding, our manifestation here on Earth. The crown of head *chakra* is the energy center for spirituality, the final step before liberation. Through the process of liberation, the ancient yogis could free themselves from earthly connections to ascend upwards into universal consciousness. Thus, with our standing postures, we build them from ground up. First starting with the grounding of the feet into the earth, and building the posture, activating the body and letting energy flow from the earth up to the sky. In a sense, through this process, we achieve liberation from our inauthentic selves. Thus, a soft passive body fails to generate both spiritual and physical energy. Whatever the particular standing *asana* we assume, one can experience that energy by always actively engaging the muscles of the arms, legs and core.

*Tadasana**

The Mountain

Everyone wants to live on top of the mountain, but all the happiness and growth occurs while you're climbing it.

Andy Rooney

I guided you through *tadasana* in the second part of this book. As was mentioned, *tada* is the Sanskrit word for mountain, such that *tadasana* means, "the position of the mountain." As was previously discussed, *tadasana* is the foundation of all of the other standing poses. Part of the mastery of *tadasana* lies in an understanding of the importance of grounding. Being well-grounded in life creates stability, safety and balance. Grounding in yoga achieves the same result. In *tadasana,* we begin with an awareness of the position of the feet. The feet should be parallel and a hip distance apart, which is about six to eight inches. By placing the feet directly below the hips, single vertical lines of support are formed all the way from the feet to the hips that promote stability and balance. That verticality is lost if the feet are too close or too wide apart. The weight of the body should be evenly distributed on all parts of the soles of the feet: the heels, balls and toes. If the weight is uneven, either more towards the balls of the feet or on the heels, once again instability and imbalance ensues. The toes should be spread wide apart to better grip the mat. One might think of the feet as similar to the hands with fingers widely spaced for better gripping.

As grounding is a downward force in *tadasana,* the opposing upward force creates elongation of the spine. Relaxing the shoulders down the back allows for more length in the neck. Subtlety lifting the chest promotes feelings of pride. It is often the perceived simple postures that are the most difficult to master. By mastering grounding, the lower body from the hips to the feet becomes like a strong pedestal of a statue, providing the stability needed to enjoy the freedom and grace of movement of the upper body.

As was summarized previously, the position of the body in *tadasana*:

1. The feet, parallel and at hip distance apart, grounded on the mat with the body's weight evenly distributed on all parts of the feet.
2. The leg muscles are engaged, especially the quadriceps, wrapping around the femur and drawing the kneecaps up.
3. The pelvis is leveled by dropping the tailbone and raising the pubic bones.
4. The shoulders are soft and down the back causing the sternum to move forward and up and the neck to elongate.
5. The spine is elongated from the sacrum to cervical spine with one long line of energy extending from the feet to the crown of head. Imagine that there is a string attached to the crown of head, pulling it up toward the sky.

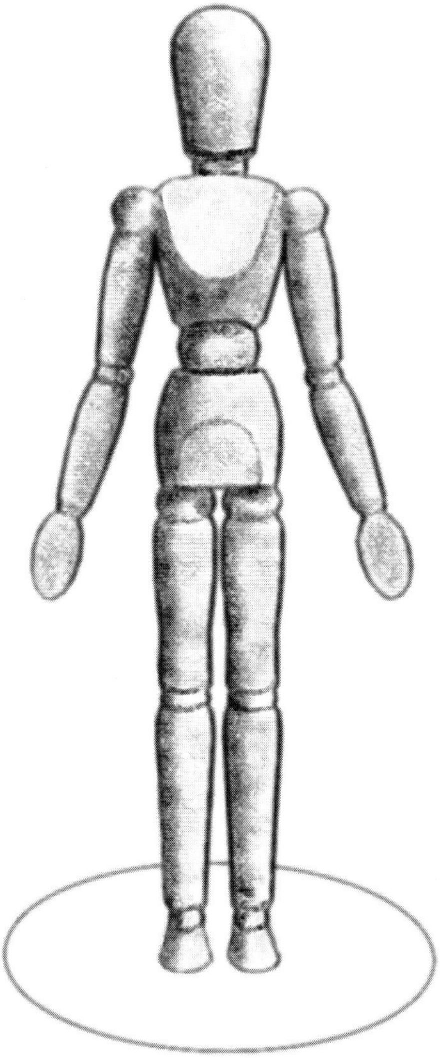

Tadasana ~ The Mountain

Indudalasana
Standing Crescent Moon Pose

Shoot for the moon, you might just get there.

Buzz Aldrin

The name of this posture is a combination of three Sanskrit words, *indu* or moon, *dala* or fragment, and *asana* or position. The full expression of the pose is exactly as its English name describes. To assume the crescent shape, lateral flexion of the spine is required.

1. The *asana* begins in *tadasana.* Once again, *tadasana* is the foundation for all of our standing postures. The feet are parallel, hip distance apart, and grounded on the mat with all the weight of the body evenly distributed on all parts of the soles, from heel to toes.
2. The quadriceps muscles are then engaged, pulling the kneecaps superiorly.
3. The arms are raised overhead to either side of the ears. As the arms sweep up, the spine elongates from the sacrum to the cervical spine and the crown of the head extends up toward the sky. Raising the arms gradually and slowly overhead achieves a greater focus on the elongation of the spine. As with most things in life, taking one's time and not rushing opens up opportunities to be better aware of what is happening in the moment.
4. The hands are brought into a steeple *mudra,* fingers clasped except for the index fingers, which point upward.

5. As one breathes in deeply, the index fingers are pulled skyward, eliminating the bend in the elbows. The upward pull of the index fingers is opposed by the grounding of the feet into the mat, thereby creating maximal stretch of the body and elongation of the spine. Notice the resulting upward lift of the chest and abdomen. The body is now fully engaged, creating a single line of energy that originates in the ground, courses through the body and exits from the fingertips into the sky.
6. Inhale into the active stretch and, without releasing the engagement and lengthening of the body, with exhalation, arch over to the right or left as instructed and shift the hips toward the opposite side. The upper body should lateral flex or bend in a single horizontal plane, imagining the body is between two plates of glass. As one arches to the side, make sure to maintain engagement of the muscles in the legs, particularly the quadriceps muscles, and the upward pull of the index fingers away from the body. The posture should not become a passive lateral flexion, but an active stretch. By contracting the thigh muscles, grounding the feet and stretching through the fingertips, the spine will elongate to a much greater degree and the stretch in the side body will be maximized.
7. To exit the pose, the upper body is brought back to center. The clasp of the hands is released. The arms are then brought back down to the sides of the hips. Letting the arms drop slowly and gradually, affords a greater appreciation of the resolution of the stretch.

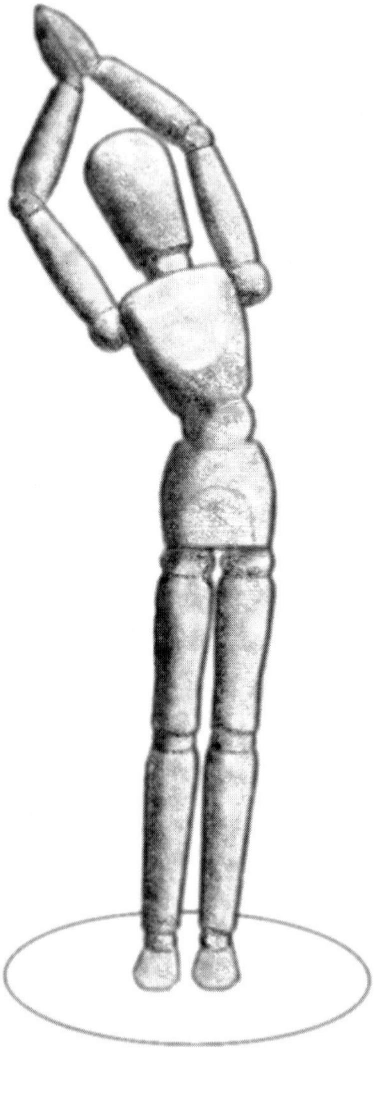

Indulasana ~ Standing Crescent Moon Pose

A variation of this pose is performed with one hand on the hip and the other arm extended next to the ear. As one bends to one side, the fingertips should be actively pulled away from the body to intensify the side stretch. Don't let the arm just float passively in space.

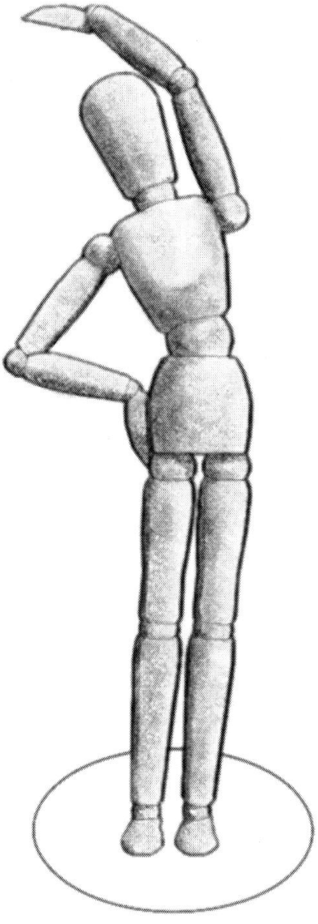

Indudalasana ~ The Standing Crescent Moon Pose Variation

*Utkatasana**
The Chair Pose

Every chair should be a throne and hold a king.

Ralph Waldo Emerson

The Sanskrit word *utkata* has many meanings including "powerful", "proud" and "fierce". The English name of this posture simply reflects the appearance of sitting in a chair, an imaginary one in this instance.

The *asana* has its origin in Hindu mythology, specifically from the *Ramayana,* an epic poem written several thousands of years ago. It follows the struggles of Rama, a divine prince from the Kosala Kingdom following his exile from the kingdom by his father, King Dasharatha. With courage and strength he overcomes many struggles and challenges as he travels across the Indian subcontinent with his wife, Sita, and brother, Lakshmana. After fourteen years in exile, Rama returns to his birthplace, Ayodhya, to be crowned king and assume his rightful place on the throne. The main theme of the myth is *utkata;* the power, courage, and ferocity embodied by Rama. With regard to *utkatasana,* one might consider a throne as a type of chair reserved for the powerful. Perhaps as we assume *utkatasana* we might access feelings of pride and the power of positive affirmations and gratitude. Yoga provides an opportunity to connect with our true selves and passions, allowing us to embrace life. Tapping into that power can be quite liberating.

Utkatasana ~ The Chair Pose

1. Start in *tadasana.*
2. The arms are then raised to shoulder height.
3. As we never want to lose any opportunity to activate and strengthen muscles, rather than holding the arms up passively, pull the fingers away from the body while simultaneously pulling the shoulders back into their sockets. This action engages the arm muscles.

4. Begin to sit down into your imaginary chair. Just like the standing crescent moon pose, try to maintain the muscular engagement in the arms and legs. The action of sitting begins by pulling the hips and knees back as weight shifts onto the heels, while at the same time, hinging forward with a flat back. A challenge of this posture is to shift the points of grounding from the entire sole of the foot in *tadasana* to just the heels. As you hinge forward at the hip creases, try not to lean too far forward, as this will shift the weight away from the heels.
5. Look down at your knees. Try to bring the knees directly over the ankles so that you can see your toes.
6. One can raise the arms to either side of the ears, but be cognizant that this can place a strain on the neck, may cause the torso to hinge too far forward, the back to round, and a forward shift of weight on the feet.
7. Exiting from the posture is typically done by slowly extending the legs to assume an upright position as the arms follow overhead. Once again, in the interest of enjoying the moment, let your arms drop slowly and gradually downward, as if you are moving the arms through honey or a dense fog. As the hands reach the level of the hips, release all of the engagement in the body and enjoy a nice deep breath. Transitioning from activity to rest is an opportunity to reconnect with the breath and check in to any sensations in the physical body and thoughts or emotions in the mind that you might be experiencing.

Allow *utkatasana* to be more than just an imaginary chair, but rather a symbol of pride that is realized from your yoga practice.

*Virabhadrasana**
The Warrior

The two most powerful warriors are patience and time.

Leo Tolstoy

There are three distinct warrior poses in a typical Hatha yoga practice: warriors I, II and III. Warrior III is an advanced balance posture, but I will touch on it nonetheless so you can have a full understanding of all three. It always seemed odd to me that a peaceful practice like yoga that stresses *ahimsa* or nonviolence should incorporate a pose called the warrior. The origin of all three warrior poses, however, comes from ancient Hindu mythology through a story of violence, revenge, remorse, sorrow, compassion and love. The symbolism of that myth has been transformed into the *asanas* we do today.

Sati, the daughter of the powerful King Daksha, marries Shiva, one of the principal deities of the Hindu religion, known as the destroyer and transformer. The King does not approve of the marriage as he cares not for the reclusive god Shiva who meditates on mountain tops rather than being an active part of society. He also knows of Shiva's history of questionable behaviors, such as the decapitation of one of the five heads of Brahma. King Daksha hosts a *yagna*, a religious sacrifice and celebration to which he invites all beings of heaven except Shiva and his daughter, Sati. An enraged and slighted Sati goes to the *yagna* anyway. There, through yoga, she enters into a deep state of meditation and rage, which fuels her inner fire to such a degree that it totally consumes her physical body. Hearing of his wife's violent demise, Shiva rips off his clothes and tears out his hair. One of his torn locks of hair is transformed into the malevolent warrior Virabhadra.

Shiva instructs Virabhadra to go to the *yagna*, kill everyone there, behead the king and drink the king's blood.

Virabhadra enters the *yagna* chest forward with two swords, one in each hand, raised above his head. Virabhadra's initial posture becomes *virabhadrasana* I, in which the hips and chest are squared forward with arms raised above the head and the front knee bent forward, ready for battle. In *virabhadrasana* II, we are positioned like warriors poised to attack, with an unwavering gaze directed over an extended sword in our front hand and our front knee bent forward, ready to thrust the sword into the king. Finally, in *virabhadrasana* III, the body becomes extended parallel to the ground with both arms extended forward next to the ears while balancing on one leg. It is as if we are holding two swords directed downward. Balancing on one leg symbolizes the final commitment to drive the swords through the neck of the king. After Virabhadra kills the king and everyone else at the celebration, Shiva arrives and witnesses all of the death and destruction resulting from his warrior's actions. Feeling remorse and compassion, he absorbs Virabhadra back into his body and restores life back to everyone, including King Daksha. Sati, his wife, is reincarnated as Parvarti, the goddess of fertility, marriage, strength and devotion.

The meanings and messages of this myth are up to individual interpretation. One might reflect on the importance of restraint in order to avoid the remorse and sorrow that may result from rash and reflexive actions in emotionally charged situations. More importantly, all of the warrior poses afford an opportunity to consider how each of us may be a proud warrior in life, having overcome or presently facing life's challenges with determination and courage.

*Virabhadrasana I**

Warrior I

This *asana* exemplifies two of the most important principles of yoga: grounding and balance. For *virabhadrasana* I, balance follows grounding. Correctly entering into the pose necessitates firm grounding into the mat to produce stability, as the lower body from hips to feet become like the pedestal of your statue. Stability and strength of the lower body allows for a greater variation of upper body movements. Warrior I is all about grounding, balance and stability; desired qualities of the warrior we often need to better meet life's challenges.

1. Come to the front of the mat. Once again start in mountain pose with feet hip distance apart and hands on hips. Inhale into a straight torso and elongated spine as you relax the shoulders.
2. As you exhale, take a large step directly back with your right foot. Plant the foot on the mat at about a forty-five degree angle, while at the same time bending the left knee forward over the ankle.
3. Very important for optimal stability and balance is for the feet to remain hip distance apart. Look down at your feet. The distance between two parallel lines drawn from the feet to the front of the mat should be about six to eight inches or slightly wider apart. Balance is compromised if the two parallel lines are too close together. One should imagine that he or she is standing on two train tracks rather than on a tightrope. The hips should also be square to the front of the mat, chest facing forward. From an anatomical perspective,

it is physically impossible to square the hips forward if one's feet are in one straight line on that tightrope. Look down at your hands on your hips. The hands should align horizontally. If the hands are on a diagonal, swing your back foot out wider toward the edge of the mat to allow the hips and chest to become square to the front of the mat.

4. Draw your attention to the feet. Notice if the weight of the body is evenly distributed on both feet. You can gently rock forward and back to experience the weight shift from foot to foot. Then return back to the point of even grounding. Push both feet firmly into the mat, imagining them pulling the mat apart in opposite directions.
5. Sweep both arms overhead into a gentle "V" shape in order to relax the shoulders and relieve any tension in the neck that comes from positioning the arms too close to the ears. The "V" shape is also a symbol of victory in our warrior pose.
6. To exit the warrior pose, bring the hands back to the hips, shift weight forward onto the front leg as you step the right foot forward to meet the left.
7. The *asana* can then be done on the opposite side.

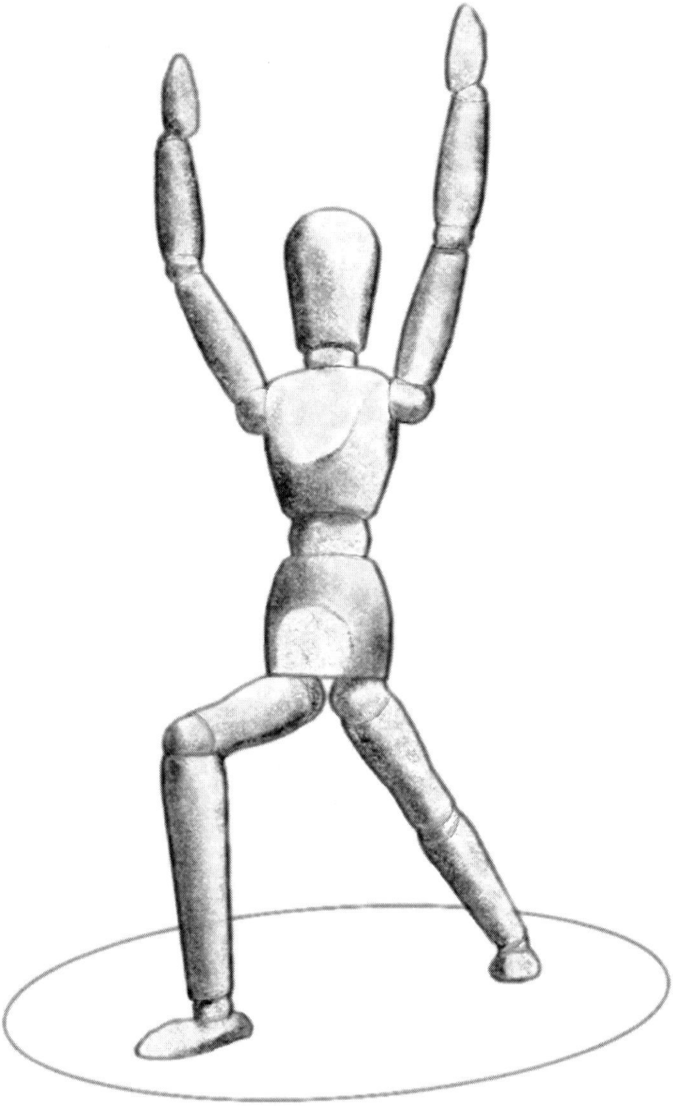

Virabhadrasana I ~ Warrior I

The Humble Warrior

Establishing firm grounding and stability in the lower body creates the balance necessary to allow us to position the upper body in whatever position we desire. One such position is known as the "humble warrior," accomplished by hinging forward at the hip creases from warrior I, with a common variation often encountered in classes that adds a spinal twist.

The Humble Warrior

1. From *virabhadrasana* I, bring the hands together in *anjali mudra* at heart center.
2. Hinging forward occurs at the hip creases, not at the lower

back. You can practice this by placing the middle fingers over the hip creases. Imagine the middle fingers are the axis that the hip creases rotate around as you hinge forward. Hinging forward is done with a flat back.

3. Success at the humble warrior pose is realized by maintaining equal grounding on both feet. As we hinge forward, our upper body weight shifts forward with a concurrent shift of weight off of the back foot. The force of the weight of the upper body hinging forward should be counteracted by deliberately pressing the back foot firmly into the mat.
4. To add a spinal twist, the upper body is rotated to the left as the right elbow nears or comes to rest on the left knee or upper thigh and vice versa for the opposite side.
5. More commonly, from the humble warrior one returns back to *virabhadrasana* I.

Another variation of Warrior I involves back extension. From the warrior the fingers are interlaced behind the back. By pushing the hands downward, the shoulders are pulled back, the scapulae are drawn together and the pectoralis muscles are stretched.The degree of arch in the back can be increased by turning the gaze upward towards the ceiling. In this position, the upper body weight will shift backward, so be cognizant of maintaining even grounding of the feet on the mat, as well.

*Virabhadrasana II**
Warrior II

Virabhadrasana II ~ Warrior II

There are many different ways of entering into *virabhadrasana II.* Positioning of the legs and feet properly is best understood by beginning facing towards the long edge of your mat.

1. As you place your hands on both hips, step the feet about a leg length apart. Look down at your feet. Both feet should be parallel or slightly pigeon-toed.

2. Notice how your chest is facing the long edge of your mat. Our goal is for the chest to maintain this orientation and relationship to the long edge of the mat throughout the full expression of the *asana*.
3. Rotate the right foot ninety degrees. Again, look down at your feet. The feet are in the correct position if you can draw an imaginary straight line from the heel of the front right foot to the arch of the back left foot. At this point, maintain full extension in both legs, not allowing the right knee to bend.
4. Raise both arms to shoulder height, palms facing downward. Look at both arms to assure that they are at shoulder height. There is a tendency to drop the back arm. The arms should be in a straight line that is parallel to the floor.
5. Without rotating the chest, but only the head and neck, turn your gaze over your right hand.
6. Pull your fingertips away from the body, imagining two friends on either side of you gently pulling your arms in opposite directions. Activating the arms results in a gentle pull of the humeral heads from their sockets at the shoulder joints. Another tendency in classes is to passively hold both arms up at shoulder height. Among the many benefits of yoga is the development of muscle strength. Once again, we don't want to miss an opportunity to engage muscles; in this case the muscles of the arms, from shoulders to fingertips. This engagement will also activate the core. Often we are unaware of the engagement of the muscles of the core. Simultaneous contraction of the arm and leg muscles always results in the contraction of the muscles of the core. To experience this, release any tension in the muscles of the

arms and legs. Focusing your attention on the chest and torso, notice what happens to the muscles of the core when you re-engage the muscles of the extremities.

7. Bend the right knee to bring it directly over the ankle. Another tendency is to allow the torso to tilt forward away from vertical as the knee is bent. The torso should be fully upright with full elongation of the spine, shoulders directly over hips as much as possible. In order to assure the proper position, before bending into your front knee imagine that your torso and arms are completely frozen in space. Now, as you bend your knee, only allow your legs to move. Concentrate on the shoulders remaining over the hips. Use the power of the mind to prevent the upper body from changing its relationship to the ground. As the knee bends forward, imagine that the upper body is being translated forward as if on a conveyor belt at the supermarket checkout.
8. Look at your right knee to assure that it is directly over the ankle. If the knee is collapsing inward, pull the knee out laterally such that it obscures the visualization of the pinky toe of the right foot.

Congratulations! You are now in your full expression of warrior II. Do a full body scan. Are both feet firmly and equally grounded on the mat? Imagine the feet trying to pull the mat apart in opposite directions. Is your front knee positioned over the ankle? Are your arms at shoulder height and engaged? Is your chest facing the long edge of your mat? Many teachers will instruct you to square your hips to the long edge of your mat instead of the chest. This is physically impossible as some rotation of the hips is necessary for the perpendicular relationship of the feet. Concentrate only on the chest position, not the hips. Is your torso, neck and head upright? Finally, notice the muscular engagement and energy surging through all parts of the body and feel the strength of your warrior. Turn inward and try to tap into your inner strength. Life is full of challenges. Yoga may not be the answer to overcoming them, but yoga can promote introspection and clarity that are valuable tools in any attempt.

Before entering into the warrior II on the opposite side, straighten the front leg, place your hands on your hips and rotate the right foot such that it is again parallel with the left. You are now in the position where we began; feet parallel, about a leg's length apart. Rotate the left foot ninety degrees and enjoy the process of becoming the warrior once again.

Reversing the Warrior

Quite often an instructor will guide you into a reversed warrior. Starting in warrior II, the front hand is rotated, palm facing up. With a deep inhalation, the front arm is swept up overhead and back. The back hand slides down the back of the thigh of the rear leg as the spine extends and twists backwards, opening up the chest to the sky. Reversing the warrior is not just a spinal extension, but also a spinal twist. To create the twist, pull the top shoulder behind you and direct your gaze upwards as you open your chest up to the sky. Entering into the reversed warrior requires only movement of the upper body. The legs should remain stationary and grounding should remain evenly distributed on both feet. To exit the reversed warrior pose, windmill the arms back to shoulder height, returning to warrior II.

Viparita Virabhadrasana ~ Reverse Warrior

Utthita Parsvakonasana
Extended Side Angle Pose

Utthita Parsvakonasana ~ Extended Side Angle

From Warrior II, we can create a counter twist of the spine to that experienced in the reversed warrior by hinging forward, placing the forearm of the front arm onto the thigh of the front leg, and extending the top arm forward overhead. A diagonal line can be drawn from the foot of the back leg to the fingertips of the top arm. The spinal twist comes from pulling the top shoulder back to stack the shoulder joints vertically. For some with rotator issues, extending the arm above the head at a diagonal can be uncomfortable. Another option is to bend the elbow and bring the forearm of the top arm behind the back. Regardless of where the arm is positioned, most important is stacking the shoulders vertically to create the counter twist in the spine. Focus your gaze wherever it creates the least amount of strain on the neck. Similar to the humble warrior, it is important to maintain equal grounding in both feet as this pose results in a shift of the weight of the upper body forward. By maintaining equal grounding of both feet, stability is more easily achieved, allowing us to have the freedom of movement of the upper body.

A variation of the extended angle pose is to bring the front hand down to the mat inside the front foot rather than placing the forearm on the thigh.

*Trikonasana**
The Triangle Pose

> *Learn how to see. Realize that everything connects to everything else.*
>
> *Leonardo Da Vinci*

The sides of a triangle connect to each other. There are many different classifications of triangles based on the lengths and relationship of the three sides and the value of each of the three angles formed. An equilateral triangle has three congruent sides and three congruent angles. It is balanced in its symmetry. An isosceles triangle has two congruent sides and two congruent angles. A right triangle possesses one right or 90 degree angle. The relationship of its three sides is described by the Pythagorean theorem. Pythagoras was an ancient Greek philosopher who was the first to articulate this relationship centuries ago. Triangles can also be acute and obtuse. As you will see, as we assume *trikonasana* we try to create two adjacent triangles that connect us to the earth and to ourselves. The following description of this *asana* represents just one of many different ways to enter into the posture.

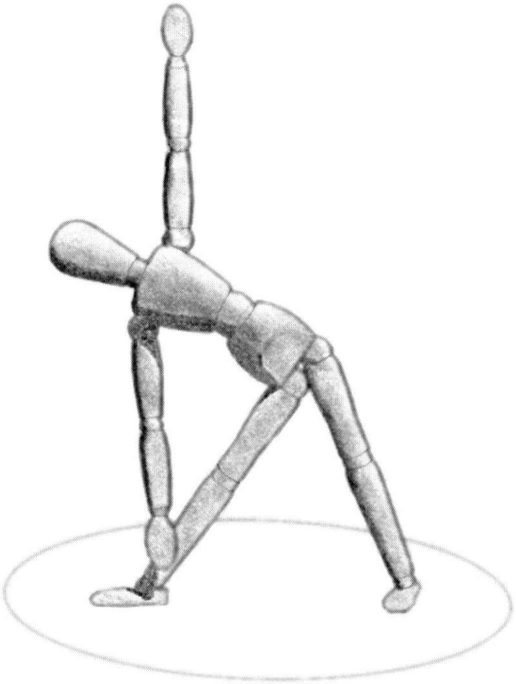

Triokonasana ~ The Triangle Pose

1. Begin by facing the long edge of the mat.
2. Bring your hands to your hips and step the legs apart so that the feet are approximately a leg length apart. Look down at the feet. Make sure they are parallel or slightly pigeon-toed.
3. Rotate the right foot ninety degrees toward the front edge of the mat. If more comfortable or if it affords greater balance, the back heel could be slightly pushed back to an angle less than 90 degrees.
4. Bring the arms to shoulder height, gaze over the right hand.
5. Reach the fingers of the right hand forward while shifting the hips backward.
6. With straight arms like hands on a clockface, begin to rotate the upper body forward so that the left arm raises toward the sky and the right down towards the mat. The back of the right hand can rest on the right calf or a block positioned next to the calf. Try to pull the left shoulder back in order to stack the shoulders vertically, maintaining the arms in a tee at shoulder height. Stacking the shoulders vertically creates the desired spinal twist in *trikonasana.* More important than how close to the mat you bring the right hand is assuming a position that allows for the stacking of the shoulders.
7. In the full expression of the *asana,* two triangles are created. If the feet are a leg length apart, the line drawn on the mat between the feet and the two legs forms an equilateral triangle. The right leg, the right side body and the right arm form the second triangle.
8. To exit *trikonasana,* while maintaining straight arms, rotate the torso upright, bring the hands to the hips, and rotate the right foot ninety degrees so that the feet once again are

parallel. By rotating the left foot ninety degrees, you can begin to enter the posture from the other side.

As we assume *trikonasana,* we can reflect upon and explore the geometric relationships that exist in the world around us. The position of our bodies reflect complex mathematical relationships and our movements are governed by the laws of physics. Yoga affords us a multitude of opportunities to consider the world from different perspectives that can expand our horizons and enrich our lives with new meaning. It is felt that *trikonasana* stimulates the sacral or *svadhisthana chakra,* the energy center for creativity, sexuality and pleasure. Our freedom of expression is a wonderful complement to the constraints and constancy of the physical laws of nature.

Prasarita padottanasana

Wide Angle Standing Forward Fold

We all come from the same root, but the leaves are all different.

John Fire Lame Deer

In Sanskrit, *prasarita* means "extended", *pada* "foot", *utta* "intense" and *asana* "pose". Forward folding with the legs spread wide apart can at times be intense, so practice vigilance and don't exceed your edge. Another important proviso is to exit this posture slowly with care. This *asana* constitutes an inversion. An inversion is any pose that requires the head to be below the level of the heart. Raising the head too quickly creates a potential for orthostatic hypotension, which essentially is becoming faint from "the blood rushing out of the head".

Gradually lifting the head makes this drop in blood pressure less likely. In addition, inversions should be avoided for people with glaucoma, high blood pressure and other cardiovascular conditions. *Uttanasana,* the Standing Forward Fold, described in this chapter, and *Adho Mukha Svanasana,* the Downward Facing Dog, described in chapter sixteen, are also examples of inversions.

1. Once again, begin facing the long edge of your mat with your hands on your hips.
2. Step your feet about a leg length apart, feet parallel or slightly pigeon-toed.
3. Come to a straight torso and elongated spine.
4. Hinge over at the hip creases with a flat back.
5. Bend forward to a point where your flat back and legs form a ninety degree angle.
6. Begin to round the back as you drop your head to bring your gaze between your legs. The final position of the hands will depend on individual flexibility. Some may be able to bring the palms flat on the mat, others on the shins or knees. As always, inability to bring the hands to the mat does not represent a failure to perform the posture correctly. Wherever your hands rest represents your own personal expression of the *asana.* There is no right or wrong to personal expression.
7. Exiting the *asana* should be done slowly and gradually. As you bring your hands to your hips, straighten the back and hinge up at the hip creases. Once your torso is upright, heel-toe your feet back to center.

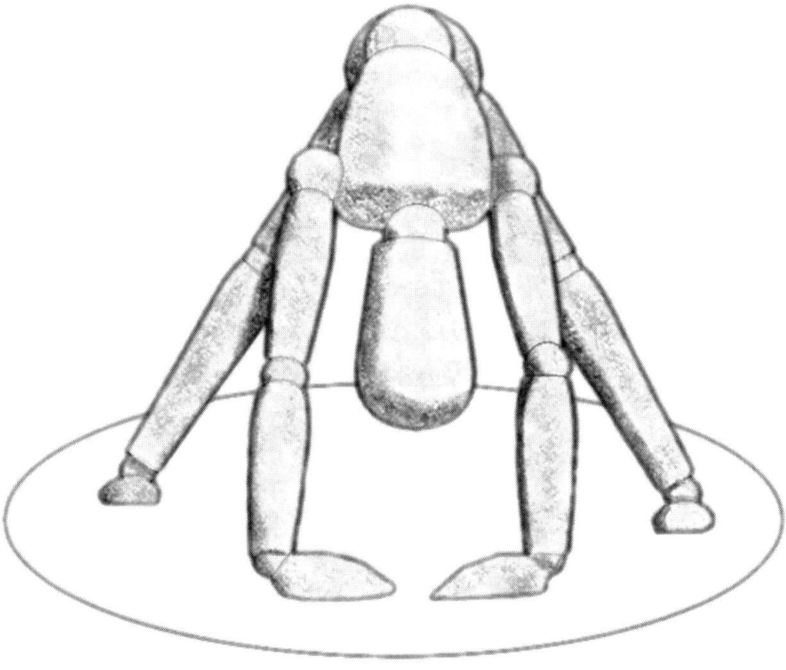

Prasarita Padottanasana ~ Wide Angle Standing Forward Fold

Utkata Konasana
The Goddess Pose

It is within you that the divine lives.

Joseph Campbell

We have already come across the Sanskrit word, *utkata,* in the previous discussion of *utkatasana,* again meaning powerful, proud and fierce. This *asana* is about harnessing the power, pride and ferocity of a goddess. The goddess might be considered to represent the femininity of *ida,* the moon energy channel, coupled with the active masculine characteristics of *pingala,* the sun energy channel. There exists a similarity between *utkatasana* and *utkata konasana* in that in both postures, the hips and sitz bones drop as if one is sitting on an imaginary chair. For the Goddess pose, the feet are more widely spaced, which results in stretching of the hip adductor or inner thigh muscles.

1. The initial steps to enter into the posture are similar to *Prasarita Padottanasana,* except the feet flare out to the sides at about forty-five degree angles, rather than the feet being parallel or slightly pigeon-toed.
2. The arms are then raised to shoulder height with elbows bent. This position of the arms is often referred to as "cactus" or "goal post" arms. I prefer to use as little imagery as possible in describing particular positions as it may distract one from a single-pointed focus on something else, such as the breath.
3. Concentrating on keeping the torso straight, spine elongated, and shoulders over the hips, begin to bend the

knees to drop the hips and sitz bones toward the mat. Imagine you are sitting down on a stool. The inner thigh adductor muscles responsible for adduction or pulling the thighs toward the center of the body are stretched as the hip joints flex and externally rotate.

4. Exiting the pose is accomplished simply by extending both legs, bringing the hands to the hips and heel-toeing the feet together.

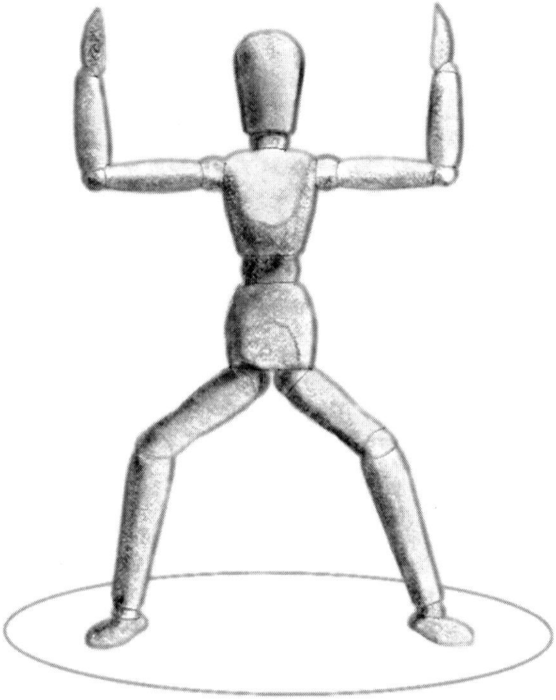

Utkata Konasana ~ The Goddess Pose

Utthita Tadasana
The Star Pose

It is not in the stars to hold our destiny but in ourselves.

William Shakespeare

The Sanskrit word *utthita* means "extended", such that *utthita tadasana* is the "extended mountain pose." The English descriptor refers to the star shape that is created with the body.

1. Similar to the Goddess pose, the Star pose is entered with feet wide apart and flared out to the sides.
2. For the Star pose, both legs remain straight and extended. The arms are outstretched straight at about forty-five degree angles with the fingers stretched wide apart.
3. To gain the most benefit from this posture, pull the fingers away from the body and actively press the feet into the mat. Engaging all of the arm and leg muscles will secondarily activate the core. Focus on maintaining an elongated spine. Imagine four lines of energy extending through the fingertips and feet to intersect at the solar plexus *chakra,* the energy center for strength and wisdom.
4. Exit the posture by bringing hands to hips and heel-toeing feet together.

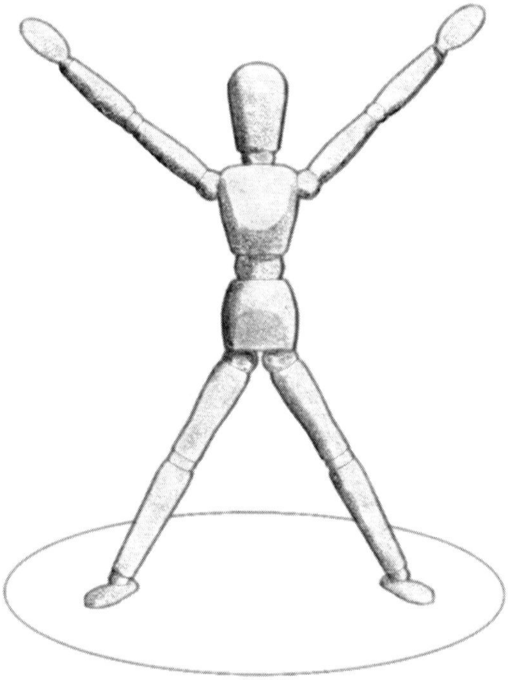

Utthita Tadasana ~ The Star Pose

The Star and Goddess poses can be integrated by alternating extending and bending the arms and legs, respectively. Focus might be turned to the stretch and relaxation of the inner thigh muscles that occur with knee flexion and extension. One might also honor the inner deity that we all possess while in the Goddess pose and the infinite universe that we are all a part of while in the Star.

Uttanasana*

Standing Forward Fold

In a gentle way, you can shake the world.

Mahatma Gandhi

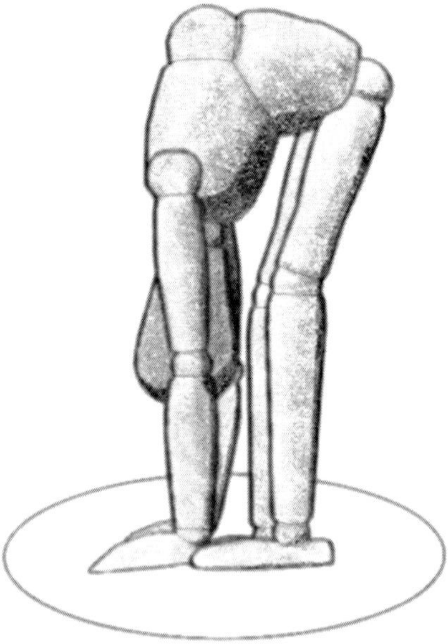

Uttanasana ~ Standing Forward Fold

The standing forward fold is an asana that is usually done as part of a *surya namaskar* series or sun salutation, however, it can be done as a transition between any positions or postures. The posture is usually entered by "swan-diving" from a standing position or by walking or hopping the feet forward between the hands from a downward facing dog. I like to refer to this posture as a gentle forward fold since the entire body is soft and released. It is important not to lock the knees, but rather bend them as much as is most comfortable. Bending occurs at the hip joints. The body above the hip joints and the head become heavy, surrendering to the effects of gravity. If they reach, the hands can be placed on the mat. If they don't, or even if they do, the arms can simply dangle in space as you enjoy the force of gravity tugging on the hands and arms, gently pulling the upper arm bones down from the shoulder joints. Small micro-movements with the torso allow the arms to sway as if being blown by the wind. One might also grab the elbows and let the arms sway as a single unit. Exiting this pose can be accomplished by reverse swandiving to a standing position or possibly by planting the hands and stepping back into a high plank or downward facing dog.

*Ardha Uttanasana**
Half Forward Fold

Similar to *uttanasana, ardha uttanasana* is part of a sun salutation sequence. It is almost always entered from the forward fold. Quite simply, while in *uttanasana,* the legs are extended by removing the bend from the knee joints, as one hinges up from the hip crease to a flat back, leading forward with the sternum and head. The arms are fully extended. The hands can rest where they reduce the most stress in the arms and legs, possibly on the shins. One then typically drops back down into *uttanasana.*

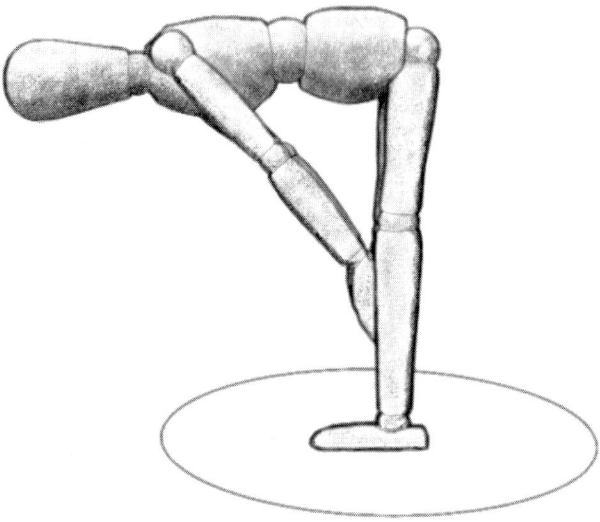

Ardha Uttanasana ~ Half Forward Fold

14
THE BALANCE POSTURES

Life is like riding a bicycle. To keep your balance you must keep moving.

Albert Einstein

Of course, unlike riding a bicycle, the balance postures in yoga require a still body and a quiet mind. The act of balancing on one leg is contrary to the functioning of the brain. Our brains react to states of corporeal instability. Secondary to impulses traveling to the brainstem from the labyrinths of the inner ears and proprioceptors throughout the musculoskeletal system, the brain directs the movements of the body to bring us back to stability. Quite simply, the brain does not want us to stand on one leg. Arguably, the balance postures represent some of the most challenging *asanas* to master. The challenge, however, is not a physical one. Success does not lie in the ability to stand on one leg. The ultimate goal is the attainment of an unwavering, undistracted focus on a single point. It requires being in the moment, clearing the mind of thoughts. Never look at a balance posture as a physical challenge, but rather a challenge of the mind. If success is defined as the creation of a single point of focus that quiets the mind, arguably a balance posture could be performed with both feet on the ground or in a chair. Unlike many other postures, there are many opportunities for distraction, especially in a class, such as thoughts turning to wobbling coupled with negative self-judgments regarding the inability to balance, as well as an awareness of fellow students.

In yoga, we try to establish a balance between mind and body and the energies of the sun and moon. Off the mat, we strive for balance in our lives; balance between work and play, activity and rest, company and solitude, and sympathetic and parasympathetic neural tone, to name a few. The balance postures are an integration of the body and mind. Grounding into the mat and proper positioning of the torso and limbs are necessary for balance, but success will not come without accessing the mind and achieving undistracted concentration. As was discussed previously, *santosha,* one of the *niyamas* meaning contentment, is more easily attained through non-attachment. Not attaching oneself to the outcome of any endeavor relieves the pressure to worry about that outcome. Many of us, including myself, have tendencies to lament about perceived past failures and worry about future events. Neither the past or future is in our present control. If we can have control, it can only exist in the present. Non-attachment to the outcome of a balance posture, that is balancing in stillness versus wobbling or falling out of the posture, is necessary to establish clarity of mind and a single point of focus. The mind is distracted by negative self-judgments arising from a failure to physically balance or positive self-judgments from success. Clarity of mind and consequent physical balance comes from sole concentration on a *drishti,* or focal point, found either on the floor or wall. The *drishti* exists in the present moment.

One might argue that focusing on a *drishti* merely creates a distraction from what is occurring in the physical body. In a sense it does, as it preoccupies the mind and diverts attention away from thoughts about the potential outcome of wobbling or falling out of the pose, and for some, the self-fulfilling prophecy put forth by their inner critic regarding their inability to balance. But, it is much more than a distraction. The act of focusing on a *drishti* is a way to hone the tool of mindfulness. It is a practice of observing a single visual point to achieve an understanding of what exists in the present moment. For the ancients, the elimination of all other thoughts to gain a comprehensive knowledge of the object of meditation led some to *samadhi,* the final limb of Pantanjali's eight limbs of yoga.

Through the firing of proprioceptive receptors throughout the body, the brain receives neural information as to the position of the limbs, head and torso in space. The physical body can fade from awareness by supplying the brain with a single piece of information to which it can react. The *drishti* represents that single quantum of data. Although quite challenging, the physical body can come into stillness and balance with closed eyes using a technique called internal gazing. Normally, when we close our eyes, the eyes continue to move. Even though the eyelids are closed, the eyes can be kept motionless by directing them to the third eye *chakra.* The third eye *chakra* becomes the *drishti* on which one can focus without distraction.

Many times, as one attempts to balance on one leg, there is a tendency to hold the breath as the physical body tenses up. One can experience this effect by simply making a very tight fist and then noticing what happens to the breath. It is quite difficult not to hold your breath, especially if your focus is on the fist. Deepening the breath with expansion of the belly promotes balance. The act of expanding the belly while breathing triggers the parasympathetic response in the body with consequent relaxation of skeletal muscles. Relaxation promotes balance.

Most importantly, like the rest of your yoga practice, always practice self-kindness in the balance postures. Practice self-observation without judgment. Leave out the word "and" from any observation. Instead of, "I am wobbling *and* I can't balance," change your thought to, "I am wobbling." If you do wobble, it is actually a wonderful thing. Since the neural centers of balance engage when you enter into a state of instability, wobbling indicates that your brain is functioning normally, attempting to bring you back to a safe place. I, for one, am always overjoyed to be reminded that my brain is working. Be a friend to yourself. A friend would tell you that it doesn't matter if you wobble. It has no consequence. Substitute positive affirmations for automatic and reflexive negative self-judgments that might generalize to everything that one attempts in life. Balance in life is so important. Let one side of your scale be laden with kindness and the other light of negative self-judgments. If you do find yourself wobbling or falling out of a balance posture, smile. The act of smiling triggers physiological responses in the body that promote relaxation. It is also important to realize that one need not take the practice of yoga seriously at all times. Feel free to smile, even laugh.

Before delving into the more common balance postures you may encounter in a yoga class, let me once more stress the importance of the *drishti.* Establishing single-pointed focus while breathing deeply must precede the entry into any balance posture. Optimizing concentration without distraction is achieved by coupling auditory awareness of the breath to the visual awareness of the *drishti*. As an exercise, while sitting or standing, find any single point at which to stare. Do not let your vision waiver. Imagine that the point is being drawn towards your eyes, that the distance between you and the point is progressively diminishing. While continuing to stare at that single point, deepen the breath and begin to listen to it coming in and out of the nose. Also imagine that you are breathing into the *drishti*, that each inhalation is drawing it closer and closer to you. As we will discuss later, using the yogic breathing technique or *pranayama* known as the *ujjayi* breath increases the awareness of the breath and minimizes distraction. For about a minute, simply stare and listen. After a minute, notice how you feel. Was your concentration broken at any time? Did any thoughts arise? Meditation through focused concentration can clear the mind of chatter. It takes time to acquire the ability to meditate. The mind must learn and experience the meditative state so that eventually it can be easily accessed. Your *drishti* coupled with the auditory focus on the breath comes into the foreground of consciousness, while the awareness of the physical body fades into the background. Just as muscle strength and flexibility are acquired progressively and gradually over time, such is true of the ability to easily access a meditative state. Once developed, it can then become part of your tool box to minimize life's stresses. This state of introversion becomes a sanctuary, a safe place that you can always enter, a place of relaxation and peace. You have the power to spend as much or as little time as you wish in that sanctuary. Knowing of its existence is often enough to cope with whatever challenges arise.

With regard to the practical aspects of the balance postures and practicing self-kindness, be open to using a wall or props to aid in physical balance. A wall is a wonderful and valuable tool to establish feelings of stability and safety that can allow you to divert attention away from the physical body. Don't shy away from moving next to a wall with the fear that others will think less of you. Instead, be proud of yourself for practicing self-care and creating your own special individual yoga experience. Also, if options or modifications are offered by the teacher, know that options are not challenges. Options are merely different ways of positioning the body to come into a steady and comfortable position that will enhance one's experience. Success at a balance posture is achieving a single point of focus. Balancing on a toe rather than fully lifting a foot off of the mat may facilitate the realization of that goal rather than becoming distracted by physical instability. Balance self-kindness with nonattachment and stability will follow.

*Vrikshasana**

The Tree Pose

A tree with strong roots laughs at storms.

Malay Proverb

The Sanskrit word, *vrikshasana,* translates to "tree pose". Like all of the *asanas*, grounding into the earth is a prerequisite for success. For the tree pose, grounding is accomplished by creating a single vertical line extending from the sole of the foot of the standing leg to the hip. With the tree pose, you might imagine your foot as the roots of your tree. Spreading out the toes widens the reach of your roots into the earth. Your leg becomes your strong, supportive trunk and the upper body and arms your branches.

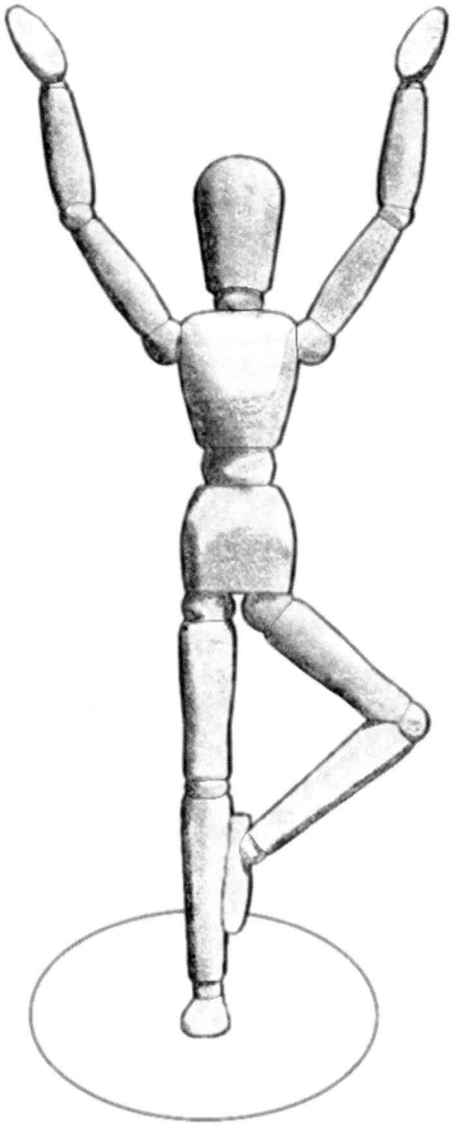

Vrikshasana ~ The Tree Pose

1. Establish your *drishti* and deepen, lengthen and listen to your breath.
2. With the hands on the hips begin to shift your weight onto one foot, let's say for this example, the right foot. Spread your toes and notice if your weight is evenly distributed on all parts of the foot; the toes, ball, and heel.
3. Slowly begin to lift the left heel off of the mat. Rotate the heel and bring the sole of the foot to rest on the right calf. Some with greater flexibility will be able to bring the foot to rest on the inner thigh. An important proviso is that the foot should never rest on the knee as this could lead to an undue varus stress on the knee joint that could result in ligamentous injury, especially if quickly falling out of the posture. If the foot cannot rest on the thigh above the knee, lower it to rest against the calf. Balance can be facilitated by pressing the sole of the foot into the leg.
4. Once the legs come into stillness, the arms are raised overhead to form your branches. As with all yoga postures, it is important to make them your own. Tap into your own self-expression to become whatever version of a tree you wish to be. Your elbows could be straight or bent, wrists flexed or extended, and the fingers spread out wide. Once you have mastered single-pointed focus, you might experiment with moving the arms as if your branches are blowing in the wind. As a variation, you might bring prayer hands together in *anjali mudra* at heart center. Ideally, the hips should be square to the front of your mat. Once square, the bent left knee may not be parallel to the hips. This is fine. Once again, it is your tree. In a forest, no tree looks like any of the others.

5. Success at a balance posture is achieving single-pointed focus, and as such, can be attained with modifications of the full expression of the *asana*. One modification is to rotate the left heel onto the right ankle, allowing the toes or big toe to maintain contact with the mat for extra support. Unfortunately, you will often hear teachers refer to this modification as the "sapling pose", as if implying that you are less than a fully developed tree.
6. To exit the tree pose, bring the left foot fully onto the mat and drop the arms to the sides as slowly and gracefully as possible. Before entering into the tree on the other side, it is wonderful to close the eyes, reset the brain and reestablish your intention for your balance posture before once again finding your *drishti.*

*Garudasana**
The Eagle Pose

One can never consent to creep when one feels an impulse to soar.

Helen Keller

The Sanskrit word *garudasana* translates directly to "eagle pose". The Garuda is a bird in Hindu mythology, as well as in Buddhism and Jainist lore. He is the avian protector of the Hindu god Vishnu, able to transport him anywhere. Garuda is the king of birds, portrayed as either a bird or a man-bird creature.

Garudasana represents a greater challenge than *vrikshasana,* but the fundamentals to achieve success are the same.

1. A *drishti* is established coupled with awareness of the breath
2. Hands are placed on hips and weight is transferred onto one leg.
3. Lift the other foot off of the mat, again let's say the right. As you begin to bend the left knee, cross the right thigh over the left. Ideally, to come into the full expression of eagle legs, the right foot wraps around the left calf, but just leaving the thighs crossed is sufficient. Wrapping the foot around the calf is facilitated by putting a greater bend in the knee of the standing leg.
4. Raise the arms and pass the right arm under the left. Typically, the arm that passes underneath corresponds to the same sided leg that crossed over on top. Again, ideally, to come into full eagle arms the palms of both hands touch and the elbows are brought to shoulder height. Modifications of eagle arms include the back of the hands touching, the hands on both shoulders or the hands in *anjali mudra* or prayer hands at heart center. Modifications are valuable for people with shoulder pathology such as rotator cuff issues or arthritis, as full eagle arms open up the shoulder joints, distracting the humeral heads forward from the joints. In full eagle arms it is difficult to maintain a *drishti* since the arms can obstruct one's view, but a small space between the forearms through which to peer can be used. For the other side, the left leg crosses over the right and the left arm comes under the right.

5. To exit from the pose, gracefully and slowly unwind the arms and then legs.

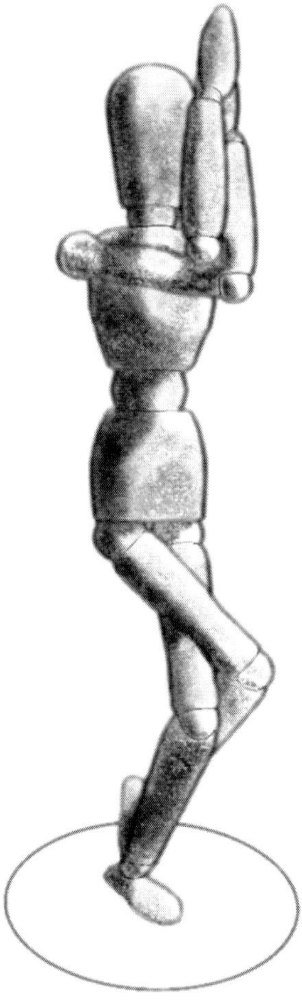

Garudasana ~ The Eagle Pose

Virabhadrasana III*
Warrior III

The world of reality has its limits; the world of imagination is boundless.

Jean-Jacques Rousseau

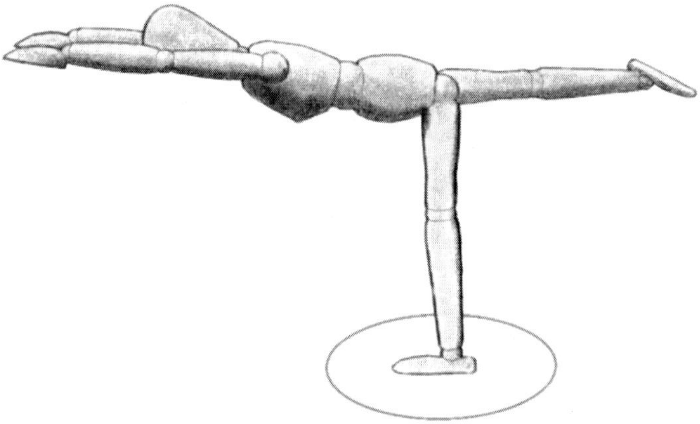

Virabhadrasana III ~ Warrior III

Warrior III is an advanced *asana.* Warriors I and II are positions of strength. *Virabhadrasana III* explores balance as another necessary attribute to become the warrior. Creating balance in life helps to better face life's challenges, while at the same time practicing non-attachment to any outcome.

1. One begins this pose in Warrior I.
2. Select a *drishti* on the floor or the edge of your mat so that when you hinge forward and vision is directed downward there is no need to find a new focal point.
3. Bring all of your weight onto your front foot.
4. Hinge forward at the hip creases with a flat back, while at the same time you lift your back leg.
5. Extend the front leg, taking any bend out of the knee, but without locking the knee.
6. With the full expression of this *asana,* the body and the planted leg form a tee-shape. The fingers and toes of the lifted leg are stretched in opposite directions to maximize the elongation of the body.
7. To exit the posture, simply drop the lifted leg and return back to Warrior I.

The Half Moon Pose or *Ardha Chandrasana* can be entered from Warrior III, by rotating the torso to the side of the planted leg and extending the arms out in a tee at shoulder height, one arm extended upward and the other down to the mat. For either the warrior III or half moon, using a block to support a hand facilitates maintaining the body parallel to the floor and adds support and stability.

Natarajasana

The Lord of the Dance or Dancer's Pose

> *We are travelers on a cosmic journey, stardust, swirling and dancing in the eddies and whirlpools of infinity. Life is eternal. We have stopped for a moment to encounter each other, to meet, to love, to share. This is a precious moment. It is a little parenthesis in eternity.*
>
> *Paulo Coelho*

Nataraja is one of the names given to the Hindu deity *Shiva,* referring to him as the cosmic dancer. The Sanskrit word *nata* means "dancer" and *raja,* "king". The dancer's pose is portrayed in many of the statues of *Shiva* found in *Nataraja* temples.

For this example, the right leg will serve as the foundation for balance.

1. Find your *drishti* and couple it to the awareness of the breath.
2. Shift your weight onto the right foot.
3. Straighten the right leg without locking the knee.
4. The pose now requires grabbing the left foot or ankle behind the buttocks with the left hand, which is a challenge of flexibility.
5. Now, begin to kick the left foot back into the left hand as you arch the back, trying to keep the torso as upright as possible.
6. Finally, the right arm and hand are raised into a graceful curve.
7. To exit the posture, simply release the left foot and slowly

bring it back to the mat as the right arm is lowered and the spinal extension resolves.

Natarajasana ~ The Lord of the Dance or the Dancer's Pose

We strive to tap into our grace as we become the dancer, creating beautiful arcs in the back and the arm lifted up toward the sky. Accessing your grace, however, can be accomplished in all of the *asanas.* In yoga, as well as life, grace is an outward manifestation of one's inner beauty.

15
THE SEATED POSTURES

A seated posture should be steady and comfortable.

Patanjali

As was discussed previously in the chapter on yogic philosophy, Pantanjali described the eight limbs of yoga in his seminal work, *The Yoga Sutras.* One must master each limb before stepping on to the next rung of the ladder. Living a moral and ethical life according to the precepts of the *yamas* and *nyamas* must be realized before attempting to master *asana* and *pranayama.* Pantanjali defines *asana* as a posture that is comfortable and steady. What if a posture is unsteady and uncomfortable. Any hope for clarity is lost if the mind becomes clouded with thoughts of discomfort. Balance of mind and body is disturbed by unsteadiness.

From a practical perspective, most of the seated yoga postures can become more comfortable and steady by sitting on the edge of a yoga bolster or a rolled blanket. As noted in the following discussion, elevating the hips, dropping the knees and elongating the torso and spine with the use of a prop facilitates breathing. For many, sitting directly on the mat results in a rounding of the back and stress on the lower lumbosacral spine. Sitting on a bolster or rolled blanket straightens out the back and removes stress from the spine. The stress on the spine can be exacerbated in the seated *asanas* requiring folding forward. When sitting on a bolster or rolled blanket, because the hips are elevated, hinging forward can occur at the hip creases rather than the lower back, thereby lessening lumbosacral strain. It becomes quite difficult to fold forward at the hip creases when sitting directly on the mat.

If you elect to use a prop, may it be a bolster, blanket, strap or block, always remember that props are not crutches. Rather, they are wonderful tools to enhance one's practice. As was mentioned in the chapter regarding overcoming obstacles, societal pressures result in competitiveness, especially in oneself. Near the beginning of my foray into yoga, when a teacher suggested the option to use a prop, my self-competitiveness ignored that option, thereby negating its value in increasing both my comfort and safety. This attitude worsened when I saw no one else in the class using the suggested prop. I don't wish to presume that others in the class possessed a similar attitude as mine. They may have felt comfortable and steady without it. I have a suspicion, however, that not everyone necessarily did. Learning the *asanas* is important. But even more important is to learn to practice self-kindness on and off the mat. In your seated postures, make sure you are sitting with a good friend: yourself!

*Sukhasana**
The Easy or Pleasant Pose

*Padmasana**
The Lotus Pose

*Virasana**
The Hero Pose

It is easy to sit up and take notice. What is difficult is getting up and taking action.

Honoré de Balzac

I have chosen to group these three postures under one heading as they all represent postures in which *pranayama* is often performed. For some, all three present different physical challenges with regard to inflexibility and discomfort, but can be modified to meet each one's individual needs.

In Sanskrit, "*sukh*" literally means "pleasant". In childhood, we all sat cross-legged or, what was once called, "Indian style". The "easy pose" is a bit of a misnomer for many practitioners who possess relatively inflexible inner thigh or hip adductor muscles. In *sukhasana,* inflexibility of those muscles prevents the knees from dropping below the level of the hips. The elevated position of the knees is accompanied by a rounding of the back. As an instructor guides a class through *pranayama,* most students will assume *sukhasana.* Maximal lung capacity and the ability to breathe to complete fullness required in these yogic breathing techniques is facilitated by elongating the spine and straightening the torso to increase the space in the abdomen for the downward movement of the diaphragm. Rounding the back "scrunches up" the abdomen and limits inferior movement of the diaphragm and the ability to breathe deeply. Further, when we are in sympathetic overload and the fight or flight response, we tend to breathe solely with the chest. The act of belly breathing induces physiologic responses in the body that promote relaxation and a shift to parasympathetic tone, optimized by a greater degree of inferior diaphragmatic movement. Autonomic responses in the body occur under the so-called "radar". Conscious awareness of tension and discomfort in any part of the musculoskeletal system can prevent introversion and centering through *pranayama*. In *sukhasana,* discomfort in the lower back or hip adductor muscles can flood the mind with undesirable, negative thoughts.

One solution to optimize breathing capacity and alleviate lower back and hip adductor muscular discomfort while in *sukhasana* is the use of a bolster or a block. By sitting on a block or the edge of a bolster, the knees are able to drop downward toward the mat and below, or at least closer to, the level of the hips. As the knees drop, the spine and torso straighten and elongate in the opposite direction, in turn, maximizing the inferior translation of the diaphragm. I prefer a bolster, which is softer and more stable than a smaller block.

Padmasana ~ The Lotus

Assuming *padmasana* or the lotus pose necessitates a degree of hyperflexibility, as the expression of the posture requires the feet to rest on top of the thighs. The lotus blossom is an important religious symbol in Hinduism and other eastern religions that is associated with various deities. The Buddha is often depicted in Far Eastern sculpture and painting sitting in the lotus pose. Although someone that is capable of sitting in lotus position more likely has the flexibility to maintain a straight back, he or she may choose to sit on the edge of a cushion or bolster to lower the knees downward to touch the ground, creating a greater sense of comfort and steadiness. *Pranayama* is more effective by establishing three points of grounding to create a "tripod" effect. For the lotus, the three parts of the tripod are the sitz bones on the bolster and both knees on the mat. This condition creates comfort and steadiness for the physical body that is a prerequisite for the practice of *pranayama,* as professed by Pantanjali. In chair yoga, the tripod is formed by both feet firmly on the ground and the sitz bones on the seat of the chair. The spine is free to elongate with the support of the back of the chair, once again creating a comfortable and steady position. For most practitioners sitting in *sukhasana,* even with the help of a bolster, it is difficult to lower the knees to touch the mat, and the stable tripod configuration cannot be realized.

Virasana or the hero's pose is assumed in an upright sitting position, typically with the sitz bones between or on the heels. The tripod is formed once again by the sitz bones and both knees contacting the mat. "*Vira*" in Sanskrit translates to "hero". The origin of *Virasana* comes from the seated position of Hanuman at the feet of Lord Rama, one of the incarnations of the god Vishnu seen in Hindu art. Hanuman, a central character in the ancient Hindu epic, *Ranayama,* and often depicted in a simian form, performs numerous heroic feats as a servant of Lord Rama.

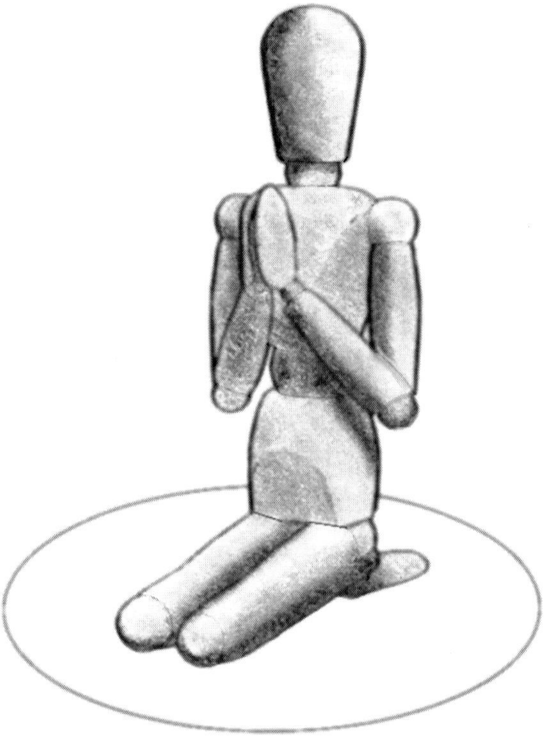

Virasana ~ The Hero's Pose

For novices, as well as for many advanced practitioners, sitting between or on one's heels is uncomfortable. An option is a supported Hero's Pose, whereby one sits on two stacked foam yoga blocks at their lowest setting placed between the thighs. Alternatively, one could straddle a yoga bolster to come into the same position. Again, the end result is a tripod formed by both knees on the mat and the sitz bones sitting on the blocks. I would highly recommend the supported Hero's

Pose for the practice of *pranayama,* especially for beginners. It satisfies the requirements of comfort and steadiness. More so than the other seated poses for *pranayama,* it allows for the greatest lengthening of the spine and the most space in the abdomen for downward translation of the diaphragm during inhalation.

Always keep in mind that you are in the driver's seat (speaking of seated poses) when it comes to finding a position that provides comfort and stability, eliminating any distraction stemming from tension in the physical body. When I began my journey towards a regular yoga practice, *sukhasana* was so uncomfortable and, at times painful, yet I felt compelled to sit in that *asana* because everyone else in the class was doing the same. Due to my competitive mindset and observation of others, I also shied away from the use of props, such as a bolster. My attention was focused on the wrong things; others in my class, discomfort in my inner thighs and tension in my lower back. Learning about the supported Hero's Pose changed my practice for the better, allowing me to focus on more positive things.

Modifications and options suggested by a teacher for any of the *asanas* are not challenges. Options are merely different ways of positioning the body, which may enhance one's experience of an *asana* through greater balance and strength. One variation of a pose that is best suited for one person may not be the best for another. It is up to each one of us to find what works best. A good teacher can facilitate that search.

*Dandasana**
The Staff Pose

Paschimottanasana
Seated Forward Fold

Janu Shirshasana
Head to Knee Forward Bend

Matsyendrasana
Lord of the Fishes Pose or Seated Spinal Twist

Whatever sound the mind is drawn to, settle on it, adhere to it, and become absorbed in it.

The Hatha Yoga Pradipika

Sitting on the edge of a cushion or bolster is especially beneficial to relieve lower back strain for *dandasana, paschimottanasana, janu shirshasana* and *Matsyendrasana. Dandasana,* the staff pose, is the starting point for the other three *asanas* in this section. It is assumed by sitting with an upright flat back with legs fully extended, inner edges of the feet touching, toes pointing up and both palms face down on either side of the hips. The goal is to create a ninety degree angle between the torso and legs. Actively pressing down onto both palms pulls the humeral heads down from the shoulder joints and increases elongation of the spine and straightening of the torso. Sitting with your back against the wall can give you an appreciation for the proper relationship between your legs and torso.

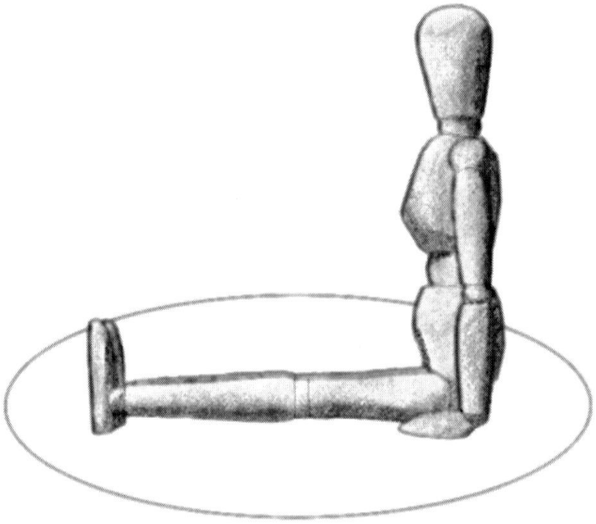

Dandasana ~ The Staff Pose

Starting from *dandasana,* you can enter into *paschimottanasana,* the seated forward fold, by hinging forward at the hip creases with a flat back as you extend your arms out in front of you. The posture creates a stretch in the posterior leg muscles, including the hamstrings in the thigh and the gastrocnemius and soleus muscles in the posterior calf.

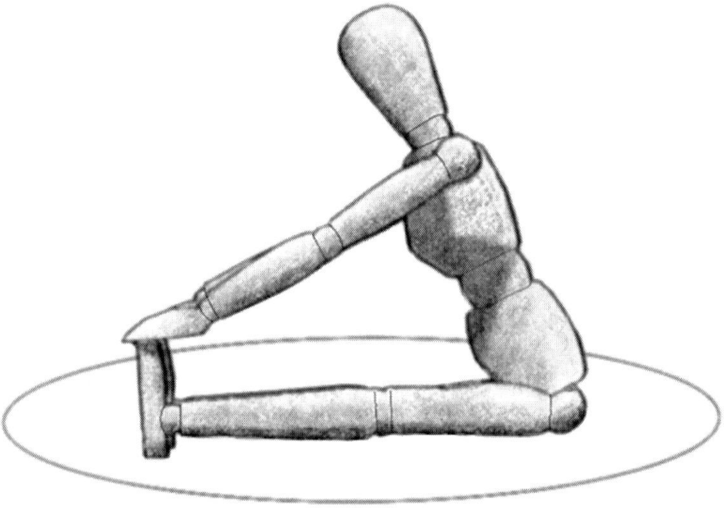

Paschimottanasana ~ The Seated Forward Fold

For a more intense stretch, you can begin to round the back, reaching the chest and crown of the head forward towards the toes as you bend. Dorsiflexing the ankles to point the toes up toward the ceiling while pushing the heels away from the body adds to the intensity of the stretch. Try not to lock the knees, which puts more stress on the tendons of the hamstring muscles behind the knee. In a yoga class, you may see someone who is quite flexible grab their toes as they hinge forward, and even draw their forehead towards their knees as they round the back. Aside from the fact that one should not be comparing oneself to others, for many less flexible people with tight hamstrings, the amount that they can hinge forward may not be very far, possibly just an inch or two. All that matters is to achieve the goal of the long posterior leg muscle stretch. Remember to practice at your edge. The goal is to experience a stretch. Comparison to fellow classmates does not serve one well. Once again, sitting on a cushion or bolster can facilitate folding forward.

Janu translates to "knee" and *shirsha* is the Sanskrit word for "head". As one might surmise, for this *asana,* the head is drawn toward the knee. *Janu shirshasana* is similar to *paschimottanasana,* but performed with one knee bent with the sole of the foot of that leg pressing against the inner thigh of the other extended leg. The ankle of the extended leg is dorsiflexed with toes pointing to the ceiling. Some perform this posture with the extended leg directly in line with the hip, while others move the extended leg out to an approximate forty-five degree angle.

Similar to *Paschimottanasana,* initially hinging forward occurs at the hip crease with a flat back, then with the option to round the back, drawing the head closer to the knee and intensifying the stretch. The goal in assuming this posture is also to create posterior leg muscle stretch, so once again the degree to which you hinge forward may not be much at all for the desired effect.

Props are wonderful to use in yoga. Looping a strap under both soles of the feet for *paschimottanasana* or under the foot of the extended leg for *janu shirshasana* offers support and increases one's ability to hinge forward, while at the same time lessens the stress on the lower back. As the strap is used for support, one should only gently tug on the strap rather than forcibly using your full arm strength to pull your upper body forward, which can be stressful on the back.

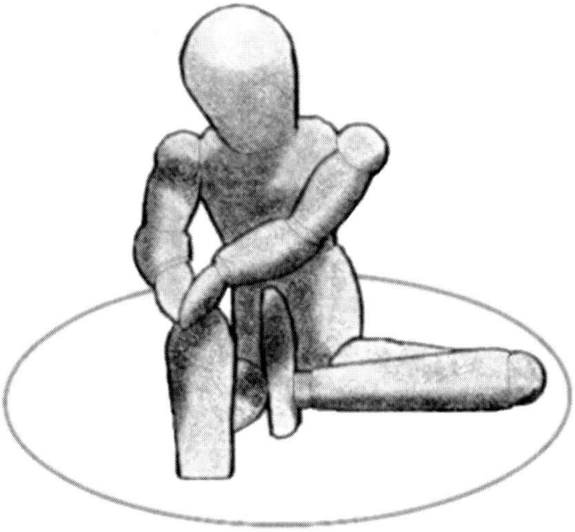

Janu Shirshasana ~ Head to Knee Forward Bend

Matsyendrasana, the Lord of the Fishes pose or the seated spinal twist, also begins in *dandasana.* As mentioned previously, Matysendranath was a sage and author who lived in the 10th century, CE, credited with writing many texts. He is an important figure in Hinduism. His name literally translates to "Lord of the Fishes". According to Hindu mythology, Matsyendranath was swallowed by a fish after his parents, fearful of the omen of an ill-fated star, tossed their baby into the ocean. One day, the fish swam to the seabed where Matysendranath overheard the god Shiva revealing the secrets of Hatha yoga to Parvati, the Hindu goddess of fertility, beauty and love, among other things. In possession of those secrets, Matysendranath practiced yoga in the fish for many years, ultimately emerging as a spiritually aware yogi, and ultimately the Lord of the Fishes. His words were eventually written down in the *Hatha Yoga Pradipika*.

To perform *Matysendrasana,* using the right side as an example:

1. Start in *dandasana*. Once again, consider the use of a bolster.
2. Bend the right knee and slide the right foot next to the thigh of the extended left leg. The pose can be done either with the foot on the inner or outer side of the left thigh.
3. Bend the left ankle to point the toes towards the sky so that the muscles of the extended leg engage. Many let the leg be passive, which is a lost opportunity to strengthen and stretch muscles.
4. Wrap the left elbow around the bent right knee. If this is difficult to accomplish due to shoulder or elbow sensitivities or simply your arm is short, the right knee can be alternatively held with the left hand.
5. Windmill the right arm overhead and plant the right hand on the mat behind the back. This action will cause the spine and torso to twist toward the right.
6. Elongation and straightening of the spine are paramount and can be achieved by moving the right hand closer to the back so that the right arm assumes a more vertical position and by hugging the right thigh into the belly with the wrapped left elbow or hand. Traditionally, the *asana* is done with a bent elbow resting on the outside of the knee, but I find a straight spine is better achieved with the ability to pull

the thigh into the belly, which cannot be done in the traditional posture.

7. Shoulders should remain soft and neck elongated. The degree of twist of the spine will vary per individual. Begin by twisting the lumbar spine, followed by the thoracic spine. If you don't suffer from neck issues or limitations, the neck can be twisted to bring your gaze over the right shoulder. Imagine that your spine is like a corkscrew winding about a central axle.
8. To exit the pose, unwind the spine from cervical to lumbar as you bring both arms forward and extend both legs back into *dandasana*. The pose can then be repeated on the other side.

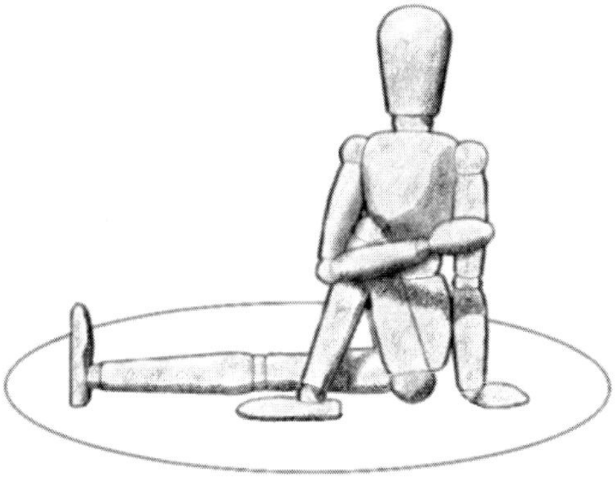

Matsyendrasana ~ The Lord of the Fishes Pose or The Seated Spinal Twist

One variation of this posture is *ardha* (Sanskrit for half) *Matsyendrasana.* It consists of bringing the right foot to the outside of the left thigh. Rather than remaining straight and extended, the left leg bends at the knee, the left heel coming near the right buttock. The left elbow can rest on the outside of the right knee, fingers of the left hand spread wide and pointing towards the sky. The pose can then be done on the other side.

*Navasana**

The Boat Pose or Upward Boat

> *You must decide where you want to go. Do not let the winds of life determine your life's outcome. Set your sail, and use the winds of life to get to where you want to go.*
>
> *John Whitton*

"*Nava*" is the Sanskrit root for "boat". I will take a moment to digress off topic, as this is a good opportunity to discuss languages. Interestingly, in Latin, the root for "boat" is "nav". We find this root in English words, such as navy and navigate. Although no direct evidence exists, many linguists believe in the existence of an ancient, common Proto-Indo-European (PIE) language spoken several thousands of years ago, possibly earlier than 4000 BCE, which evolved into more modern languages through diasporas, migrations and interactions of different populations. Other examples of root similarities are the Sanskrit root for foot "pado" as in the *asana, prasarita padottanasana,* the Greek root "pod" and the Latin root "ped", as in pedal and pedestrian, and the Sanskrit root for knee "janu", as in the *asana, janu shirshasana,* and the Latin root "genu" as in genuflect. Since the language was only oral and never written down, no direct evidence exists for PIE, but the theory would certainly explain the similarity of many of the roots shared between Sanskrit, Greek and the Romance languages.

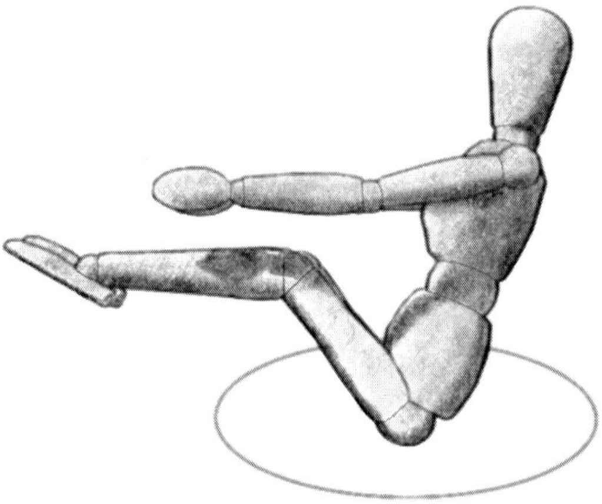

Navasana ~ The Boat Pose

1. The starting position for *navasana* is sitting with knees bent, soles of feet flat on the mat and hands holding the backs of the thighs just above the knees. In this position, you are sitting on a triangle formed by the sitz bones and the sacrum/coccyx. The challenge of this posture is to remain sitting on that triangle when lifting the feet off of the mat rather than rolling backwards onto the sacrum. This is

accomplished twofold, by drawing the thighs into the chest and pulling the chest forward.

2. Start by actively pulling one thigh towards the chest as you lift the foot off of the mat, followed by the other side. Use your arm strength to pull the thighs toward the belly to prevent rolling back on to the sacrum. Concentrate on maintaining contact of both sitz bones on the mat.
3. If it is accessible, you can release the thighs and draw the arms out at shoulder height, pulling the fingertips toward the feet and the chest towards the thighs. These actions also prevent one from rolling back onto the sacrum. One can experiment with arm positioning, possibly drawing arms behind the shoulders, which helps bring the chest towards the thighs, as well as leg positioning, possibly keeping knees bent or fully extended.
4. To exit the pose, simply regrasp the backs of the thighs and lower the feet back to the mat.

Baddha Konasana

Bound Angle Pose

My humanity is bound up in yours, for we can only be human together.

Desmond Tutu

Baddha konasana directly translates to its English name. As with all of the seated postures, sitting on a blanket or edge of a cushion raises the hips, elongates the spine, creates space in the abdomen for downward diaphragmatic movement and is more gentle on the lower back.

Baddha Konasana ~ Bound Angle Pose

1. To enter into the posture, begin in *sukhasana* or easy pose.
2. Bring the soles of the feet together to touch as the knees fall downward to either side. A decreased range of motion from inflexible hip adductor muscles results in the knees positioned relatively high in the air.
3. Grab your big toes with both hands, or alternatively the feet or ankles, as you draw the heels towards the pelvis. Ideally, the back remains straight and the spine elongated, but rounding of the back may be unavoidable if the hip adductors are tight. Sitting on the edge of a bolster or folded blanket can partially drop the knees and remedy a rounded back.

16
THE PRONE POSTURES

Until one has loved an animal, a part of one's soul remains unawakened.

Anatole France

The love for all living creatures is the most noble attribute of man.

Charles Darwin

I use the word "prone" in this chapter loosely, referring to the belly either resting on the mat or above the mat, facing downwards. This definition is one of convenience and practicality for the discussion of these *asanas.* I begin this chapter with the above quotes since the prone *asanas* in the following discussion are mostly named for animals. As the owner of a wonderful, sweet yellow lab named Bella, I often think that the unconditional love I receive from such a peaceful soul is a more powerful stress reducer than any yoga I might practice. She takes me away from my thoughts to a place of love and gratitude.

Bhujangasana*

The Cobra Pose

Salamba Bhujangasana

The Sphinx Pose

Urdhva Mukha Svanasana

The Upward Facing Dog

The Sanskrit for all three of these postures translates directly to their English names. All three of these poses begin prone, resting the head either on the chin or forehead.

1. *Bhujangasana* begins in a prone position with the palms face down on either sides of the shoulders or slightly below and with the thumbs at the level of the upper ribs. The tops of the feet rest on the mat.
2. Hug the sides of the ribs tightly with the elbows and forearms.
3. Create length in the legs by reaching the toes away from the body.

4. Spread the fingers wide in order to feel the palms contacting the mat as if the hands are like suction cups.
5. While rooting down through the pubic bone and tops of the feet and legs, press into the palms to raise the chest off of the mat as you come into a backbend, pulling the shoulders back, lifting and opening up the chest and bringing the gaze forward. Ideally, each elbow joint forms a ninety degree angle.
6. A common tendency is to allow the elbows to flare outward as one lifts the chest. As the chest rises, be sure to continue to hug the sides of the ribs.
7. To exit the pose, lower the chest back down to the mat.

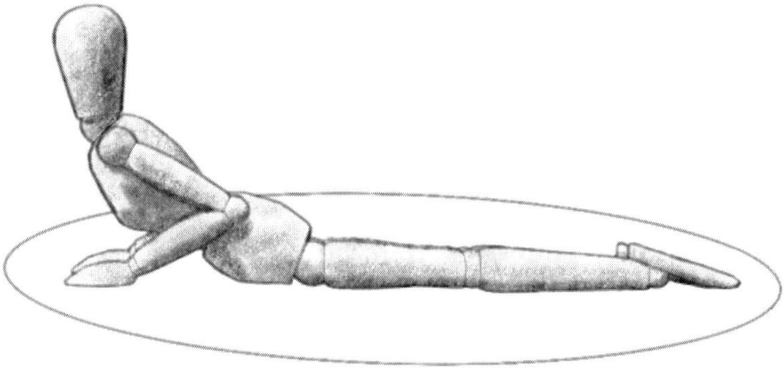

Bhujangasana ~ The Cobra Pose

In yoga classes, instructors commonly lead students through a baby cobra pose, either by itself or preceding the full expression of the cobra. In the baby cobra pose, the chest is lifted without the use of hand or arm strength, forming a lesser back bend. Unlike the full expression of the cobra, in the baby cobra the gaze remains down toward the front edge of the mat, the neck straight and in line with the rest of the spine. This position places less stress on the neck. In the baby cobra, a teacher might ask you to let your hands hover above the mat to confirm that you are indeed not using any arm strength.

Relative to the cobra, the sphinx pose, *salamba bhujangasana*, represents a more gentle backbend.

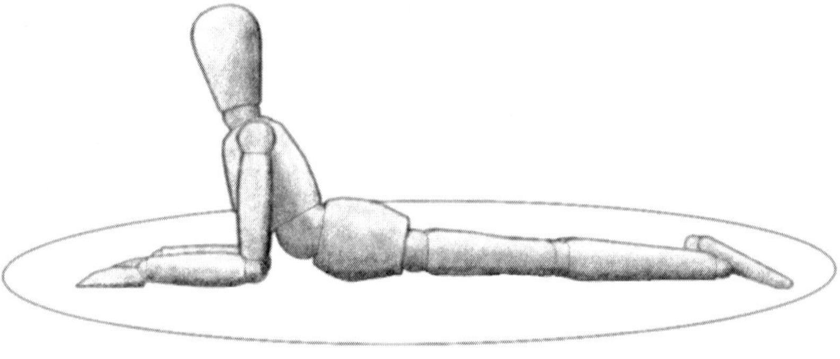

Salamba Bhujangasana ~ The Sphinx Pose

1. Position the elbows on the mat directly under the shoulders, forearms extending out parallel on the mat, fingers spread wide.

2. While rooting into the pubic bone and tops of the feet and legs, press firmly down from the elbows to palms to lift the chest, coming into a gentle backbend, gaze forward, and of course, emulating the position of the great sphinx of ancient Egypt.
3. To exit from the posture, lower the chest to the mat.

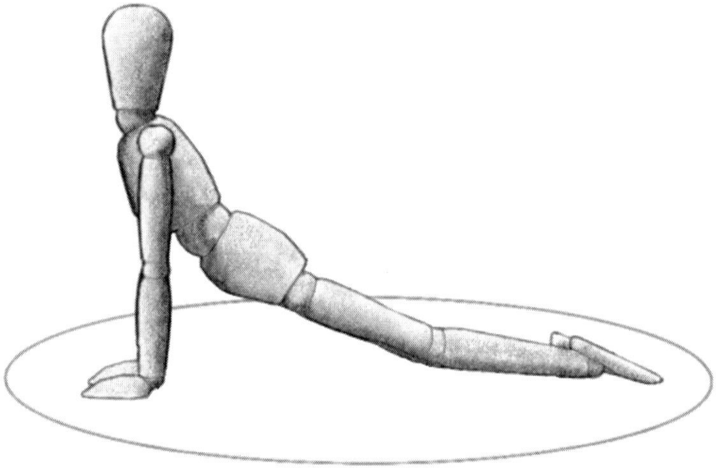

Urdhva Mukha Svanasana ~ The Upward Facing Dog

The initial position for the upward facing dog, *urdhva mukha svanasana,* is the same as the cobra. The two main differences are the hips are lifted off the mat and the elbow joints completely extend as both arms straighten.

1. Start in a prone position with hands under the shoulders, palms face down.
2. Rooting into the tops of the feet, press through both hands to fully extend both arms, thereby lifting the hips and the chest to create a backbend with gaze forward, hands directly under the shoulders.
3. The backbend is intensified by actively pushing into both hands, which will draw the shoulders down, gently pushing the sockets of the shoulder joints superiorly relative to the humeral heads, while allowing the belly to drop towards the mat.
4. The pose can be done with or without the knees lifted off of the mat. The former requires greater rooting into the tops of the feet and greater leg and core strength.
5. To exit the pose, lower the chest, hips and legs back down to the mat.

The upward dog and cobra are often performed as part of a *vinyasa* flow, as will be discussed in the next chapter, or as individual *asanas.*

Salabhasana

The Grasshopper or Locust Pose

Once again, the Sanskrit name corresponds directly to the English name of the pose. Names of the *asanas* can differ from one school of yoga to another. I certainly prefer "grasshopper" over "locust" as it evokes a more peaceful image of an insect.

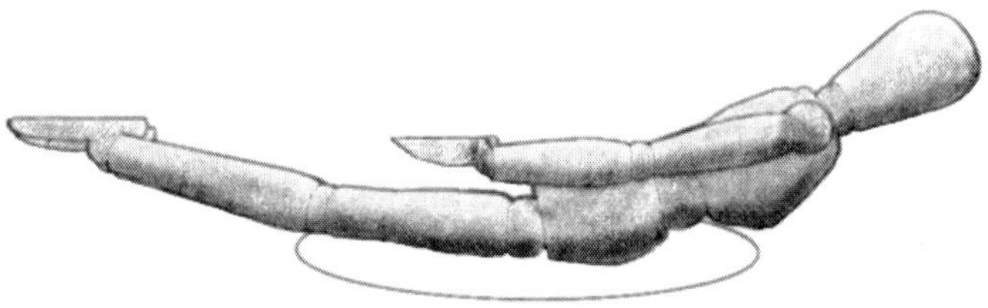

Salabhasana ~ *The Grasshopper or Locust Pose*

1. Lying prone, the head rests on the chin or forehead, legs are extended with tops of feet on the mat, arms are at the sides and palms are face down at the level of the hips.
2. It is beneficial to establish elongation of the body and spine before lifting any body parts. This is accomplished by pulling the toes and fingers towards the bottom of the mat and elongating the neck in the opposite direction while taking a deep breath in.
3. On the next deep inhalation, while rooting down into the pubic bone, the chest is lifted off of the mat with the neck in a neutral position; the cervical spine in line with the thoracic spine. Many have a tendency to hyperextend the neck, bringing the gaze forward. This, however, creates stress on the neck and shoulder muscles. Gaze should be down, focused on the edge of the mat or a point just off of the mat.
4. Continuing to push the pubic bone into the mat, the arms are then lifted and finally the legs. Ideally, the arch created in

the back is such that the majority of the rib cage and the thighs come off of the mat. But even more optimal is to find your edge and personalize the posture to make it your own.

5. To exit out of the posture, the legs, arms and chest are all dropped down to the mat. Often a teacher will instruct you to rest the face on one cheek, in a sense coming into a position of release and recovery from this vigorous posture.

Like most of the *asanas,* variations exist for *salabhasana.* Clasping hands behind the back, pulling the shoulder blades together, can open up the shoulder joints. By grabbing both feet, one can enter into the bow pose.

Often, when we assume and sustain strenuous postures in yoga we lose awareness of the breath. Maintaining and drawing your focus to deep breathing will allow you to sustain the posture for longer periods of time, drawing thoughts away from any straining in the body. Alternatively, one can focus on a *drishti,* possibly a point on or just off the edge of the mat. We typically associate *drishtis* with balance postures, but they are wonderful tools to clear the mind of other thoughts regardless of the posture. Another way to enjoy *salabhasana* is to transition from a static position to a dynamic one, letting the arms and legs pulsate every so slightly up and down with the breath, injecting living energy into your grasshopper.

I typically transition from *salabhasana* into child's pose to realize the benefits of pose and counterpose. The grasshopper is a posture of back extension accomplished through the contraction of posterior back muscles with the relaxation and stretching of anterior muscles of the core. Child's pose reverses those relationships as the back flexes through the contraction of anterior muscles with the stretching of muscles across the back. The importance of pose and counterpose lies in the creation of balance between muscular contraction and relaxation.

Bharmanasana

The Table Pose

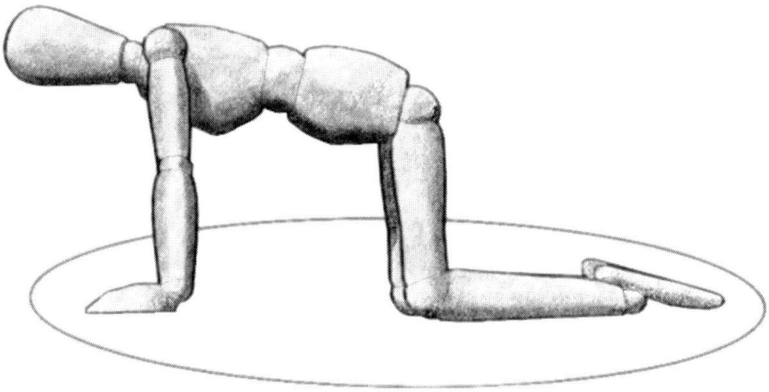

Bharmanasana ~ The Table Pose

The table pose is a common starting pose for many of the other *asanas,* including the cow, cat and sunbird. The table pose is assumed on hands and knees. The hands are directly under the shoulders and knees under the hips. The four legs of the table are the arms and thighs and, just like the legs of a table, should be vertical. Peer down to assure that your

wrists and knees are properly positioned so that your table legs are not tilted and unstable. The fingers should be spread nice and wide. This is a good rule to follow for all of the *asanas* where the hands are on the mat. Spreading the fingers wide drives the palms downward such that the hands become like suction cups on the mat, both increasing arm strength and promoting balance. If one has wrist sensitivity or issues such as carpal tunnel syndrome, resting on the knuckles is more gentle on the wrist joints. While in the table, the back is flat and the neck is in a neutral position, in line with the rest of the spine.

Bitilasana

The Cow Pose

Marjaryasana

The Cat Pose

The cat and cow poses are complementary poses that are typically done together, alternating from one to the other. Similar to the grasshopper and child's pose, the integration of the cat and the cow illustrate pose and counterpose, one of the important guiding principles of yoga. Back extension is accomplished in the cow and flexion in the cat; once again the process of activation and rest is directed at specific muscle groups.

One enters into the cow pose from the table by lifting the tailbone, chest and gaze, all to create extension in the back. One might imagine the shape of the back of an old cow. Then, dropping the head, directing gaze to the knees, pressing down through both hands to round the back and dropping the tail bone brings one into the cat pose. One might imagine a frightened or angry cat with its back in the air. The cat and cow are a wonderful way to warm up the spine in flexion and extension, respectively.

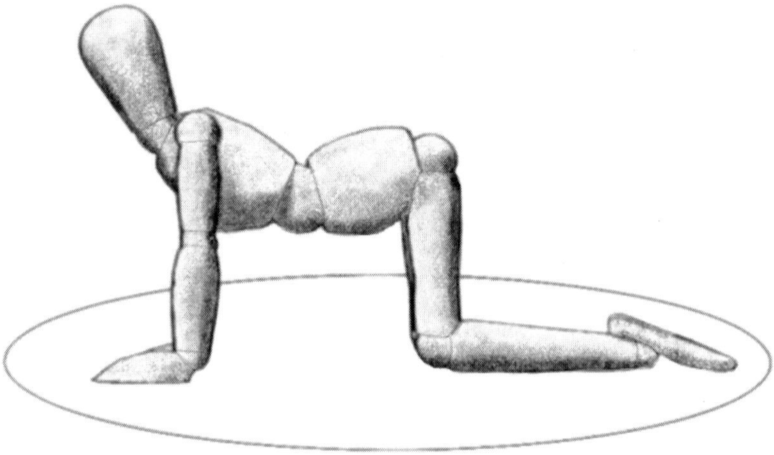

Bitilasana ~ The Cow Pose

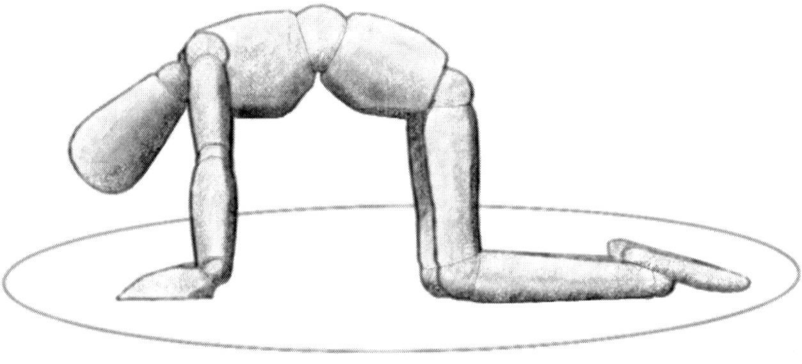

Marjaryasana ~ The Cat Pose

Inwardness can be better achieved by connecting the breath to the movements. In table position, deepen and lengthen the breath. Let the breath begin with the expansion of the belly and like a wave spread up to the collar bones. Then, exhale out all the air that you can. On the next inhalation, as the belly expands the tailbone is lifted to the sky. As the breath spreads up into the chest, the sternum is lifted forward, and then the gaze comes up last. Imagine that you are creating two connected waves; the breath that spreads from belly to collar bones and the physical movement that spreads from tailbone to the crown of head. Upon exhalation, the two waves then spread back from the crown of head to tailbone, as the head first drops, then the back rounds, and finally the tailbone drops. Closing the eyes can heighten awareness of the connection of breath to movement. To take it one step further, imagine that it is the breath that is directing the movement, not the mind. The inhalation opens the body in the cow and the exhalation closes the body in the cat. Single-pointed focus is not on the physical movements or the breath alone, but on the connection of the breath to the movement.

Chakravakasana
The Sunbird

One also enters into the sunbird pose from the table. From the table, one arm is extended out at shoulder height with a neutral neck, such that the upper arm is near the ear. At the same time, the leg on the opposite side is extended out at hip height, typically with the toes pointing toward the mat. The hips should remain parallel and square to the ground. By pushing the heel and pulling the fingers in opposite directions, elongation of the spine and body is achieved. This is a wonderful stretch that creates a long line of energy from feet to hands. Experiment with pointing the toes away from the body to notice if that changes the stretch and energy you experience. Teachers may also guide you through modifications of the sunbird with various limb positions, joint flexions, back arching and spine twisting.

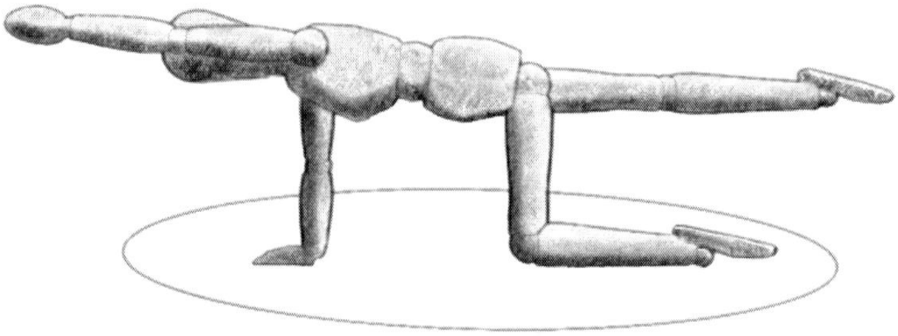

Chakravakasana ~ The Sunbird

Phalakasana

High Plank

The high plank can be entered into several different ways. One can come into this posture from the table position, planting hands and stepping back from a standing forward fold, or shifting forward from the downward-facing dog.

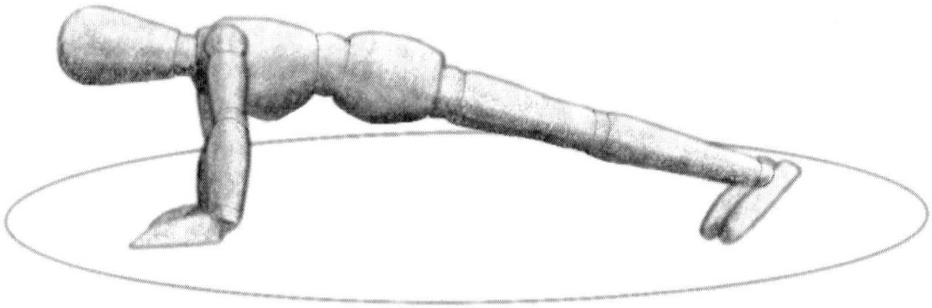

Phalakasana ~ High Plank

1. From the table, step one foot back and then the other, planting the balls of the feet onto the mat, and extending both legs with the knees lifted off of the mat.
2. By entering into a high plank from the table, the hands and wrists are already in proper position, directly below the shoulders. The high plank requires a lot of arm strength, and as mentioned, facilitated by spreading the fingers wide to feel the inner palms touch the mat.
3. While in this posture, actively pushing into both hands will draw the shoulders down, gently pushing the sockets of the shoulder joints superiorly relative to the humeral heads.
4. At the same time, the legs are engaged by actively pushing the balls of the feet towards the back of the mat.
5. The neck is kept in line with the rest of the thoracic spine with the gaze down towards the mat.
6. The body in high plank is linear, however, lifting the hips just a bit to create a small angle between the back and legs

can be more gentle on a sensitive back. Letting the hips sag will create stress on the lower lumbosacral spine.

7. Exit the pose by dropping the knees and returning to table position or push into both hands to lift the hips back and upward into downward-facing dog.

From a high plank, one can transition into a side plank. This is a strenuous pose for many. Starting in high plank, bring one hand, say the right, to center as you rotate the body ninety degrees to the left. The left arm and hand are then raised to the sky. The left foot can rest on or in front of the right foot. A less vigorous option is a supported side plank. From high plank, drop the right knee under the right hip. The left leg remains extended. The right lower leg rotates ninety degrees as the sole of the left foot is placed on the mat. The right hand is again centrally placed on the mat as the left arm and hand extend either straight up or over the ear. One has the option to lift the left leg up from the mat. Always remember that in yoga, options are not challenges. They are merely different ways of experiencing yoga.

*Chaturanga Dandasana**
Four Limb Staff Pose or Low Pushup

Chaturanga dandasana is almost always performed following a high plank. More often in yoga classes it is referred to as "*chaturanga*" or as a low pushup. The challenge of *chaturanga* is to maintain a single line from the crown of the head to feet as the body lowers toward the mat.

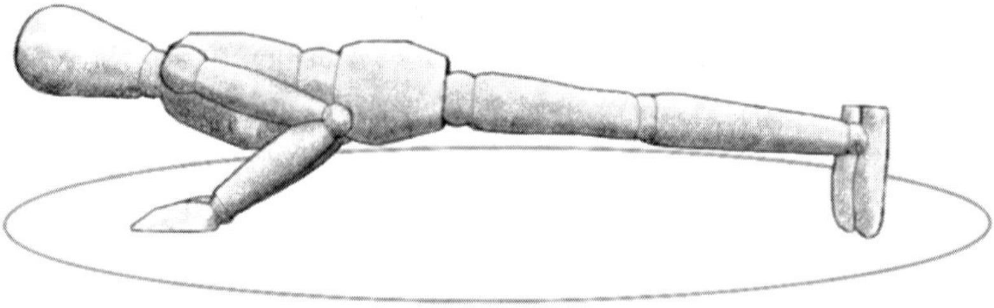

Chaturanga Dandasana ~ Four Limb Staff Pose or Low Pushup

1. Start in high plank.
2. Drop the hips slightly to remove any angle between the back and legs that was created in high plank.
3. As you begin to lower the body, keep the elbows close to the body and begin to come forward onto the tips of the toes.
4. As the body lowers down toward the mat, the elbows bend back towards the hips. At the same time, lead with your sternum in the opposite direction, towards the front of the mat.
5. The body is lowered all the way to the mat resting the head on the chin or forehead. Sometimes a teacher will suggest that you allow your body to hover just above the mat as a core strengthening exercise before fully lowering it.

*Adho Mukha Svanasana**

Downward Dog or Downward Facing Dog

Several ways to enter into downward-facing dog include from table position, upward-facing dog, high plank or standing forward fold.

1. From table position, widen the fingers and curl the toes, then using your arm strength push the shoulders back and hips back and up toward the sky.
2. As the shoulders move back, the arms lengthen.
3. The distance between the shoulder blades should be widened by rolling the shoulder blades downward toward the sides of the chest, which can be facilitated by moving the hands further apart on the mat and externally rotating the arms. Pressing down into all parts of the hands also helps to widen the distance between the shoulder blades.
4. Ideally, the legs are extended without locking the knees and the soles of the feet are placed flat on the mat. This ideal is not available to many practitioners and it is fine to come onto the balls of the feet with bent knees.
5. Regardless of the knee and lower leg position, the desired end result is the creation of an approximate ninety degree angle between a flat back and the upper legs.
6. The head is in a comfortable position that minimizes stress on the neck, gaze back toward the feet.
7. Exit the pose by dropping the knees and returning to table position.

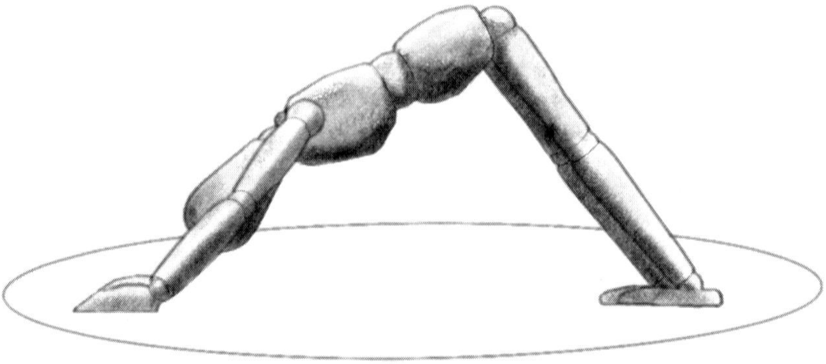

Adho Mukha Svanasana ~ Downward Dog or Downward Facing Dog

Often, the teacher will instruct the class to "walk the dog" or "pedal out the dog" by alternating dropping and lifting the heels of both feet. This is a wonderful way to warm up the muscles along the back of the leg, including the hamstrings and the posterior calf muscles, as well as the Achilles tendon. Many yoga instructors will suggest maintaining downward dog for several breaths, suggesting that this is a position of rest. I have never appreciated that particular opinion. This *asana* is strenuous for me because of my relatively tight hamstrings and my lack of affinity for dropping my head below my heart for an extended period of time. Always remember that the yoga instructor is just a guide. Giving yourself permission to come out of a pose to alleviate discomfort can be quite liberating.

*Kapotasana**

The Pigeon Pose

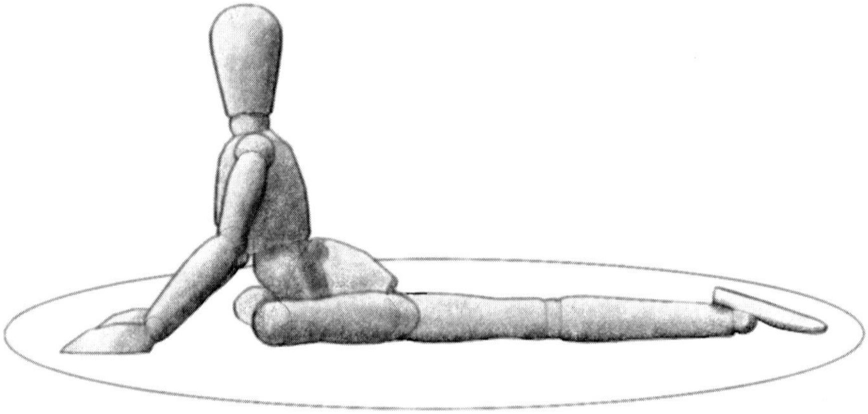

Kapotasana ~ The Pigeon Pose

If you search Google images for *kapotasana,* the results include two vastly different postures. One is an extreme backbend that, on the face of it, seems accessible only to contortionists. The posture illustrated here and described below is a gentle hip opener and back bend available to most practitioners.

The Sanskrit word "*kapota*" means pigeon, but also has significance in Hindu mythology. Kapota is one of the myriad names for Lord Shiva. An ancient text, the *Skanda Purana,* tells the story in which the Lord Shiva shrinks to the size of a pigeon while living solely on air, hence the moniker *Kapota.*

Similar to many of our *asanas, kapotasana* can be entered from many positions, especially from downward-facing dog and the table position. I will describe the latter, which is a simpler way to enter the pose.

1. Start in table position, hands under shoulders and knees under hips.
2. Slide a knee, let's say the right knee, forward to as close to the right wrist as possible.
3. With the right knee bent, swing the right heel under the left hip.
4. Extend the left leg behind you, possibly walking the foot back using curled toes to achieve maximum extension, eventually resting the top of the foot on the mat.
5. Look behind you to assure that the left leg is in line with the left hip.
6. Press your hands into the mat in order to lift the chest up and forward and shoulders up and back resulting in back extension.
7. For many, the hips will not be on the mat, but lifted in the air. If this is uncomfortable, one can consider supporting either hip with a cushion or block.
8. To exit the posture, curl the toes of the left foot, press into the hands to lift the hips and slide the right leg back, returning to table position.
9. Repeat the posture on the other side.

Eka Pada Rajakapotasana
The Sleeping Pigeon Pose

Very often in a class, a teacher will suggest that you can transition from the pigeon pose to a sleeping pigeon. This is simply accomplished from the pigeon pose by lowering the head toward the mat, rounding the back and either allowing the forehead to rest on the mat or on stacked hands or forearms. While in this position, a gentle sway of the hips side to side can feel wonderful as you pass back and forth through the stretch of the hip joint.

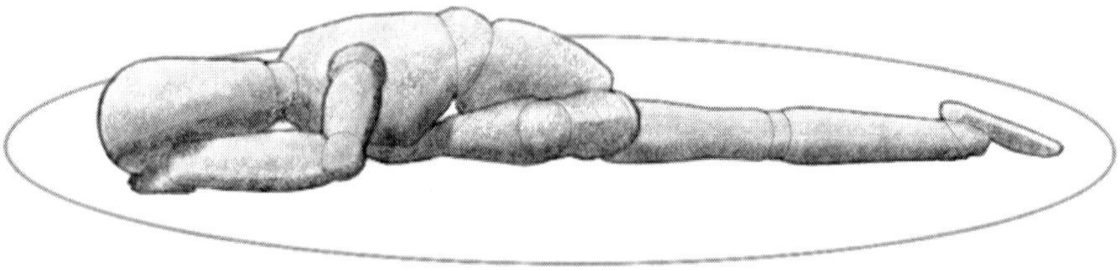

Eka Pada Rajakapotasana ~The Sleeping Pigeon Pose

Balasana or Garbhasana
Child's Pose

I feel fine about including this posture in this chapter, as a child, a young homo sapien, qualifies as an animal. The child's pose is truly a position of rest. It is an opportunity to take a respite from the activity of the practice to re-establish a connection with the breath. It creates a balance between activity and rest and between the energy of the sun and moon. Child's pose harnesses the cool energy of the moon as you become the observer of your experience.

Child's pose can be assumed from the table by using the hands to push the sitz bones back toward the heels as the head is dropped towards the mat. From downward-facing dog, the knees are dropped before pushing back into the posture. There are several variations of this *asana*. One common variation brings the feet to touch, knees wide apart, and elbows, forearms and forehead resting on the mat. One can also position the feet and knees together to touch, drawing the arms back next to the feet as the forehead drops to the mat. Whatever expression you choose, it should be a position to decrease muscle tension as much as possible, especially in the neck. The forehead must be supported to fully relax the muscles of the neck. The head weighs ten to fifteen pounds. Having the equivalent of a bowling ball floating in the air and pulling on the neck can elicit tension, discomfort and even pain. If one is unable to relax the forehead on the mat, relaxing the neck muscles can be facilitated by resting the forehead on a block, stacked hands or stacked forearms. Even if you are able to rest the forehead directly on the mat, experiment with making a pillow with stacked hands or forearms to see if you experience a lessening of any neck strain. In addition, if it is not physically possible to fully bring the sitz bones to rest on the heels, then a blanket can be inserted between the two. Any sensations of physical discomfort will interfere with the enjoyment of a time of stillness, rest and relaxation, one where you can be with yourself and your thoughts. Perhaps, it is the child within us that must be rediscovered or revisited; that time of innocence before our minds were usurped by the stresses of life.

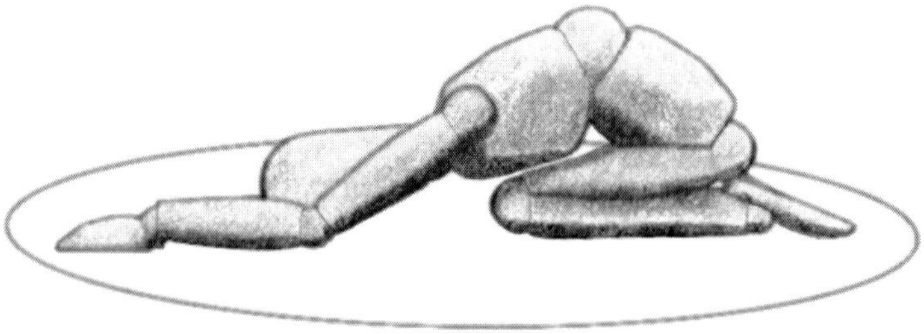

Balasana or Garbhasana ~ Child's Pose

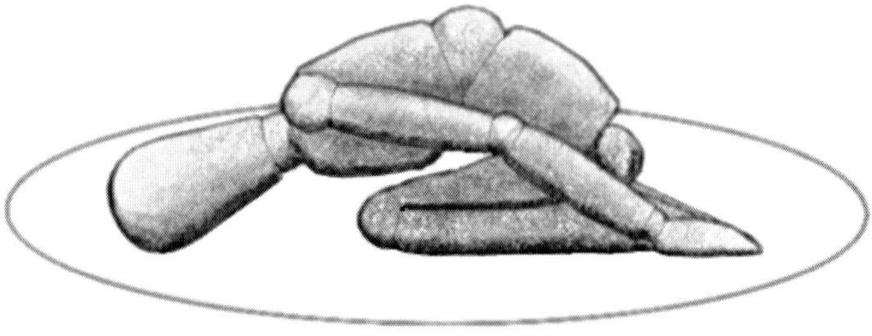

Balasana or Garbhasana ~ Child's Pose Variation

17

SUN SALUTATIONS AND VINYASA FLOW

Keep your face always toward the sunshine ~ and shadows will fall behind you.

Walt Whitman

What I love most about rivers is you can't step in the same river twice. The water's always changing, always flowing.

Pocahontas

The sun salutations and the *vinyasa* flow sequences of *asanas* are frequently encountered in yoga classes, especially in those, as you can imagine, described as "*Vinyasa Flow*" classes. The Sanskrit word, "*vinyasa*" means "to place in a special way". In yoga, *vinyasa* is a sequence of poses that are linked to the breath to create a continuous flow of movement. Although not necessarily always the case, inhalation is more commonly connected to upward, open movements, while exhalation is more often linked to downward, closing movements. This makes intuitive sense since movements that open the body tend to create more space in the chest and abdomen, promoting greater air intake as the diaphragm has more room to move downward. Movements that close the body can occur concurrently with the collapse of the chest and abdomen that occurs with exhalation. As an example, sweeping the arms overhead in *tadasana* creates length in the body and space in the torso and is most suited for inhalation. Swan diving down into a forward fold crunches the abdomen and is not only more suitable for exhalation, but can even facilitate greater air release through a relative forced exhalation. Remember, breath is not only deepened through a full inhalation, but also through complete exhalation.

Before delving into the wonderful experience of the sun salutations, I will briefly touch on the concept of *vinyasa* flow. Many teachers will instruct students to "go through your flow" or "go through your *vinyasa,*" referring to a sequence of four *asanas* that are part of the sun salutation sequence. Those four postures done in succession are the high plank, the low pushup or *chaturanga,* the upward-facing dog and the downward-facing dog. It is important to realize that this is just one variation of a *vinyasa* flow, which can be any sequence of *asanas* that is linked to the breath resulting in a continuous flow of movement. On the other hand, however, communication between teachers and students is key. From a practical standpoint, if everyone in a class accepts the definition of *vinyasa* as referring to those four postures, transitions between poses arguably might be more fluid.

In a vinyasa flow, each movement in the sequence is linked to either inhalation or exhalation. Learning to focus on this connection of the breath to a flow of movement can make a *vinyasa* practice very satisfying and gratifying.

*Surya Namaskar**
The Sun Salutations

The Sanskrit word *surya* in Sanskrit means "sun" and *namaskar,* "salute". Like many ancient religions, Hindus were sun worshippers. *Surya* is the Hindu sun god, often depicted driving a chariot drawn by seven horses, each representing a color of the rainbow and the seven *chakras.* He is considered the creator of the universe and the source of all life who brings light and warmth to the world. The sun salutations are also energizing and heat-producing, activating the *pingala nadi,* the sun energy channel. As such, sun salutations can have more impact if they are followed by the stillness of a cooling *asana,* such as child's pose or a fully relaxed and released standing posture, in order to balance the *ida nadi,* the moon energy channel, with the *pingala nadi.*

There are many variations of the sun salutations that consist of many different types and sequences of *asanas.* I will describe two of the more common sequences that you might encounter in your yoga classes: sun salutations A and B.

Sun breaths are an integral part of the sun salutation. They also can be performed separately, either in a standing or seated position. In a standing position, the sun breath should be active and generate heat by engaging the arms, legs and core. I usually guide my students through sun breaths by starting in *tadasana* with forearms crossed.

With a deep inhale, the arms are swept up overhead, ending with forearms again crossed. It is important that the arms aren't just passively swept overhead, but rather the arm muscles are active by pulling the fingers away from the body as the arms rise. With the arms above the head and the forearms crossed, the fingers are pulled to the sky, imagining that they are trying to pull you up off of the mat, as the weight is lifted off of the heels. The body not only becomes long, but also is completely stretched and full of energy that surges from toes to fingertips. As you swan dive, all of the energy can be released in exhalation, possibly breathing out the mouth, as you bend over into *uttanasana,* the gentle forward fold. The cycle begins again by crossing the forearms and reverse swan diving the arms back overhead with inhalation. Additional energy can be harnessed by bringing the gaze overhead and gently arching the back as the arms are swept overhead.

As mentioned, sun breaths are an integral part of *surya namaskar* A and B. The connection of the inhalations and exhalations to each posture drives the flow of the sun salutations. The following is a common sequence for Sun Salutation A:

1. Begin in *tadasana,* the mountain. As described before, weight should be evenly distributed on both feet, thigh muscles engaged, pelvis level, shoulders relaxed and spine elongated.
2. On a deep inhalation, a standing sunbreath is performed as described above, ending in *uttanasana,* the standing forward fold, following a long exhalation. The forward fold is described as gentle, meaning that the knees can bend to a comfortable position and the hands may rest on the mat, the shins or simply dangle.
3. Inhale to *ardha uttanasana,* a flat back and straight legs, leading with the chest, gaze coming forward. The shape of the number "7" is approximated between the back and legs.
4. Exhale back down into *uttanasana.*

5. On the next inhale, step one leg and then the other leg back to come into a high plank.
6. Exhale as you flow through *chaturanga* down to the mat. To alleviate any potential straining in the upper body, *chaturanga* can be performed by first dropping the knees and then the upper body to the mat.
7. Uncurl the toes and come onto the tops of the feet as you inhale into upward-facing dog.
8. Curl the toes and exhale back into downward-facing dog.
9. Inhale and then on the next exhale, step or hop the feet forward between the hands, coming into a forward fold.
10. Inhale to reverse swan dive, sweeping the arms above the head.
11. Bring the palms together and on a complete exhale gradually bring them down to heart center, possibly watching them slowly pass over the crown of the head, third eye and throat *chakras*.
12. Relax the body, soften the muscles and come into stillness.

This sequence may be repeated several times in succession. Notice how the breath is connected with each posture, typically inhaling as the body opens and exhaling as it closes, not only facilitating deep breathing, but also drawing *prana* inward to activate and energize the body.

One variation of Sun Salutation A is done standing; inhaling arms overhead, exhaling into a gentle forward fold, inhaling to a flat back and straight legs, exhaling into a forward fold, inhaling into *utkatasana,* the chair pose, exhaling into a forward fold, inhaling to reverse swan dive, and slowly exhaling hands in *anjali mudra* to heart center.

Sun Salutation B builds on Sun Salutation A with the addition of postures to the framework of Sun Salutation A. The added postures tend to make *Surya namaskar* B more challenging and strenuous. A teacher might insert a high crescent lunge after the downward-facing dog into the above "A" sequence by instructing students to inhale into a three legged dog by sweeping one leg upwards from downward-facing dog, exhaling the raised foot forward between the hands to come into a low runner's lunge, and then inhaling to sweep the arms to either sides of the ears, as one rises to the high crescent. The arms might then be windmilled forward onto the mat to frame the front foot. The front foot is then stepped back to meet the other foot, returning to downward-facing dog. The teacher might then instruct you to walk the feet forward between the hands to come back into a folding fold before reverse swan diving to stand. The sun salutation sequence may be repeated to include performing the high crescent lunge on the other side. In addition, while in the high crescent lunge, all possibilities exist from hinging forward and twisting, planting the back foot and coming into warrior II, or hinging forward to enter into warrior III. The sky's the limit and it is up to the creativity of the teacher to find a *vinyasa* sequence that is interesting, novel and fresh.

A class that is advertised as a "*vinyasa* flow" class may spend the majority of time in these sun salutation sequences. The postures may be challenging and rigorous. It is usually a good idea to be familiar with the basic yoga sequences beforehand as the pace of the class can be relatively fast. A good teacher will establish a pace that remains slow enough to connect the breath with the movements. Again, to create balance, I prefer periods of rest in child's pose or relaxed standing interspersed between sun salutations. Time to observe, reflect and connect is a wonderful luxury.

There are two important points to keep in mind during *Surya namaskar* B. One is the realization that when a teacher instructs you to step one foot forward between the hands from downward-facing dog to enter into a low runner's lunge, for many, this can be a multi-step process. A limber teacher may be able to take one step forward between the hands. It is fine to use your hand to push the leg forward, rise up a little bit to take the step and/or readjust before coming into the low runner's lunge. The second is the realization that the teacher is not a drill sergeant. Sometimes, it is wonderful to take a rest when needed, maybe slipping into a comfortable child's pose or reaching over for your water bottle for a drink instead of pushing up into a downward dog. Always remember that you are there for yourself. Like any vigorous practice, periods of rest and hydration can be valuable in increasing the effectiveness of the exercise, allowing the muscles time to recover. I appreciate a teacher that affords me the time to rest, as well as one that winds down the class with less physically demanding postures.

As you practice *Surya namaskar,* become aware of the energy of the sun, *the pingala nadi.* The vigorous nature of the sun salutations can fuel the *agni* and stir up emotions, and even past traumas. Make sure to take the time to enter into a position of stillness to balance the energy of the moon with that of the sun. Experiencing the cooling energy of the moon affords an opportunity to be the witness to those feelings stirred up in an active *vinyasa* flow. Once again, yoga is a balance. The challenge of *Surya namaskar* is to find your balance between the sun and the moon and the mind and body, done with self-kindness and compassion.

18
THE SUPINE POSTURES

Lie down on the ground and feel the planet's heart beating.

Paul Coelho

I choose to place this exploration of the supine postures immediately before the next chapter on *shavasana* since, more often than not, you will find yourself on your back as a class begins to wind down towards its conclusion. Once again, I discuss those postures that you are more likely to encounter in a class. The Sanskrit names you might hear are designated as such with an asterisk.

*Setu Bandhasana**
The Bridge Pose

We build too many walls and not enough bridges.

Isaac Newton

Setu translates to bridge and *bandha,* bound. As will be discussed later on, we come across the word *bandha* in the practice of *pranayama.* It is important to note that the goal of the bridge pose is back extension. Also, a bridge is typically supported in two places. Our bridge is supported by our arms and legs. Like much of yoga, we never want to miss an opportunity to strengthen muscles and, as such, we wish to activate all four limbs.

1. While lying supine, arms at the sides, and palms face down adjacent to the hips, bend the knees and walk the heels as close to the sitz bones as possible. For some, the fingers might contact the back of the heels.
2. Begin by grounding the arms, from shoulders to fingertips, into the mat. Allow a wave of muscular contraction to spread from the shoulders, distally to the fingertips.
3. Now push firmly into the feet to drive the hips and pelvis up to the sky.
4. Try to create more back extension by actively elevating the lower rib cage.
5. Become aware of the weight shifting onto the shoulders as both hips elevate and the back bends.

6. Protect the neck by elongating and softening it, possibly with a small tilt of the chin towards the chest.
7. To exit the posture, beginning from the top of the spine, slowly lower the back down to the mat one vertebrae at a time, until finally the sacrum makes a soft landing. One might imagine the spine as a metal chain, laying each link individually onto the ground.

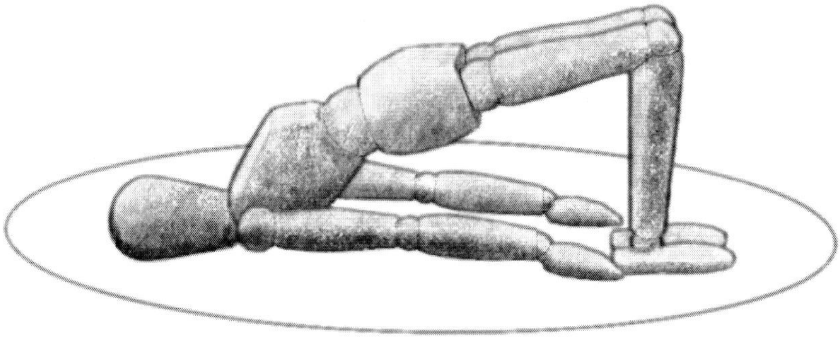

Setu Bandhasana ~ The Bridge Pose

There are many variations available to you in the bridge pose. One might walk the shoulders under the back and interlace fingers. Other options include drawing the arms overhead to either side of the ears, pulling fingertips away from the head, or raising the heels and pressing into the balls of the feet. Both actions can provide greater hip and pelvic elevation with a resultant greater degree of back extension.

Often, we follow a pose with a counterpose. Commonly, a teacher will instruct the class to grab the knees to the chest after exiting the bridge; following back extension with back flexion. With the knees toward the chest, one might gently rock back and forth or circle the knees in the air to experience a lower back massage. If there is no neck sensitivity, one might also lift the shoulders off the mat, drawing forehead to knees, rolling up into a ball.

Ananda Balasana

Happy Baby Pose

Each night, when I go to sleep, I die. And the next morning, when I wake up, I am reborn.

Mahatma Gandhi

There is not much to say about this pose. Quite simply, on your back, rocking back and forth, with legs in the air you physically resemble a happy baby. Whether you are happy or unhappy in this pose may be related to flexibility and comfort. Never have the expectation in yoga that every pose that is suggested will feel good. This pose is a great hip adductor or inner thigh muscle stretch.

1. While lying supine, bring your knees to the chest.
2. Grab your big toes, feet, ankles or the backs of the thighs just above the knees.
3. Spread the legs apart and bend the knees to bring the lower legs vertically in the air, soles of feet parallel to the ceiling.

4. Pull the knees towards the armpits to experience the hip adductor stretch.
5. Option to rock side to side.
6. If you wish to minimize neck strain, choose the option to hold the backs of the thighs. As it bears to be repeated, options are not challenges. Options are different ways to position your body to enhance your experience of yoga.
7. Exit the pose by releasing the legs and bringing the feet to the mat.

Ananda Balasana ~ Happy Baby Pose

Supta Eka Pada Utkatasana
Supine Figure Four Pose

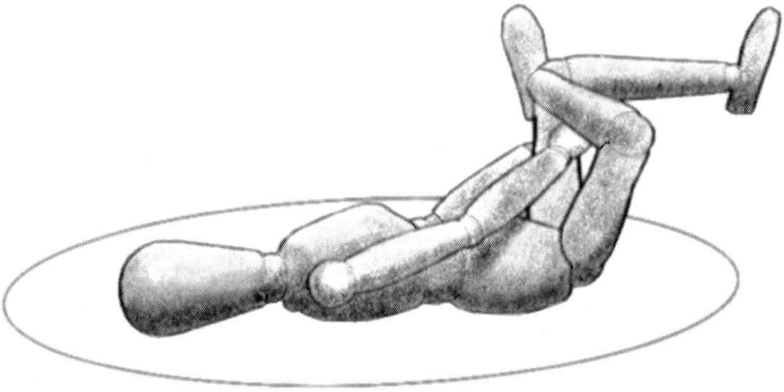

Supta Eka Pada Utkatasana ~ Supine Figure Four Pose

This *asana* is a comfortable way to open and stretch the hip joint. As you may remember, *utkatasana* is the chair pose. The Sanskrit word, *eka*, means "one" and *pada* means "foot." Therefore, *eka pada utkatasana* is the one-legged chair pose, a balance posture in which one resembles a person sitting in a chair with one ankle resting on the other thigh just above the knee. The Sanskrit word *supta* means "reclined" or "supine". If you could take that person in the one-legged chair balance pose and place him or her on their back, they would end up in *supta eka pada utkatasana.*

1. Start supine with knees bent and both feet on the mat.
2. Extend one leg, say the right leg, straight up, toes pointing to the sky.
3. As you then bend the right knee, externally rotate the right hip to bring the ankle on top of the left thigh, just above the knee.
4. Lift the left foot to bring the left lower leg parallel with the mat.
5. If it does not result in neck or shoulder discomfort, interlace the fingers of both hands behind the left thigh.
6. Exit the posture by releasing the interlace and dropping both feet back down to the mat.
7. Repeat on the other side.

If interlacing the fingers behind the left thigh is uncomfortable, feel free to cradle the lower leg or gently push the right knee away with the right hand to enjoy a nice opening of the hip. Variations of this pose include extending the left leg straight or leaving the left foot on the mat, not lifting the left leg. Occasionally, you may hear the figure four pose referred to as *supta kapotasana,* the reclining pigeon pose.

Supta Matsyendrasana
Supine Spinal Twist

When the breath wanders, the mind is also unsteady.

Hatha Yoga Pradipika

The Hatha Yoga Pradipika is the seminal book on the practice of

Hatha Yoga, believed to have been written in the 15th century, in part representing the teachings of Matsyendraneth. As you might remember from the chapter on the sitting postures, Matsyendraneth is credited with disseminating the secrets of Hatha yoga, which he overheard from the god Shiva. I include the above quote, because *supta Matsyendrasana* is a position of total release that allows one to reconnect with the breath. We often lose awareness of the breath during more active and vigorous postures in our practice. In *supta Matsyendrasana* we let the body become heavy and sink into the mat, surrendering the physical body to quiet an active mind.

1. Start supine, knees bent, feet on the mat.
2. For this example, shift the hips all the way over to the right edge of your mat.
3. Bring the arms out into a T-shape position on the ground at shoulder level, palms facing either up or down.
4. Draw the right knee and then the left to the chest.
5. Keeping both shoulders on the mat, let the knees drop over to the left. The right hip will lift off of the mat.
6. If there is no neck sensitivity, twist the neck to the right, gaze directed to your right hand.
7. Exit the posture by untwisting and placing both feet on the mat.
8. Bring the hands to the sides in order to shift the hips to the left and repeat on the other side.

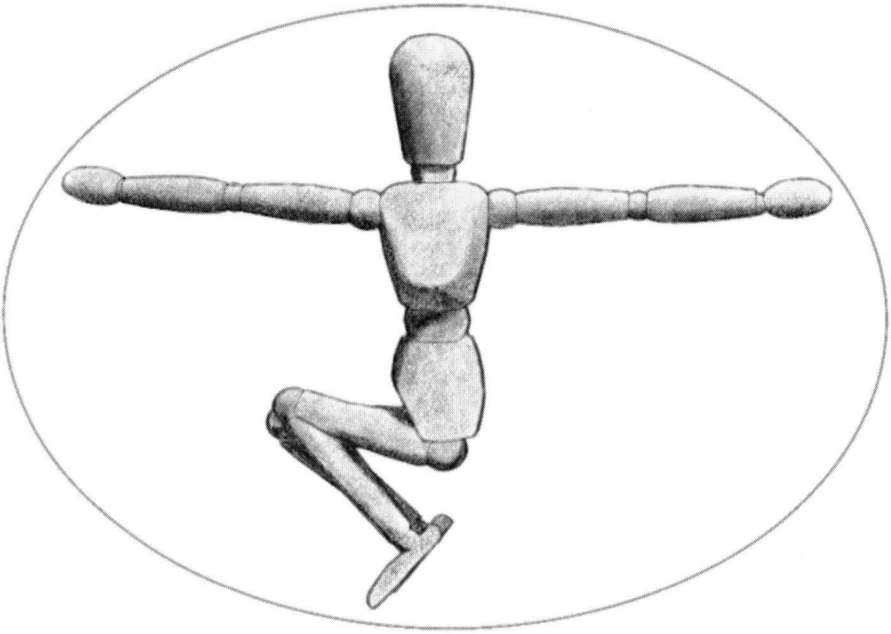

Supta Matsyendrasana ~ Supine Spinal Twist

As was mentioned, *supta Matsyendrasana* is a posture of release. Tension in the body is not welcome. For many, the knees may not fully rest on the ground without lifting one shoulder off of the mat. Keeping the knees hanging in the air engages the leg muscles. Readjust the position of the legs to remove all tension. As is true of all of the *asanas,* to paraphrase Pantanjali, find a position that is "steady and comfortable."

The realized feelings of surrender and release makes *supta Matsyendrasana* a wonderful way to prepare for *shavasana,* the ultimate state of peaceful unawareness of body and mind.

19
SHAVASANA

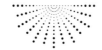

Within yourself is a stillness, a sanctuary to which you can retreat at any time and be yourself.

Herman Hesse

Shavasana literally translates to "the corpse pose". I never mention the English translation in my classes as it can evoke undesirable thoughts and disturbing imagery. Many say that of all of the *asanas, shavasana* is the most challenging and difficult to master. What makes *shavasana* so challenging is that it requires both total unawareness of the physical body and a clearing of the mind of all thoughts. For all of the other *asanas,* we strive to have an awareness of the breath, mind and body. In *shavasana* we must let everything go. Clearing the mind of thoughts, however, is easier said than done. Rather than deliberately trying not to think, relieve that pressure by recognizing that it is normal to have thoughts. Resting the mind comes from acknowledging those thoughts as they arise, letting them disappear into the air and returning back to relaxation and stillness.

Before entering into *shavasana,* a teacher typically will invite you to take any additional movements or stretches before settling into the pose. Some may suggest performing any additional *asanas* that were not included in the class that a student might desire to do.

Shavasana is traditionally done supine, legs extended, arms gently angled from the body, and palms face up. In yoga, palms facing toward the sky is considered a receptive posture. Although the desired goal is consciously clearing the mind of all thoughts, entering into *shavasana* receptive to new ideas and perspectives can maximize its benefits on a subconscious level. It is so very important to remember, however, that there is only one rule as to how to be positioned for this *asana*: to be comfortable in order to be able to forget about the physical body. Tension in any of the muscles or across joints must be eliminated so that thoughts of discomfort don't activate the mind. It might create less tension in the arms to lie with the palms face down or less stress to the lower back to have knees bent. Putting a bolster under the knees is a wonderful way to lessen any lower back strain. Internal body temperature may be increased from the physical activity of your practice. A blanket over the body during *shavasana* can keep the body warm as evaporative cooling through sweat glands occurs. For some, an eye pillow helps eliminate strain in closed eyelids. Placing a rolled blanket under the neck can relieve tension in the cervical muscles and ligamentous and bony structures of the cervical spine. Placing a bolster or block on the belly can create a sense of heaviness in the body that for some creates a sense of safety. Further, *shavasana* need not be done supine. Some assume a fetal position or a supine spinal twist, among other possible positions.

Perhaps even more challenging than losing awareness of physical sensations in the body is clearing the mind of all thoughts. It is the mind chatter that we all experience that is so very difficult to suppress. *Shavasana* is an opportunity to allow oneself a few moments to rest the mind in a safe space. It is giving yourself permission to create distance from worries and stress through a realization that for those few moments during *shavasana* nothing bad will happen if you just let go. Equally important is to not beat yourself up for failing to quiet the mind of chatter and unwanted thoughts on a particular day. Some days are different from others. If the mind remains active, at the very least, you are resting the body after an hour or so of physical activity.

In my classes, I begin *shavasana* with a short guided meditation aimed at diverting attention away from the room, the body and thoughts. I also choose to play a calming piece of music, which I believe adds an additional layer of diversion from noisy mind chatter. Some yoga instructors prefer to lead *shavasana* in silence.

In a typical yoga class, due to time constraints *shavasana* typically lasts five minutes or so. If practicing at home with or without an online video, you can take advantage of a longer period of *shavasana,* which can enhance your meditative experience. After a period of time in *shavasana,* the teacher begins to awaken you from relaxation, possibly telling you to become aware of the breath and aware of the body, creating movements that start small in the fingers and toes and evolve into larger stretches with a deepening of the breath. The teacher will then guide you to draw the knees to the chest and roll over into a fetal position. Traditionally, the fetal position is assumed with the right side down so that the heart in the left chest is not compressed. It is interesting that one transitions from a corpse pose into a fetal position, from death to life. One might consider self-discovery from one's yoga practice as a rebirth to new possibilities.

There are some who have suffered a prior trauma who are not comfortable closing their eyes in a room full of other people or lying supine with an instructor watching. Once again, there are no rules regarding *shavasana.* The eyes may remain open, as meditative states arise from single-pointed focus, which can be visual. Comfort can be achieved in a chair or in any position on a mat. Yoga is a completely personal experience, uniquely performed by each one of us to best meet our needs. It is important in a yoga class to be in a safe space, both for the physical body and the mind.

Most importantly, *shavasana* is an opportunity to rest; rest the body and rest the mind. It is a few moments to give yourself permission to release the unwelcome weight of stressful or disturbing thoughts by saying that it is alright to just be. Some say that one reaches the ultimate level of relaxation by falling asleep. For some, *shavasana* will induce sleep. The hope is that you will arise from *shavasana* refreshed and energized with a healthier perspective to take on whatever lies ahead in the day.

Often in life we experience opposite extremes. Knowing the sensations and feelings evoked by one extreme gives one an appreciation for the other. The warmth of a house is better appreciated when coming in from the frigid outdoors. The resting of the mind and body in *shavasana* is much more appreciated after a period of activity and engagement. Each *asana* affords an opportunity to stretch and contract muscles and increase the flexibility of the joints and spine. Each *asana* also activates emotions and thoughts as we interpret and explore the movements of the body and their connection to the breath. Enjoying the full experience of an active mind and body leads to a much better appreciation of the rest and peace that comes from *shavasana.* It is most appreciated when taking *shavasana* to the extreme; complete loss of awareness of the body and mind. It is the ultimate challenge of *shavasana* that when realized will be as comforting and relaxing as the warmth of a house on that cold winter day.

20

PRANAYAMA

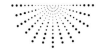

Yogash chitta vritti nirodhah ~ Yoga is the quieting of the fluctuations of the mind.

Patanjali

Prana is considered the life force that surrounds us all and permeates the universe of which we are all a part. If you recall from the chapter on yogic philosophy, the Sanskrit word "*yama*" translates to restraint. For *pranayama, yama* refers to the restraint or control of the *prana*. *Pranayama* is more than just yogic breathing techniques, but the practice of breath control. There are a range of techniques that differ in intensity and heat, ranging from channel activating techniques like *bhastrika* that fuels the *agni,* the inner fire, activates the energy of the sun and stirs up emotions buried deep in the pelvis, to energy channeling techniques like *sitali* and *sitkari,* which cool the mind and body and activate the energy of the moon, allowing one to become the witness to any uncovered emotions. A practice of *pranayama* consists of a sequence of different breathing techniques designed to approximate a wave that progressively creates more and more emotional and physical heat until it ultimately crests, eventually subsiding with cooling and self-reflection to bring the *pingala* and *ida nadis* into balance. Similar to the practice of the *asanas, pranayama* takes time to master for it to be emotionally impactful. Mastery is realized through dedication to a regular practice. Both *pranayama* and the *asanas* represent two vehicles to access the spirit and create clarity of mind. They are complementary and both important to the practice of yoga.

Unfortunately, in most yoga classes, most, or even all of the emphasis is placed on the performance of the *asanas* at the expense of time in *pranayama. Pranayama* has become a lost art in the Western world. A teacher may guide the class through a short round of *pranayama* at any point in a class, possibly two to five minutes, more often at the beginning, and less so at the end. At the beginning of the class, *pranayama* serves to center the class and allow for a transition from thoughts of the day to thoughts of one's practice. Centering is bringing oneself into the center of the room, into the center of self and into the moment. It is also a way to establish the breath in anticipation of its connection to movement. If performed near the end of a class, *pranayama* can serve as a bridge from physical activity to the quiet and relaxation of *shavasana.*

Pranayama is the fourth of Pantanjali's eight limbs of yoga found in his *Yoga Sutras*. As his teaching professes, the mastery of *pranayama* is necessary to enter into *pratyahara,* the fifth limb and the first stage of introversion. As mentioned previously, many schools of yoga assert that one must master the *asanas* before learning the breath control techniques of *pranayama*. In the Kripalu tradition, *asanas, pranayama* and meditation are integrated in the attempt to master all three concurrently.

Unlike the expression of the *asanas,* which differ from person to person and are dependent on both acquired and genetically-based flexibility and strength, the practice of *pranayama* has a more level playing field. Except for people afflicted with pulmonary, muscular or neurological diseases, we all have a similar capacity to breathe. Through *pranayama,* the optimal balance and distribution of *prana* throughout the body can be established. Physiologically, breathing is the mechanism whereby oxygen is brought into the body and carbon dioxide removed. Oxygen is also a life force. Without it, our cells would lose the ability to produce energy. Whether from a yogic philosophical perspective or on a physiologic basis, optimizing and controlling the flow of breath nourishes the body with the life force. As was discussed previously, lengthening the spine in a sitting position by raising the hips above the knees, maximizes the efficiency of the breath as the diaphragm has more room to move downward.

Deep diaphragmatic breathing also stimulates the parasympathetic nervous system, promoting states of relaxation. If we return back to our proverbial caveman, we find him back at home in his cave with his family after fleeing the saber-tooth tiger. During his flight to safety, his breaths were short, primarily just involving the movement of the ribs to expand the lungs. Now that he feels safe, he breathes with his diaphragm, as his breath slows and deepens. The decreased frequency and increased depth of the breath tells his brain that now is the time to rest and digest. Parasympathetic tone increases as sympathetic tone wanes. Learning to consistently use the diaphragm to breathe triggers the relaxation response over the long term. I am sure at one time or another someone observed you were stressed and told you to take a deep breath and relax. You will see most professional basketball players take a deep breath to relax the body and increase their focus right before attempting a free throw at the foul line. *Pranayama* has a dual purpose. One is to promote feelings of inwardness and introversion by increasing conscious awareness of the breath. The second is the induction of the physiological-mediated relaxation response.

Pranayama is primarily performed by inhaling and exhaling through the nose, which intensifies the awareness of the breath. This can be accomplished through a focus on the sound or feel of the breath or the physical actions of the body used to control the breath specific to each technique.

In Pantanjali's *Yoga Sutras,* the term *asana* refers to assuming a steady, comfortable position in which to perform *pranayama.* Any discomfort will flood the mind with negative physical sensations that will disrupt the creation of a single point of focus on the breath. With regard to the positioning of the body, two conditions should be met. One is sitting without physical discomfort or strain. The other is sitting in a position that allows for the greatest downward excursion of the diaphragm with inhalation. As previously discussed, but bears repeating, the diaphragm is a dome-shaped muscle that divides the chest from the abdomen. With inhalation it moves downward into the abdomen. Limitations to maximizing breath control arise more so from incorrect posture than the ability to breathe. Rounding of the back "crunches" and crowds the abdomen, as the intestines and abdominal organs are pushed together. With less room in the abdomen, downward movement of the diaphragm is limited, resulting in a decrease in lung capacity. Elongation of the spine and relaxing the shoulders down the back affords more space in the abdomen, greater inferior diaphragmatic movement and a more optimal breath. Elongation of the spine is best accomplished by sitting on the edge of a cushion in order to bring the hips above the level of the knees, thereby lessening the tendency to round the back. Sitting in a chair or on two blocks while kneeling in a supported hero's pose are also effective ways to elongate the spine. Once the elongation of the spine and torso are realized, the ability to perform *pranayama* transcends age and physical limitations.

As is true of performing the *asanas,* safety is paramount in the practice of *pranayama.* Precautions and contraindications exist, especially for the more vigorous and heat-producing forms, such as *anuloma viloma, kapalabhati,* and *bhastrika,* all more often done with breath retention. Contraindications include pregnancy, recent abdominal surgery, abdominal or pelvic hernias, glaucoma, uncontrolled hypertension and pulmonary and/or cardiovascular diseases. Some consider menstruation a precaution. Of course, nasal congestion and resistance to breathing due to a deviated septum could pose difficulties to the practice of *pranayama.*

Dirga Pranayama
The Three Part Complete Yogic Breath

The Sanskrit word *dirga* translates to "full" or "complete." Many consider *dirga pranayama* the foundational breathing technique as it serves as a warm-up to much more vigorous and activating *pranayama.* Other techniques are layered and built upon the framework of *dirga pranayama.* As discussed above, if at all, a yoga class may have a short period of *pranayama.* As such, *dirga* breathing is often the type of breathing that is led. *Dirga pranayama* warms up the mind to be more receptive to new perspectives and self-discovery, as well as the muscles of respiration. The muscles of respiration include the diaphragm, the intercostal muscles or muscles between the ribs, and other core muscles of the chest and abdomen. Similar to other skeletal muscles, the muscles of respiration optimally function after progressive stretching of muscle fibers. As such, *dirga* breathing should become progressively deeper and longer with each inhalation and exhalation, until you are breathing into complete fullness and exhaling into complete emptiness.

During inhalation, the three parts of the breath sequentially occur in the abdomen, the rib cage and the upper chest. The challenge is to add all three together into a single deep wave of motion. In order to learn this technique, however, it is useful to consider each part separately before combining them into a single deep complete breath. Resting one hand on the belly and one on the chest is useful in understanding the complete three part breath.

Part I ~ The Abdomen

Begin by taking a deep inhalation to expand the belly alone. The lower hand resting on the belly is pushed out away from the body as you breathe in. Exhale out as much air as you can in order to draw the lower hand and belly button as close to the spine as possible. Take another deep inhalation allowing the belly to expand out like a balloon. Exhale to let the balloon collapse to complete emptiness.

Part II ~ The Ribcage

Now, inhale to expand the belly and let the breath travel up into the ribs as they flare out in all four directions. As you exhale completely, the ribs are drawn together and the belly collapses. Take another deep inhalation to first expand the belly and then the ribcage, imagining that the ribs are spreading apart like the gills of a fish.

Part III ~ The Upper Chest

Finally, inhale to expand the belly and let the breath travel into the ribs and all the way superiorly into the upper chest, causing the collar bones to lift up and out. Exhalation can occur in reverse from the upper chest to the lower belly. An attempt should be made to make the exhalation longer than the inhalation if possible. Take another deep inhalation and notice how the lower hand on the belly first rises away from the spine, and as the breath travels upward, the upper hand is then pushed out. Breath retention is considered a component of more advanced *pranayama,* but inserting a very short pause at the very top of the inhalation and bottom of the exhalation can afford a few moments to appreciate stillness before reactivating the respiratory movements of the chest and abdomen.

Now the three parts of the breath can become one. Imagine the breath is a wave that spreads from the bottom of the belly all the way up to the collar bones. The wave pulls the belly from the spine, draws the ribs apart and then expands the chest. The wave ebbs and recedes during exhalation from the upper chest down to the lower belly. The full expression of *dirga pranayama* is realized by making smooth transitions between the three parts, as well as between inhalation and exhalation.

Once establishing the rhythm of the breath, see if each breath can be slower and deeper than the one before. Let the gentle, yet full waves of breath become long. As the complete breath is established, attention can be brought not just to the sound of the breath, but also to the rhythm of the wave-like movement of the chest and abdomen. Eventually, as one falls into deeper meditative states one can be less deliberate in their observations.

We can analyze what is occurring anatomically during the three parts of *dirga pranayama.* During the first part, expansion of the belly is caused by the downward excursion of the diaphragm as it displaces the moveable abdominal contents outward and downward. Inhalation occurs with a vacuum-like mechanism. One might imagine the downward pull of the diaphragm analogous to the inner stopper of a hypodermic needle. As the stopper is pulled back, in this case air is sucked inside the lungs. During the second part, as air expands the lungs, the ribs are pushed outward and the intervening intercostal muscles are secondarily stretched. Finally, during the third part, air completely fills all of the air spaces of the lungs. The filling of the upper lobes of the lungs outwardly expands the upper chest and pushes the collar bones outward and upward. Exhalation occurs by the contraction of the intercostal muscles, pulling the ribs together to actively push air out of the lungs. Concurrently, there is upward relaxation of the diaphragm.

Although an instructor may guide you through only a short period of *dirga pranayama,* ideally maintaining long and deep diaphragmatic breathing throughout a class and connecting that breath to the movements of the body during the *asanas* can help achieve the desired integration of *asanas, pranayama* and meditation. And certainly, *dirga pranayama* need not be limited to a yoga class. It is a wonderful, meditative experience to enjoy at any time. Even just taking a few moments out of a hectic and stressful day to pause, close the eyes and take a deep, three part, diaphragmatic breath can relax the mind and reset the brain for the remainder of the day. Yoga is not just reserved for a class or studio. It is best practiced on and off the mat, ultimately becoming a way of life.

Ujjayi Pranayama
The Victorious Breath

The *ujjayi* breath is also called the ocean sounding breath. It is created by breathing in and out of the nose while partially constricting the muscles in the back of the throat surrounding the glottis. You can experience this by bringing a palm up close to your open mouth as you exhale, as if you are fogging up a mirror or cleaning your eyeglasses. This will create a "hah" sound. That "hah" sound is a result of the constriction of the throat. Now, see if you can replicate that sound with inhalation. Once you feel comfortable with this breath, close your mouth and breathe through the nose while continuing to constrict the muscles of the throat. You will notice that the breath sounds like the waves of the ocean coming in to shore and back out to sea with each inhalation and exhalation. Once you have settled into the relaxing sounds of the ocean waves, see if you can increase the forcefulness of the breath. The resultant increase in sound volume facilitates single-pointed concentration on the breath. In *dirga pranayama,* the repetitive motions of the body throughout the respiration cycle add to the meditative effects of the breathing technique. This is also true of the *ujjayi* breath, with an added focus on the sensation resulting from the resistance to air flow caused by the constricted muscles at the level of the glottis responsible for the unique sound of the breath.

The *ujjayi* breath can be layered upon *dirga pranayama.* In this regard, *dirga pranayama* is initially established, followed by the addition of the *ujjayi* breath. In addition, similar to *dirga pranayama,* the *ujjayi* breath need not be limited to just a period of centering and *pranayama.* In many yogic traditions, such as Ashtanga yoga, *ujjayi* breathing is done throughout a practice. Regardless of the particular yogic tradition, the increased and peaceful sound of the breath becomes a constant reminder to connect the breath to movement.

The Sanskrit word, "*ujjayi*" translates to victorious. How one's yoga practice is a victory is up to each one of us to determine. If the relaxing effects of *ujjayi pranayama* help better face the challenges of life, then it is truly a victory.

Nadi Shodhana

Alternate Nostril Breathing or the Channel Clearing Breath

The *nadis* are considered to be energy channels through which *prana* flows throughout the body. Ancient Hindu texts differ as to the number of *nadis* present in the human body, some describing as many as 350,000 *nadis.* Many of the *nadis* directly connect to the *chakras.* *Nadi shodhana* is a yogic breathing technique designed to clear these energy channels, allowing for optimal flow and balance of *prana* throughout the body. Metaphorically, one might imagine the *nadis* clogged or obstructed by negative energy arising from thoughts that don't serve us at the present moment. *Nadi shodhana* is a practice of mindfulness that clears those obstructions to allow for the flow of positive energy. Being in the moment diminishes the awareness of habitual negative thoughts. For *nadi shodhana,* the object of mindfulness is the breath. The focus is not just on the sound of the breath, but also on the rhythm of the hand and finger movements alternately opening and closing the nostrils. The sound of the breath is the primary point of focus for all of the yogic breathing techniques, but what makes each form of *pranayama* unique is the actions of the physical body used to generate the sound.

As with all forms of meditation, starting in a comfortable and steady position is paramount. Traditionally, *nadi shodhana* is performed with the right hand in *vishnu mudra. Vishnu* is known as the Preserver, preserving the order in the universe. In yogic philosophy, the right hand is symbolic of receiving. *Vishnu mudra* is created by bending the index and third fingers inward towards the palm. The extended ring finger is placed adjacent to the left nostril and the thumb next to the right. Begin by inhaling through both nostrils. Next, occlude the right nostril with the thumb as you exhale through the left. Then, inhale up the left nostril, open up the right, occlude the left and exhale through the right. Breathing continues as such, alternating from nostril to nostril.

Once you have established the alternating rhythm between nostrils, begin to slow and deepen the breath into *dirga* breath. You can also layer on the *ujjayi* breath, again to increase the sound volume of the breath and create the relaxing sounds of the ocean waves. Feelings of inwardness are deepened by bringing awareness to the sound of the breath, as well as to the rhythm of the fingers moving back and forth to occlude and release alternate nostrils.

As is true of many things in yoga, as well as in life, there are no hard and fast rules as to how to perform *nadi shodhana* and modifications are welcome. The *Vishnu mudra* is uncomfortable for some. The sustained flexion of the second and third fingers toward the palm requires continued contraction of the flexor muscles in the forearm, which can lead to muscle fatigue and discomfort. A modification that releases the engagement of the flexors involves extending the index and third fingers to rest on the forehead at the third eye center. One can also use the left hand and arm to support the right elbow if the right arm becomes fatigued. One can even do a hands-free version of *nadi shodhana* whereby one simply imagines alternately breathing in through one nostril and breathing out through the other. Taking it one step further, one might imagine energy flowing from the foot to the crown of head on one side of the body with inhalation and energy flowing in the opposite direction on exhalation. The focus becomes the long lines of energy flow alternating from one side of the body to the other.

Typically in a yoga class time does not allow for an extended period of *pranayama. Nadi shodhana* is much more effective and powerful as a meditative tool when performed over a longer period of time. The focus on the rhythms that one creates can be hypnotic.

As was discussed in the chapter on yogic philosophy, the purpose and goal of *nadi shodhana* is to balance the *ida* and *pingala nadis,* the lunar and solar energy channels. It is through this balance between the moon and the sun, rest and activity, heat and cooling, receptivity and irrationality, and the feminine and masculine that the barriers to self-discovery, realization and personal growth dissolve.

Anuloma Viloma
Alternate Nostril Breathing with Breath Retention

Anuloma viloma translates to "with the hair or grain and against the hair or grain". Imagine grooming a horse. Brushing the horse against the grain of the hair causes dirt, shedded skin and other particulate matter to be jarred loose from the horse's body. Brushing with the grain then smooths out the disturbances and mess. *Anuloma viloma* is similar to *nadi shodhana* with the addition of a *kumbhaka or* breath retention of variable length. The longer the *kumbhaka,* the more heat is produced and the more activating the *pranayama* becomes. Just like brushing against the grain, *anuloma viloma* stirs up emotions and past traumas. Like brushing with the grain, one can bear witness to what has been stirred up in order to smooth out one's life experiences.

The uncovering and witnessing of repressed emotions and trauma that comes with more vigorous *pranayama* that employ a *kumbhaka* may not initially be accessible. Just like a practice of the *asanas,* gradual realization of the benefits of a regular *pranayama* practice takes time and patience. *Anuloma viloma* is considered a more advanced practice and should be reserved only after the more basic, less activating forms of *pranayama* are mastered. Unlike *dirga, ujjayi* and *nadi shodhana pranayamas,* which are relatively safe with few precautions, contraindications exist any time a *kumbhaka* is used. As mentioned previously, these include uncontrolled hypertension, pregnancy, glaucoma, recent abdominal surgery, hernias and pulmonary and cardiovascular diseases. Some consider menstruation a precaution. I mention these contraindications again to stress the importance of establishing a personal safe space in which to practice yoga.

Kapalabhati Pranayama

The Skull Shining Breath or The Breath of Fire

Kapalabhati is a Sanskrit compound word made up of *kapal* meaning "skull" and *bhati* meaning "shining" or "enlightening". *Kapalabhati pranayama* is a purification technique. It results in clearing the cranial paranasal sinuses of mucus and secretions. With an explosive quality, the breaths of fire also activate and energize the body and mind, stirring up repressed emotions and past traumas deep in the pelvis. It awakens the *kundalini,* followed by the flow of energy up the central *sushumna nadi* in the process of liberation. One has the capacity to bear witness to hidden feelings and emotions through the activation of the *chakras* as energy ascends toward spirituality.

To learn *kapalabhati* breathing, place both hands, one on top of the other, on the belly. Both the inhalations and exhalations occur quickly and at a rapid pace. The exhalation is a short, powerful burst created by forceful contraction of the abdominal muscles. The inhalation occurs passively as the abdominal muscles release thereby sucking air into the lungs. The contraction of the abdominal muscles will cause the stacked hands to move in toward the spine during exhalation and, with relaxation, outward during inhalation. Once you become accustomed to the action of the abdominal muscles, you can release the hands down to the thighs or lap. Frequency of the inhalations and exhalations and duration of *kapalabhati* breathing varies from practitioner to practitioner. One example of the frequency of the breathing cycle that might be used is one to two breaths per second for eight to ten cycles. Often, continued *kapalabhati* breathing will begin to clear mucus and secretions from the nose and sinuses so it is a good idea to have a tissue nearby.

There are many contraindications to the performance of *kapalabhati pranayama.* This breath of fire can be physically dangerous. It can lead to hypoventilation with symptoms of lightheadedness and dizziness. As such, it should not be practiced by individuals with high or low blood pressure, heart disease, or history of prior stroke. It is felt to be contraindicated in pregnant or menstruating women. It is also contraindicated in the setting of epilepsy, glaucoma and other ophthalmologic conditions , abdominal hernias and recent abdominal surgery, among many others.

Kapalabhati pranayama is more activating and heat producing than the other more meditative forms of *pranayama,* but it epitomizes the idea of controlling the breath, allowing for the inflow of *prana* and outflow of impurities. All of the yogic breathing techniques are active and deliberate attempts to control the breath and *prana*. With time and practice, that control becomes second nature.

Bhastrika Pranayama

Bellows Breath

Bhastrika is considered the most vigorous, heat producing type of *pranayama* and should be reserved for only those that have a regular *pranayama* practice. I mention it here solely for completeness sake. It is done similar to *kapalabhati,* but instead of forced exhalations and passive inhalations, both exhalations and inhalations are actively and forcibly performed. Similar contraindications and precautions exist for both *bhastrika* and *kapalabhati.*

Both *bhastrika* and *kapalabhati* are often done in conjunction with locks or *bandhas,* the sustained contraction of specific regional muscle groups. The *bandhas* are typically performed with breath retention. External *kumbhaka,* breath retention following full exhalation, is much more rigorous and difficult than internal *kumbhaka,* done after full inhalation. There are three commonly used *bandhas.* One is *mula bandha mudra* or the root lock. This lock involves the contraction of the perineal muscles similar to a Kegel exercise. *Uddiyana bandha mudra* or the stomach lock is done exclusively during breath retention after exhalation and involves contracting the abdominal muscles and pulling them up under the ribs. The third commonly used *bandha* is *jalandhara bandha mudra* or the throat lock, a contraction of the muscles of the larynx. One performs this lock by sustaining a half swallow.

Bhastrika and *kapalabhati* can also be followed by *agni sara,* an undulation of the abdominal muscles done with an external *kumbhaka,* breath retention following exhalation. *Agni sara* translates to the essence of fire. *Agni* is the fire that burns deep in the belly.

All of the aforementioned techniques are difficult to physically master. They should be done with caution as they can result in disturbances of the mind. The intent of all of the channel activating techniques, those that generate both physical and emotional heat, is to stir up repressed emotions and past traumas. The witnessing of those past thoughts can be quite difficult to bear.

Sitali Pranayama

The Cooling Breath

As opposed to *pranayama* techniques like *kapalabhati* and *bhastrika,* which are channel activating, energizing and heat-producing, *sitali* is cooling and energy channeling. *Kapalabhati* and *bhastrika* stir up emotions deep in the pelvis, activating the energy of the sun. Subsequently performing *sitali* channels the energy to the moon pathway, allowing the more rational self to bear witness to feelings and thoughts that may not serve one well, and consequently dissolving *anhankara,* the perceived self that often can be illusory. *Sitali* is the most cooling of all of the *pranayama.*

To perform *sitali,* exhale out fully through the nose to achieve complete emptiness. Stick a curled tongue out between the lips and inhale slowly through the tube that is formed. You will experience a cooling sensation on the tongue and in the mouth. When you have inhaled completely, hold your breath and lightly touch the tip of your tongue to the roof of your mouth, either the hard or soft palate as far back as possible without causing discomfort on the undersurface of the tongue and frenulum. The frenulum is the connection of the tongue to the midline of the floor of the oral cavity. You can revert to a normal breathing rhythm or do a short round of *dirgha pranayama* before returning back to the *sitali* breath once again. The light touch of the cool tip of tongue on the palate becomes a single point of focus around which self-reflection occurs.

Sitkari Pranayama

The Hissing Breath

The Sanskrit word *sitkari* translates to "hissing". *Sitkari* is the alternative to *sitali* for those that are unable to curl their tongues; approximately one third to one quarter of the population. *Sitkari* is performed the same as *sitali* except for the position of the tongue during inhalation. For *sitkari,* the tongue remains in the mouth. The tip of the tongue is lightly touched to where the upper and lower teeth meet. Typically, the jaw is opened to separate the teeth ever so slightly. As inhalation occurs, the tongue approximates a bowl shape. Similar to *sitali, sitkari* cools the tongue. *Sitkari* may be uncomfortable for those with sensitive teeth.

Bhramari Pranayama
Female Bee Breath

Bhramari is also a cooling, energy channeling breath, often done after a round or rounds of channel activating *kapalabhati* and/or *bhastrika* . *Bhramari* is the Hindu Goddess of the Black Bees. During exhalation, a humming sound is created, emulating the sound of a bee. The tip of the tongue is firmly pressed up against the hard palate and then one inhales fully. Upon exhaling, humming is done through the nose and throat. Since this is the female bee breath, traditionally one creates a high pitch sound. One can experiment, however, with lower frequencies and observe how that changes your experience.

Bhramari is often done in conjunction with *yoni mudra.* The Sanskrit word *yoni* means "womb". *Yoni mudra* is dedicated to the female goddess Shakti. *Yoni mudra* simulates the detachment from the world and the quieting of the mind experienced by the fetus in the uterus. As such, the hand position is directed at blocking all experience of external stimuli. With both hands brought up toward the face, the second and third fingers are lightly placed over the eyelids, symbolic of the elimination of the sense of vision. The fourth fingers are placed under the nose, symbolic of the elimination of the sense of smell. Pinky fingers lie just under the mouth, within which is the sense of taste. The thumbs are then used to press the tragus of each ear to occlude the ear canals. The tragus is the small flap of cartilage protruding from each ear, just in front of the external ear canal. Occluding the ear canals intensifies the sound of the bee as it fills the head with vibratory energy. A long period of sustained bee breath is felt to be beneficial for stress reduction.

Simhasana pranayama

Lion's Breath

The Lion's Breath is done while in *simhasana,* the lion's pose. There are several ways to enter into the lion's pose. One can begin in the hero's pose. The palms are then placed face down in front of the knees, fingers either pointed towards or away from the body, as the torso leans forward. Variations include sitting on curled toes or bringing the inner edges of the feet to touch, knees out wide. Once in *simhasana,* one then sticks the tongue out from the mouth and, with a strong exhalation, creates a loud "hah" sound, the roar of the lion. The forcefulness of the lion's breath is felt to be beneficial to release anger. Creating this breath can also be quite a humorous experience. Yoga need not always be a serious pursuit. A bit of humor and laughter can go a long way to reduce stress.

A Sample *Pranayama* Practice

A *pranayama* practice is created through the sequencing of the various forms of *pranayama*. As mentioned previously, one might think of a *pranayama* practice as a wave. The wave begins to form with the performance of *dirga pranayama* and *ujjayi* that serve to warm up the muscles of respiration and begin to fuel the fire of emotions deep in the pelvis. The wave crests with the performance of the channel activating forms of *pranayama* such as *anuloma viloma, kapalabhati* and *bhastrika.* Heat and the stirring of emotions is intensified by adding *kumbhakas, bandhas* and *agni sara.* Progressive cooling then occurs as the wave subsides, fueling the lunar energy, allowing for self-reflection. A cooling sequence might consist of *nadi shodhana, brahmari,* and *sitali* or *sitkari.* Many variations for sequencing *pranayama* exist, all for the most part following a similar warmup-heat-cooling waveform. Easing slowly into a *pranayama* practice is important. Starting with a lesser number of rounds of the more heat producing forms of *pranayama* will ultimately prove to be more beneficial than jumping right into the heat. The use of *kumbhakas, bandhas* and *agni sara* should be reserved for more advanced practitioners. Progress occurs gradually. Patience is paramount.

Ultimately, the awareness of the breath that is learned through *pranayama* becomes a part of your entire yoga practice. Once you become familiar with *asanas, pranayama* and the art and skill of meditation, you can start to integrate all three. Each one can be enjoyed separately, but all together they add up to so much more. Yoga means "to unite". The act of uniting your movements, breath and mind becomes your own unique version of yoga. It is now your practice to embrace!

21
THE CODA

What I have in my heart and soul must find a way out. That's the reason for music.

Ludwig van Beethoven

The realized benefits of yoga need not end at the conclusion of a class, but of course, a yoga class that you attend must have a beginning and an end. Almost every yoga class concludes with the mutual recitation of the word, *namaste.* It is often said as one bows with hands in *anjali mudra* at heart center or on the forehead at the third eye center. The Sanskrit word *namaste* literally translates to "I bow to you". In Hinduism, *namaste* has a more specific meaning; "The divine in me bows to the divine in you." It is a recognition of the divine universal consciousness that we all share. I prefer the modified translation, "The light within me bows to the light within you," as it has less of a religious connotation. Furthermore, the idea of a light that burns within us, brightened and energized by our yoga practice, is a wonderful and powerful image. As a teacher, I humbly bow to my students to honor them for entrusting me with their safety, for their efforts done in earnest, for their attention to my words and for their kindness. In the Indian subcontinent and in parts of Southeast Asia, *namaste* is a colloquial expression of greeting, similar to aloha or shalom. It is often said with a bow and hands in *anjali mudra.*

Some teachers may end a class by leading students through the chanting of the word, *Om.* He, she or they instruct the class to inhale deeply and chant *Om* on the exhalation. The sound of *Om* is chanted in many eastern religions. It has a multitude of meanings in Hinduism and is ubiquitous throughout the ancient holy Hindu scriptures and texts. Among many other things, it is symbolic of the divine, Atman and Brahman, the cosmos, and the knowledge of the universe.· It is a holy word often chanted before and after the recitation of passages from the ancient Hindu scriptures, including the Vedas and Upanishads. Aside from its religious significance, many feel that the shared sound vibrations resulting from the chanting of *Om* are energizing and create a meaningful, shared, communal experience.

I possess a great love for music. I often look at a yoga class in musical terms. Like a symphony, there are changing dynamics, flowing themes and changes in mood and emotions. Most classical symphonies end with a coda, the final concluding musical passage. The coda is the last chance for a composer to impact the listener emotionally as the themes of the opus come to a meaningful conclusion. Similarly, the very end of a yoga class is the last opportunity the instructor has to leave his or her students with a provocative idea that connects the practice of yoga with the living of a meaningful life. The composer writes with the hope of inducing an emotional change in the listener, no matter how fleeting it might be. The yoga instructor has a similar hope by imparting profound, thoughtful words to his or her students. An instructor may say something they feel is relevant, possibly tying into a theme or intention for the class introduced at its onset, or read a personally important passage from a poem or other written work. For myself, my final words are not primarily directed at my students, but mainly toward myself. I choose to expose my own thoughts and emotions. They may resonate with some and not with others. I often speak of finding your true authentic self, not living life with an expectation of what you think someone else wants you to be. I speak of practicing self-kindness with the hope of having compassion for others. I speak of tapping into one's inner strength with a positive perspective to better face life's challenges. One does not need to practice yoga to experience any revelations. Yoga is merely a vehicle that facilitates the process. My yoga practice allows me to be introspective and gain insight. In an attempt to be an authentic teacher and not a version of what I think my students wish me to be, I end my classes with words from my heart. My words may not necessarily represent what I practice each day. Many times, they simply express an ideal that I wish I could attain, but haven't as yet realized.

Ultimately, what I speak of most is gratitude. Gratitude is felt by many to be the prerequisite for all other positive emotions. It has also been said, "It is not happiness that brings gratitude, but rather gratitude that brings happiness." Gratitude enables one to have a clear perspective of what is truly important in life. It is an acknowledgement of all the blessings that life has to offer. When you have gratitude, you can have love and compassion. When you have love and compassion, the world will be yours, and the light within you and the light that is you will burn so brightly for everyone to see!

22

EPILOGUE ~ THE TRIUMPH OF THE HUMAN SPIRIT

It didn't matter that I couldn't touch my toes. I only had to learn to touch my spirit.

Gordon Kanzer

As I hold the door open for my students to enter the yoga classroom at the local YMCA where I teach, I see a young woman, possibly nineteen or twenty, walking toward me down a long hallway. She struggles to walk. It appears that she has been afflicted with cerebral palsy. With each step, her disease causes her feet and legs to turn significantly inward, her torso to twist left and right and her arms to flail outward as she struggles to walk. Her pace is exceedingly slow. Her face appears contorted. It seems that her cerebral palsy has affected her facial muscles as well. Every step appears to require an inordinate amount of energy. I feel that she has been dealt a very bad hand in life. Since she is at the YMCA, I imagine that she is there for some sort of exercise. Maybe she is able to swim, likely without the help of her legs. Possibly she is there for some therapeutic exercise in the handicap-accessible warm pool. Why she is there doesn't really matter to me. What does concern me is how she is able to manage this horrible disease. I presume that living with her handicap elicits feelings of frustration, anger and depression. My heart goes out to her. I feel terrible about her situation. Her life must be full of misery stemming from a debilitating disease.

As she nears me, however, to my surprise she enters my classroom. As she does, she smiles at me. Her smile not only lights up her beautiful face, but everything around her. No words are necessary. Her expression is one of pure joy. Despite her handicap, one that could cause anyone to despair, her face is radiant. I can see her spirit soaring above the clouds. Perhaps, she realized at a very early age that her physical disability is not an obstacle to contentment, peace and happiness. I smile back, but as she walks past me, I begin to cry. Although probably forty years her elder, she taught me an important lesson on life that day. Despite handicaps that might limit one physically or emotionally, it is the triumph of the human spirit that makes one immune from any impediments. It is there in your soul. You just need to know how to access it. I remember her strength when I need to access my own and when I need a reminder of the importance of gratitude.

As she participated in my class, I noticed she was unable to assume many of the postures. Her movements were erratic and jerky, but at the same time full of grace. By connecting those movements to her breath she was "doing" yoga. As I watched her, all of the obstacles I had personally overcame to develop a meaningful, regular yoga practice, everything that I subsequently learned and all of the philosophy I had embraced came together in a single thought, "It didn't matter that I couldn't touch my toes, I only had to learn to touch my spirit!"

With much gratitude, I say to you ~

Namaste ~

The light that is within me honors and bows to the light within you. May your light shine brightly with all the love and compassion in your heart!

Jai Bhagwan! ~

May your life be a blessed victory! May that victory let your spirit soar!

ACKNOWLEDGMENTS

I owe much gratitude to Kirstin Pope for my cover photographs. The front cover photograph represents strength, not just of the warrior pose, but of the power of yoga to bring people together to find common meaning and joy.

You can visit Kirstin and see her many talents at her website:

~ Kirsti Out Wandering ~

https://out-wandering.com/van-girl-productions/

I am also grateful to my daughter Emily, who helped me with the illustrations in this book and taught me that their is an artist in everyone!

Finally, I am indebted to the universal kindness I received from everyone at the Kripalu Center for Yoga and Health, including my teachers, assistant teachers, and fellow students. You all touched my heart and allowed me to teach from my heart!

ABOUT THE AUTHOR

Gordon Kanzer discovered yoga after a long career as a Radiologist and medical author.

His continued desire to help people led him to the Kripalu yogic philosophy of self-observation without judgment and the practice of kindness and compassion. He writes from his personal experience of the transformative effects of yoga that helped him to overcome an inflexibility of body and mind in the pursuit of a regular, meaningful yoga practice.

He is a graduate of Hofstra University, New York University School of Medicine, and the Kripalu Center for Yoga and Health.

He lives on beautiful Cape Cod with his wife, Lauren. His two sons, daughter and daughter-in-law all live in the Boston area. His yellow lab, Bella, taught him the power of unconditional love.

You can learn more about Gordon at:

https://www.gkanzeryoga.com

Made in United States
North Haven, CT
16 January 2022

14852621R00185